EASTERN COACH WORKS
1965-1987

ISBN 1 898432 11 2

Companion Volumes

Eastern Coach Works 1946-65 (Sept 1993)
Eastern Coach Works – A Retrospect (Jan 1995)

Front Cover Illustration

The last bus to be built at Lowestoft was an Olympian double-decker supplied to London and now operating in the Selkent fleet. Its significance as a milestone in the history of British bus building has been recognised by the operator and the vehicle is kept in pristine condition. It frequently appears at rallies and has collected an impressive array of trophies. The photograph was taken by Peter Durham in the Autumn of 1993, the somewhat sombre weather being appropriate in the circumstances.

Typeset and produced electronically for the Publishers by
Mopok Graphics, 128, Pikes Lane, Glossop, Derbyshire
Printed and bound in Great Britain

EASTERN COACH WORKS
1965 – 1987

by
Maurice Doggett
and
Alan Townsin

with additional material by
Duncan Roberts

Venture *publications*

CONTENTS

FOREWORD

It is with sadness that I write this Foreword to the penultimate chapter of the long and varied story of Eastern Coach Works.

I sincerely hope that this book will inform and remind everyone of the great contribution Eastern Coach Works made to the development of bus manufacturing and for making it possible for so many people to acquire skills for which they are so rightly proud.

Ironically in 1980 it was a misplaced sense of this pride which cast a deep shadow over Eastern Coach Works which was never really to recede and culminated in a decision by Leyland not to expand manufacturing facilities at Lowestoft but to transfer their expansion plans to the Workington plant in Cumbria.

These were turbulent times. Bus Grants were being phased out and markets were changing. In conditions like these the customer manufacturer relationship is essential; all too often these relations were routed through Divisional channels which increased reaction times and did little to foster good customer relations.

In 1986 Leyland Bus was the subject of a management buy-out, but Eastern Coach Works was not included in that buy-out.

Thus the proud and profitable Eastern Coach Works passed into history. It is sadly missed !

John Bloor
Evesham
Worcestershire

INTRODUCTION

The year 1965 was a crucial one for Eastern Coach Works Ltd and its Lowestoft factory. On the one hand, an ingenious touch of commercialism released it and the corresponding chassis-producing concern, Bristol Commercial Vehicles Ltd, from the ban on sales to private enterprise or municipal operators, which had been imposed when they became State-owned in 1948, as described in the previous volume. The mechanism for this was a simple exchange of shares between the Leyland Motor Corporation and the Transport Holding Company, which then owned ECW and BCV along with other road transport interests, notably the Tilling and Scottish bus-operating groups, on behalf of the Government.

On the other hand, this also proved to be a first step towards an increasing measure of control by Leyland. At first the shareholding was 25 per cent, Bristol and ECW being free to compete for business, sometimes doing so most effectively against Leyland itself. At ECW, Alan Hunton, from Marshall of Cambridge, was appointed in 1967 to inject experience of active sales in an open market. Orders were obtained from several municipalities and some from members of the British Electric Traction group of operating companies, even before the latter agreed to sell its British bus-operating interests to THC in 1967. However, in a deal agreed in 1969 with the newly-formed State-owned National Bus Company (which took over all THC bus interests in England and Wales as a result of the Transport Act 1968) it became 50 per cent, with a Leyland appointee as Chairman, at first Ron Ellis.

By then, Leyland, already the parent company of a growing group, had become British Leyland, as a result of the merger in 1968. This brought together the British Motor Corporation, mainly involved in the manufacture of Austin and Morris cars, with the Leyland group. In terms of ECW's products, the high traditions of design and manufacture for a time continued with little obvious change. Most of the output now went to NBC and, north of the border, the Scottish Bus Group continued as an important user.

Behind the scenes, however, 'politics' of one kind or another began to intervene, among the first instances of this being the decision to phase out manufacture of the highly successful Bristol RE single-decker with standard ECW body, despite record output of the type in the 1971 programme, in favour of the Leyland National integral-construction vehicle. The latter began production in 1972, using mass-production car techniques at a new factory at Workington and needing high volume to be economic.

British Leyland's financial position deteriorated severely in the early 'seventies, influenced mainly by disastrous losses in the car division, and complete collapse was only saved by Government intervention, the combine becoming 95 per cent State-owned in 1975. The pressure to maximise profits throughout the group to recover the situation became more severe, while raising funds for investment became more difficult.

In the case of ECW, this had not been a severe problem, because the scale and nature of manufacture had been well suited to relatively simple methods and reliance on the skills of its workforce, while its success in attracting orders from municipalities in particular, where competitive tendering was usual, showed that its prices were not out of line with those ruling elsewhere.

Up to this period, ECW was regarded primarily as a supplier of bodywork designed to give long and reliable service to the bus-operating group to which it belonged, even though also building for other operators.

Continuity of methods and standards had been encouraged by the long service of ECW management. Ralph Sugden had been appointed General Manager in 1953 and was only the third holder of that office since ECW's creation as a separate business in 1936 – he had joined the firm in 1938 from Charles H. Roe Ltd, the Leeds firm from which Bill Bramham, the initial ECW General Manager had been recruited in 1936. Sugden became Commercial Manager and Deputy General Manager before taking over as General Manager.

He died in office in May 1970, being succeeded by Alfred Tattersall, another Yorkshireman who had also joined the firm in 1938. The latter became Works Manager in 1950 and it is significant that he took over the general managership just after the revised relationship with Leyland had come into effect. At that stage, ECW was still being allowed to run its business very largely on traditional lines, and indeed Tattersall belonged to the style of management where he was clearly regarded as 'the boss' yet had the respect and confidence of the workforce.

ECW was required to concentrate on double-deckers, largely on the Bristol VRT chassis, and light single-decker buses on the Bristol LH chassis, though small numbers of coaches on RE and Leyland Leopard chassis were built in 1972-5. Business for municipal fleets continued, mainly double-deckers on Fleetline or Atlantean chassis, and the latter began also to be favoured for some NBC fleets with an ex-BET background.

ECW's form of aluminium-alloy framing, first introduced in 1948, incorporating strong integration of the waist and skirt construction with the pillars, had proved exceptionally durable, allowing the Tilling group to adopt a 17-year standard vehicle life instead of the 12- or 15-year period usual elsewhere. Although no visible change to existing models was evident, there is some evidence in terms of durability of the bodies in question that constructional quality began to fall, even if only slightly. Former employees also report the beginning of a drop in morale, and it is said that Alf Tattersall disliked the increasing degree of control being imposed from Leyland headquarters, to the extent that he was happy to take early retirement in April 1976.

His successor was John Bloor, though the title of the position was changed to Plant Director. His background included the car industry, at that period apt to be a recommendation for high office within the group, but he had also worked for MCW and latterly for Park Royal, where he had been Chief Body Engineer, involved in early work on the B15 integral rear-engined double-decker, later to become the Titan. To ECW, he brought a new emphasis on mechanised methods of manufacture.

An opportunity for expansion at a period when the general future of bus sales was beginning to look less promising came early in 1980, when the impending closure of the Park Royal factory led to the proposal that manufacture of the Titan, then being built there mainly for London Transport, be moved to ECW. An unresolved dispute in regard to the position of craftsmen in relation to the recruitment of unskilled labour, echoing one that had occurred at Park Royal, led to the workforce rejecting the deal on which the move was to be based. However, there is some indication that influential forces may have been at play at very high levels on both the BL management and union sides such that neither was unduly upset at the outcome, which opened the door to taking the job to Workington.

Bodywork for the new Olympian double-decker, related to the Titan but with separate chassis, was already being developed at ECW under Leyland direction, and this was to become ECW's main product in its remaining years, largely for NBC fleets though also with some notable sales successes among municipal and Passenger Transport Executive fleets. Valiant attempts were also made to secure export business by the construction of a series of demonstrators to suit varying requirements and climates, but very few orders resulted. An attempt to re-enter the single-deck coach market was made in 1981-2 with the B51 project that seemed fated almost from the start, a combination of factors conspiring to produce structural failures of a kind quite unexpected from ECW products.

By 1983, when Peter Middleton, from Leyland, took over as Plant Director, the economic and political climate was becoming increasingly difficult, NBC having sold its shareholding in the business to Leyland in 1982. The bus market was dwindling rapidly under the effects of the Government's proposals for privatising the bus industry and this was also in mind for the BL group itself.

London Transport had been an occasional buyer of ECW products since 1951 but became increasingly important towards the end despite the Titan episode, helping to keep the factory open, at first with refurbishing work. More importantly, the biggest order for a single operator ever received by ECW was placed in 1985 for bodying 260 Olympians for London Buses Ltd, as LT's bus undertaking had become. Delivery began in 1986 but even this was insufficient to save the company and closure came after the last was delivered in January 1987.

By this time, privatisation of Leyland Bus was in hand and the deal excluded ECW, to which the final Plant Director, Michael Sheehan, was appointed, though his duties were merely to oversee the winding-down of the business. It was a sad end to what had been one of the most important bus bodybuilding factories in Britain.

These volumes have attempted to do justice to the many highly successful and the occasional less satisfactory ECW products, being based on Maurice Doggett's immense fund of knowledge and detailed records of ECW collected over almost a lifetime's study – it has been a pleasure to work with this material. My own interest in the company took on a new respect during the period from 1965 to 1972 when, as Editor of Bus & Coach, I visited the works on a series of occasions, generally to examine trend-setting new designs. In addition, we have had the benefit of the practical knowledge of Duncan Roberts, Joint Managing Director of Northern Bus Co Ltd, which operates a wide-ranging collection of ECW-bodied vehicles – some questions of a dimensional nature have been settled by him literally running over examples in the Northern fleet with a tape-measure.

In collecting relevant information, Duncan Roberts and John Senior met many former ECW managers and employees. This resulted in a much wider range of recollections, some going in depth into the complex problems which beset the company in later years, than even these volumes could accommodate. Accordingly, a further volume looking at ECW in retrospect is in course of preparation.

Alan Townsin
Steventon, 1994

PHOTOCREDITS

Thanks are due to all those who made photographs available for this volume. Apart from those identified individually below, Eastern Coach Works, or in certain cases, Leyland group, official photographs are used. From 1960 to the end of 1976, the photographic work for ECW was undertaken by Laurence Gall, also of Lowestoft, and the negatives passed to Mr Brian Ollington of Gorleston, who became the official ECW photographer from 1977, when he took over the Gall business. His co-operation is acknowledged with thanks. Over the years many prints of its photographs were issued by ECW for publicity purposes, some of which are held on a personal basis by the author and editor. Others formed part of collections which have passed to Senior Transport Archives, and examples of all of these have been used in preparing this book.

G. H. F. Atkins 49 (bottom), 50 bottom), 75 (lower), 132 (centre)

P. Bateson 109 (both)

Bristol Vintage Bus Group 15 (top), 124 (bottom)

S. J. Brown 121 (top)

A. B. Cross 127 (bottom)

M. J. Curtis 99 (top)

R. C. Davis 128 (centre)

M, G, Doggett 14, 15 (centre & bottom), 17 (both), 30 (bottom), 32 (top right), 42 (bottom), 43 (top two), 46 (bottom), 48 (lower), 49 (top), 52 (both), 57 (top), 61 (top), 63 (top right), 64 (top), 65 (both), 67 (all but top right), 70 (top right), 72 (centre), 76 (centre), 77 (both), 78 (top), 79 (all but top) 80 (bottom two), 81 (top left), 82 (bottom), 83 (both), 84 (bottom left), 89 (bottom), 90 (top), 91 (bottom), 93 (top), 94 (lower), 96 (bottom), 97 (top & bottom), 98 (all but centre), 100 (top left), 101 (both), 102, 103 (both), 104 (both), 107 (both), 108 (both), 112 (top & bottom), 113 (both), 114 (both), 116 (top), 117 (both), 118 (both), 119 (all), 120 (all), 121 (bottom), 122 (both), 123 (all), 124 (top), 126 (centre), 129 (centre & bottom), 130 (all), 131 (all but top), 132 (top)

M. G. Doggett collection 125 (second top & bottom left), 126 (bottom), 128 (top left)

P. Durham Cover

M. Fenton 92 (both), 95 (bottom), 96 (top), 97 (centre), 100 (bottom left), 115 (both)

P. R. Gainsbury 70 (bottom)

I. Lynas 129 (top)

A. MacFarlane 82 (top)

R. F. Mack 26

R. Marshall 12, 13 (both), 21 (bottom), 23 (both), 24 (bottom), 25, 28 (bottom), 29 (centre), 40 (bottom), 41 (bottom), 43 (bottom), 58 (top), 59 (bottom), 60 (top), 75 (top), 80 (top), 81 (bottom), 98 (centre left), 100 (bottom right), 106, 112 (centre)

M. R. M. New 125 (top), 126 (top)

J. A. Senior 110

R. H. G. Simpson 127 (top)

E. Surfleet 128 (top right)

A. A. Thomas 79 (top)

A. A. Townsin 132 (bottom)

M. J. Tozer 125 (bottom right)

Vectis Transport Publications 24 (centre), 84 (bottom right), 99 (bottom)

D. Wayman 63 (bottom), 71 (top), 94 (top), 116 (bottom)

Colour material was supplied by David Cole, Eastern Coach Works, John Hardey, Leyland Bus, Roy Marshall, P. D. Mitchell, Gary Nolan, Northern Bus Company, Photobus, Duncan Roberts, Duncan Roberts' collection, John Senior and the Senior Transport Archive.

ACKNOWLEDGMENTS

This volume is a continuation of my researches which appeared in Venture Publication's earlier volume ECW 1946 – 1965. It is therefore appropriate to thank those people who had helped with that volume, in addition to those who have subsequently been involved with this one. During the period that this book covers we received help and encouragement from many people in the factory and some in the Leyland organisation including Ernie Besford, Jack Lewis, John Bloor, Peter Middleton, Bernie Carr, the late Jim Irvine, Brian Wright, Alan Hunton, Bill Wybrow, the late Alfred Tattersall, the late A. W. McCall, Mrs Rita Reynolds, Bob Smith and Andrew Huddleston.

Subsequently John Senior, then of TPC and now with Venture, became involved and opened many doors within ECW and Leyland top management which increased the depth of our combined knowledge. Later still Duncan Roberts, also of Venture, but a bus operator in his own right, took a personal interest in the project which helped to clarify many aspects of the actual design and build of ECW's vehicles. Through this interest, and with assistance from Trevor Westgate of the Lowestoft Journal, came a series of interviews with Sid Wright, Stan George, Gus Halkes, Brian Ratcliffe, Gerald Vincent, Gordan Goodman, George Crisp and Alan Hunton which provided a wealth of first-hand experiences and reminiscences sufficient to fill a book in themselves. I look forward to assisting in the final volume later this year, and to the opportunity to record the contributions of many of the people who spent the whole of their working lives at the Lowestoft Coach Factory
.

Finally, as previously, I record my appreciation of Alan Townsin's efforts in converting my manuscript and many documents into the final version in which you see it.

M. G. Doggett
Purley
Surrey
August 1994

Earlier generations of Eastern Coach Works' vehicles can be seen at the many rallies and running days held throughout the country every year. These two, both originally with Hants & Dorset, were photographed in Wimborne Minster in April 1994.

In its early days, Eastern Coach Works built bodywork to varying styles to suit individual operators' requirements, though generally using a combination of standard features, especially where Tilling-managed companies were concerned, as here. This example, body number 4823 in what later became called Series 1, on Bristol JO5G chassis, was one of a batch of seven supplied to the United Counties Omnibus Co Ltd in March 1937, generally typical of deliveries to that fleet at the time. The main structure of the body was as used for several companies, but such details as the shape of destination box, the rounded front nearside window with complementary dip in the cantrail above and the 'swoop' at the rear of the waistband were all optional characteristic features which could be specified on a 'pick and mix' basis.

The story so far

The roots of Eastern Coach Works can be traced back to 4th April 1912, when United Automobile Services Ltd was registered by Mr. E. B. Hutchinson, the initial purpose being the running of motor omnibus services in the vicinity of Lowestoft, then largely a fishing port, in Suffolk. Soon, a branch was established at Bishop Auckland in County Durham, and although the 1914-18 war delayed expansion, by the late 'twenties United buses were to be found in most of the counties of England bordering the North Sea from Lowestoft as far northwards as the Scottish border, even though the territory covered never became continuous over that stretch.

Bodybuilding, largely for the company's own vehicles, was an obvious development for so ambitious a concern, and what began as a 'car fitting shop' was built at Laundry Lane, Lowestoft in 1919. From almost the beginning, work was done for sale to other operators, quite often on AEC chassis, for which United held agencies in parts of its area, as well as many other makes and for a wide variety of customers.

In 1929, United, which had been one of the largest independent operators, was taken over jointly by the London and North Eastern Railway Co and Tilling & British Automobile Traction Co Ltd (the latter itself jointly owned by Thomas Tilling Ltd and the British Electric Traction Co Ltd, the two largest groups controlling bus companies in England & Wales). The pattern of shareholdings was such that the Tilling influence on United, and its successors as proprietors of the Lowestoft factory, was dominant.

Similar patterns of ownership became common and thus United became part of the giant Tilling and BET bus-operating combine. It began supplying bodywork to some of these associated companies but in 1931, a reorganisation resulted in United's services in East Anglia, together with the bodybuilding works, being transferred to a new concern, the Eastern Counties Omnibus Co Ltd. Sales of bodywork to non-associated operators ceased and increasingly the role became one of body supply to the combine, especially where Tilling influence was strong.

It has only recently come to light that Eastern Counties was engaged in negotiations that might have led to the sale of the 'Coach Factory', as it was often called, in mid-1933. The Minutes of a Board meeting on 20th June that year record the fact without identifying the possible buyer. However, the Minutes of the Board meeting of 4th October 1933 disclose that Charles Roberts & Co Ltd, of Wakefield, had been the other party in the negotiations but had decided not to proceed with the purchase.

Roberts was a sizeable concern whose business was largely in the railway wagon field but included the manufacture of bus bodywork on a fairly modest scale, mainly for municipalities though a few small orders for company fleets were executed at about that time. It is only possible to speculate on the likely course of events had that sale gone through but it seems unlikely that the Lowestoft premises would have played the key role they did over the following half century.

The growth in breadth of supply to associated companies was already well under way before the abortive Roberts deal, but what had just begun, from deliveries made in May 1933, was a pattern of building increasingly on chassis produced by the Bristol Tramways & Carriage Co Ltd, part of the Tilling group from 1931, although this took several years before it gained full momentum.

In 1936, it was decided to create a separate company, Eastern Coach Works Ltd, as a subsidiary of Eastern Counties, to take over the Lowestoft factory. There was also a further change of policy, in that 'outside' business was once again sought, though in practice ECW's main customers continued to be the companies under Tilling control, for which bodywork was mostly on Bristol chassis, or for quite a number of those controlled by BET, in which case the chassis were more often of Leyland or other makes. Limited numbers of bodies for municipalities were built, again largely on Leyland chassis.

The threat of invasion brought ECW's production to an abrupt halt in the dark days of 1940, though it was restarted on a small scale in temporary premises at Irthlingborough, Northamptonshire, an activity which continued for a while after the Lowestoft works came back into use as the 1939-45 war ended. By that date, the complicated link between Tilling and BET had been broken by a reorganisation in 1942, Tilling increasingly adopting a policy of tight standardisation.

When ECW production restarted in 1946, the types produced were confined to one single-deck outline and a choice of two closely related double-deckers, full-height or low-height or to use the terms then widely in use, highbridge and lowbridge. Tilling companies took these with identical features, almost always on Bristol chassis and even livery variations were generally confined to a choice of red or green versions of the same style. Other customers, again largely BET companies and a few municipalities, were allowed more liberty, but the body designs were still largely uniform. In practice, there was more variety than might have been thought because of quite large-scale rebodying of chassis of various makes.

In 1948, Tilling voluntarily sold its bus interests to the British Transport Commission, which had been created by the Labour Government of the time to run the major part of the nation's public transport system which it was in the process of taking into State ownership. ECW and the Bristol concern were included, and as a result were precluded from selling their products to organisations outside the BTC. Existing non-BTC orders could be honoured, but the last of these were completed in 1950, and through the 'fifties and early 'sixties the products of these concerns were available only within the State-owned sector. As it turned out, the Tilling operating company group organisation survived, complete with its close links to both Bristol and ECW as manufacturers within the BTC set-up, the former's activities of this kind being transferred to a separate company, Bristol Commercial Vehicles Ltd, from January 1955.

Technical development was lively under the new regime, and Bristol and ECW collaborated closely on the development of the Lodekka, which was the first and by far the most successful double-decker to give the more convenient centre-gangway layout within 'lowbridge' overall height, as well as the LS integral-construction underfloor-engined medium-weight single-decker. The latter, though successful, gave way to the MW equivalent with separate chassis. There were also lighter single-deckers such as the front-engined SC and underfloor-engined SU. In 1962, Bristol introduced its RE single-decker with underfloor-mounted rear engine, and again ECW was closely involved in its development.

(A much more detailed account of ECW's history over the postwar period appears in the companion volume 'ECW – 1946-65' also published by Venture Publications Ltd.)

In the post-war period, standardisation became much more rigid. Some 1,372 examples of this style of lowbridge double-decker to the standard contemporary dimensions of 26ft length and 7ft 6in width were built between 1946 and 1950, the overwhelming majority on Bristol K-type chassis as here. They set standards of appearance which were to remain recognisable in later designs until 1981, particularly in regard to the upper deck. There were minor changes, but the basic appearance remained uniform, though a more important change from timber framing to aluminium alloy did alter the look of the interior and was in effect by the time this example was built. Body 2740 (of Series 2 which had begun at 1001 in 1946), was one of ten on Bristol-engined K6B chassis for the West Yorkshire Road Car Co Ltd. By that period a batch system had been introduced and this body was built in Batch 34, being delivered in July 1949.

Chapter Seven: **The link with Leyland**

The technical achievements of Bristol and ECW in the 'fifties and early 'sixties kept them among the leaders of bus development in Britain, despite the fact that their products were not available to operators outside the State-owned sector. The appeal of the Lodekka concept had led to a licensing arrangement with Dennis Bros Ltd in 1956, and the resulting Dennis Loline double-decker was at first virtually a Lodekka built under licence, though in later years Dennis introduced more of its own components.

On the operating side, a slightly more commercial approach to the provision of public transport was signified by the reconstruction of the nationalised transport industry by the Conservative Government in the Transport Act 1962, which resulted in the road transport interests of the British Transport Commission being transferred to the newly-created Transport Holding Company, the BTC being dissolved. Even so, at that date, there was no plan to sell-off any part of the organisation, the railways being transferred to the British Railways Board. In practice,

little change of policy in regard to vehicle supply became evident from these changes. Bristol and ECW, now among the THC subsidiaries, continued to operate in the same way, making virtually all of the vehicles placed in service by the Tilling companies in England and Wales and a substantial share of those for the Scottish Bus Group north of the border.

In addition to the Lodekka, to which the compliment of flattery by imitation had been paid in vehicles of generally similar layout made by AEC and Leyland/Albion, Bristol-ECW had created a considerable impression with the RE rear-engined single-decker. There was widespread interest in such vehicles, which extended for some years to city bus operators hitherto standardising on double-deckers. This was because of the combination of the extension of maximum permissible length to 36ft (11 metres) in 1961, and the fact that, at that date, what was still normally called one-man operation was not legally permissible on a double-decker of any kind.

The Lodekka FS-type retained the more curvaceous outline of the early production Lodekka LD, though differing from it mainly in being of the flat-floor layout to which the F prefix referred. This example with body 14690, one of a pair of FS6G for United Welsh built in Batch 371 in the 1964 programme and delivered in December of that year, did not enter service until 1965. Accordingly, 389, delivered as BWN 84B, was changed to BWN 84C as shown.

The FLF-type Lodekka reached its peak output in the 1965 programme, with a total of 351 produced. Among them were 25 FLF6G for Scottish Omnibuses Ltd, of which Roderick MacKenzie was General Manager at the time. Clearly he was favourably impressed, for, when made responsible for Scottish Bus Group engineering policy, he was to arrange for similar buses from Tilling fleets to be taken into stock by SBG in 1973/4 in exchange for VRT types which had proved more troublesome and which went south. Two of the SOL buses, AA27 and 43, with ECW 70-seat bodies 15343/59, are seen here in Edinburgh with Eastern Scottish fleetnames in May 1979, still looking very sound, though a repair of AA43 has led to black window mounting rubber being substituted for the original cream on part of the lower-deck.

The operating industry was under increasing financial pressure, on the one hand from falling numbers of passengers as more people purchased cars and on the other by steadily rising costs. Eliminating the conductor made possible a major cut in costs, since crew wages generally accounted for about two-thirds of all operating costs, even allowing for increased payments to the driver to cover the extra duties.

The 11-metre length made it possible to provide a single-decker with a seating capacity of up to about 54, comparable to double-deckers of 26ft or 27ft length, and the idea of increasing the total carrying capacity by designing the vehicle to provide room for more standing passengers, Continental-style, resurfaced.

These factors made the potential market foreseen for a suitable single-decker wider than seemed likely previously. Another, particularly related to urban operation, was the idea of a low floor level, and this made the rear-engined layout more attractive than the mid-underfloor engine position which had dominated the single-deck market since 1950.

Although the RE was not the only model of this layout, its design, coupled to the good reputation for reliability and longevity of both Bristol and ECW products made the model of particular interest.

The 'sixties' were also a time of major change in the organisation of the commercial vehicle manufacturing industry, and both Bristol and ECW became involved in a way unexpected at the time. In 1962, The Leyland and ACV combines merged (the latter's largest member being AEC but it also included the bodybuilding concerns Park Royal Vehicles Ltd and Charles H. Roe Ltd), leading to the formation of the Leyland Motor Corporation. Bristol and ECW, subsidiaries of the State-owned Transport Holding

The Bristol RE, with standard ECW 54-seat bus body, was attracting considerable attention from operators outside the nationalised sector by 1965, and was undoubtedly a factor in the move to allow sale of Bristol and ECW products on the open market by means of the link with Leyland. This example was one of eleven built for Red & White Services Ltd as part of Batch 368 in September-November 1965, one of 61 RE buses in that year's programme. Jones' Omnibus Services Ltd was an independent operator which sold out to the National Bus Company in 1969 and was put under Red & White control – GAX 6C is seen in 1973, after transfer to the Jones fleet.

It is apt to be forgotten that the Bristol MW continued to outnumber the RE among deliveries of single-deckers to the Tilling fleets until 1966. The MW had been introduced with minimal publicity in 1957 and was basically a mid-engined chassis of generally conventional mechanical design, powered by either the 5HLW or 6HLW horizontal versions of the Gardner engine and having a five-speed overdrive gearbox. The 1965 ECW programme included 135 stage saloons (15082-135/9-219), all with 45-seat capacity, built in Batches 364-6 and all delivered that year, Eastern Counties LM627 (FAH 627C), an MW5G with body 15161 seen here was typical, though alternative destination layout and types of opening window were offered.

Company from its creation as a successor to the British Transport Commission with effect from 1963, were still bound by the requirement that they could build only for other nationalised concerns.

Although not at that state nationalised itself, Leyland was involved with the Labour Government elected in 1964 in plans for industrial development, and there was interest in how Bristol and ECW could be allowed to play a larger part in this. In July 1965 it was announced that the Leyland Motor Corporation was to purchase a 25 per cent shareholding in Bristol Commercial Vehicles Ltd and Eastern Coach Works Ltd, while THC took a 30 per cent holding in Park Royal. The effect, and indeed the objective was to allow both Bristol and ECW to accept orders from other than nationalised concerns. It took a little time for potential customers to react to the new situation but both concerns began to attract quite a number of new customers during the following year or two. It is noteworthy that BET headquarters obtained copies of specifications and drawings of ECW bodies as being offered for 1966 production, including the Lodekka FS and the MW in both bus and coach forms as well as later types.

Some indication of the new circumstances came in a broadening of Bristol's range of models announced at the beginning of 1966. Among the new variants announced then were shorter RESL and RESH versions of the RE model, although it had been clear from that model's introduction and the inclusion of L for 'long' in the type designations that 'short' equivalents were to be expected. Other announcements were of a wider range of optional features, and indeed the chassis specifications offered included basic models with such features as leaf-spring instead of air suspension for the RE, plus options for many detail items which had been adopted on merit by the Tilling and Scottish companies but, it was realised, might not suit all operators' needs. The MW and SU models were to be dropped but an important new option was the availability of Self Changing Gears semi-automatic transmission. Some of these changes had implications for ECW, but more significantly, it too had now to be prepared to submit tenders for bodywork on non-Bristol chassis.

The last MWs, Lodekkas and SUs

The 1966-68 period was to prove one of change for the whole bus industry, both operating and manufacturing. At ECW, 1966 saw the end of some types that had been long familiar.

To complete the MW story, further batches of coaches were built in the 1966 and 1967 programmes, amounting to 57 and a final 22 respectively, production running from November 1965 to May 1966 and December 1966 to February 1967. The design altered slightly in that the stepped waist was eliminated but in other respects the variations were much as previously, the Crosville versions continuing with the RELH-style front grille panel but the others retaining the smaller grille.

Production of MW chassis ceased in 1966, but construction of the stage and express versions had continued almost undisturbed up to that point. It is noteworthy that MW bus production outnumbered that of the RE bus from the latter's introduction right up to the final MW year. Output of both types in the 1965 programme was swollen by the 'sweeping-up' process of bringing the production programme into line with actual output, which meant that it represented 1964-65, but the figure of 135 MW compared strongly with 61 RELL. Similarly in the final 1966 programme there were 81 MW buses and 36 RELL, though a new shorter RE was represented by six bus examples, as will be described later. The MW stage and express body designs remained little changed since early in their production apart from minor variations such as the alternative radiator designs associated with the use of the Cave-Brown-Cave heating system. However, United's final 20 of 1966 (15858-77) had a much larger high-mounted

The lightweight Bristol SU also continued in production on a small scale until 1966, when the Albion engine it used ceased to be available. All of the 1965-6 examples were of the longer SUL4A type and almost entirely for the Western and Southern National fleets. Minor changes from earlier versions included the cream rubber window surrounds and the repositioning of the front flashing indicators further forward, near the sidelights. There were twelve examples (14712-23) in the 1965 programme, built in the first three months of the year and completing Batch 369. Among them was Western National 671 (BDV 252C), with body 14720 seen here in service. The final 28 were in the 1966 programme (15981-16008), delivered in April-July of that year, and included six for United Counties, not hitherto a user of the type.

The final version of ECW coach body for the MW6G chassis was broadly to the rather controversial style built since 1962, though the 1966 programme's 57 vehicles (15714-70), built in Batches 385 and 386, differed from earlier examples in having straight waistlines rather than having the step at the fourth bay used previously. They came into line with general contemporary coach practice in having forced air ventilation, the side windows lacking opening vents. The glass cantrail windows of previous versions also had to be omitted because of the ducting required. There were minor variations in destination and entrance door layout between individual fleets, the example shown (15753) being one of eight for Southern National, painted in Royal Blue livery but having the operator's own name as fleetname – it was numbered 1418 in that fleet, and registered EDV 548D.

The 1966 programme included 28 of the express carriage version of the MW-type body, based on the bus-type outline, these being 15771-92/5-800, built in Batch 389 and delivered in May-September of the year. Of these, twelve on MW6G were supplied to the Bristol Omnibus Co and were noteworthy in having forced-air ventilation, fed by the vents on each side of the route number indicator – the side windows were not provided with vents because of this. Seen here before delivery is 2088 (HAE 271D) with body 15791.

15

The MW went out with a bang rather than a whimper, for 81 of the stage carriage version were bodied by ECW in the 1966 programme (15793-4/801-77/83-4), outnumbering the year's supply of the more recent and widely praised RE in similar form by more than two to one. They were built in Batches 390-1 in the last six months of that year, and largely followed the pattern of their predecessors.

However, the pictures illustrate two of the Eastern Counties delivery of eleven MW5G, which reflected a revival of interest in the idea of the 'standee' single-decker, accommodating a total of 60 passengers, but only half of them seated. They were both of two-doorway layout, with single-folding front entrance and double folding exit doors, the latter immediately in front of the rear axle, but the buses differed individually in internal layout. The area for standing passengers was concentrated at the rear of LM640 (KAH 640D), with body 15816, there being single seats on each side of the gangway towards the rear to provide a standing area behind the exit doorway, as seen in the centre picture. On LM641 (KAH 641D), the exterior of which is shown at the top of the page, a row of single seats were provided along the offside of the vehicle to give room for a standing area along its length. All three views also show the glazing above the cantrail, a rather coach-like feature intended here to improve vision for standing passengers. In the event, this, plus the single full-depth panes of glass in the front doors, were to prove the only lasting features, for after only a few weeks of entering service in November 1966, both vehicles were modified to standard 45-seat form.

single grille in place of the two narrow grilles previously used.

Two (15816-17) of the final eleven MW buses for Eastern Counties, fleet numbers LM640 and 641, were built as 'standee' vehicles with seats for 30 passengers and, standing space for a further 30. In addition to the normal front entrance, there was an exit door placed just in front of the rear axle rather than to the rear of it as on LS

Production of the Lodekka FS type ended in the 1966 programme, all 94 being completed within the calendar year, thus ending not only production of this model but, as it proved, of rear-entrance double-deckers altogether. The last of all was Crosville DFG238 (JFM 238D), an FS6G with body 15415 delivered on 14th December and seen here. Like all the final year's examples, built in Batches 394, 395 and 403, it had platform doors. Another feature that had been quite common on Lodekka F-series buses was the Cave-Brown-Cave heating system, with large intakes each side of the destination display. Simplification of liveries had been a widespread trend since the 'fifties, and the Tilling group was rather late in deciding to eliminate the upper-deck waistband, with its associated moulding. This took general effect for Lodekka production from the 1966 programme.

two-door models. The internal seating layouts varied between the two, 15816 having single seats each side of the gangway aft of the rear door whereas 15817 had single seats along the whole of the offside, except for the longitudinal seat over the front wheel-arch. They were delivered on 11th November 1966, but the experiment lasted only a matter of weeks, the vehicles soon being converted to standard 45-seat single-doorway form. A legacy of their original state lingered on, however, in the retention of the curved glass cant panels provided for the benefit of standing passengers.

In addition to the MW and SU, output of the FS-type Lodekka ended with a final run (15381-474) of 94 examples, all 60-seat, with platform doors, for the Crosville (35 examples), Lincolnshire (5), United Counties (21) and West Yorkshire (33) fleets, the last including some for both the York and Keighley sections. The Lincolnshire buses were noteworthy as being of the FS5G type, by then rare, and were thus the last of the five-cylinder breed of

Bristol double-decker. The body design remained unchanged over the last few years and the final vehicle with body 15415, delivered to Crosville as its DFG 238 on 14th December 1966 thus had much the same general appearances as early production Lodekka LD-type buses of twelve years or so earlier. This point was underlined by an instance of rebodying, coincidentally also a Crosville vehicle, DLG 797, new in 1955 and fitted with a new body (16054) in 1966, basically to LD design but with some FS detail features.

The FLF thus became the only Lodekka type in production, with 279 in the 1966 programme, 287 in 1967 and a final 85 in 1968. Almost all those built for Tilling fleets in this period had standard 70-seat 30ft-long bodies of similar design to their predecessors. The chassis were mainly a mixture of FLF6B and FLF6G, though both Hants & Dorset and Wilts & Dorset had batches in the 1967 programme split between FLF6B and FLF6L, the latter with Leyland engines. Another option chosen for

The numbers of FLF models in service were steadily increasing, and the 1966 programme deliveries to Tilling companies comprised 239 examples (bodies 15475-713) built in Batches 396-402 and 404 of basically uniform design with 70-seat capacity. Bristol Omnibus C7262 (GAE 883D), seen here, was typical when built, being one of 50 for that fleet and its Cheltenham District subsidiary, of which this was one of 26 on FLF6G chassis, the rest being FLF6B. It was retained when the rest were withdrawn and is seen in Tilling green with traditional scroll-type fleetname. Like most FLFs of this period, it has CBC heating, but among the minority not so fitted, Eastern Counties FLF446 with body 15546 is thought to have been unique in being built with no side opening windows on the upper deck, there being extra roof vents.

Although soon to be phased out, the Lodekka FLF was the subject of a number of significant options in its final years. One mainly associated with the Scottish Bus Group was the extension of length to 31ft 0.875in, the versions built for its subsidiaries using the extended rear overhang to increase seating capacity. However, Eastern National was alone among Tilling companies in also adopting the longer body, readily identified by the rearmost side windows, better proportioned than the usual rather 'pinched'-looking items, but retaining the normal 70-seat total capacity. though arranged differently – 40/30 instead of 38/32 upper/lower deck split because of the forward-ascending staircase. Another option was Self-Changing Gears epicyclic transmission, controlled by a miniature lever on the steering column, and Eastern National was the only operator to combine the two, 2886 (WNO 974F) seen here being one of 33 FLF6G for that fleet, powered by Gardner 6LX engines, another option which was growing in popularity. They were delivered in August-December 1967 as part of Batches 409 and 410, forming part of the 1967 programme, a further 20 similar buses being built for Eastern National in 1968. A general change made in the FLF body from the 1967 programme, though not altering the familiar outline, was the adoption of a moulded glass-fibre reinforced assembly for the front of the upper-deck. This extended from the front dome down to the cab top, including window frames. Note also the rear wheel discs, specified for a time on deliveries to Tilling fleets.

these Hants & Dorset/Wilts & Dorset buses and also by Crosville, Eastern National, Mansfield District and Midland General was semi-automatic transmission, available on the FLF in its final years. This required a modified floor design, there being a raised cover over the gearbox under a pair of passenger seats on the offside of the gangway. The Scottish Bus Group companies switched completely to the 31ft 0.875in-long version. Although 40 for Central SMT in 1966, 25 for Scottish Omnibuses and 18 for Alexander (Fife) in 1967 seated 76 (44 up/32 down), Central SMT's final batch later in 1967 were 78-seat buses. All of these had Gardner engines, as did 33 also of this extended length but seating the normal 70 for Eastern National. The final 85 examples (16949-17033) built in the 1968 programme were all for Tilling companies and again all Gardner engined, mostly 6LX, split between Eastern Counties (16), Southern Vectis (3), Thames Valley (7), United (20), Eastern National (20), Mansfield District (5) and Midland General (14). Again Eastern National favoured the longer-tailed body as well as semi-automatic transmission, five of its vehicles being 55-seat coaches.

The very last FLF, and hence the last Lodekka to be delivered, had body 17002, which went to Midland General as fleet number 313 on 4th September 1968. The registration originally allocated was TRB 580F but this was switched to YNU 351G before delivery – three of Eastern National's last batch as well as another Midland General vehicle also received 'G' registrations. Altogether, ECW had built 1,867 bodies of the FLF type and 5,218 of all types of Lodekka from the original two prototypes of 1949/50 in effectively sixteen years of production, representing an average output rate of 326 per year. It had proved both an effective answer to the low bridge problem and an exceptionally successful design in terms of efficiency and reliability.

The position in regard to possible one-person operation of double-deckers had altered completely during the last few years of the Lodekka's production, however, and this, coupled to the general trend to rear-engined layout, had undermined its position, as explained in the next chapter.

At first, the Bristol VR was to be known as the N-type and this accounts for the BN prefix to the fleet number on the first of the two prototypes bodied by ECW in 1966, this one being originally numbered NX.001 with body EX10, for service with Central SMT, that concern's Lodekka buses being prefixed BL. As well as being impressive as a fresh approach to double-deck design, the body set standards that were to be taken up in modified form for ECW bodywork on rear-engined chassis in general. Overall, the design was well-proportioned and neatly executed, with a readily-identified ECW look despite its advanced nature. The length, 33ft 1in, made it among the longest British double-deckers of the time.

Chapter Eight: **Into a new era**

The Labour Government of 1964-70 pursued policies in regard to both public transport and industry which were to have profound effects on bus operators and manufacturers. They altered ECW's position markedly, as well as, ultimately, the products it made. There were also some significant alterations in the regulations affecting bus operation which were to add to the climate of change, the whole adding up to a new era.

The VR prototypes

Even before then, double-deck bus design trends had begun to alter. Leyland had put its rear-engined Atlantean double-decker into production from 1958, Daimler following with its Fleetline, similar in general concept but with distinctive features, two years later. By the mid-'sixties, these models had built up a considerable following among both municipalities and companies outside the Tilling group, largely on the basis of increased seating capacity.

It had been realised that Bristol and ECW would need a new model of similar nature, particularly if they were to compete in the open market. A further factor was the beginning of what was to prove a remarkable change in the attitude to the operation of double-deckers without a conductor. Up to 1st July 1966, this was illegal, and not until a few months previously had any change in this position seemed likely, this perception being the basis of the tendency to favour the adoption of single-deck buses to replace double-deckers, to varying degrees, in many fleets. Even after the law was changed, it took a while before the full potential was realised across the industry and, inevitably, trade union attitudes were at best cautious, but the potential was there.

Two prototype chassis, originally designated the N-type (following on from the M that had been at the 1948 Show) were built by Bristol, these differing from the Atlantean or Fleetline in having the engine, a Gardner 6LX, mounted longitudinally, complete with semi-automatic gearbox, directly behind the offside rear wheels. The rear axle was similar to the Lodekka unit, thus allowing almost as low an overall height with normal gangway layout. The model was to be produced in alternative 33ft and 36ft lengths, anything less being

This view is perhaps the most revealing one in conveying the characteristics of the VR prototypes. Even so, the offside rear position of the engine was by no means obvious, thanks to the very neat way in which the covers giving access to it formed part of the panelling. The vehicle shown here was the second vehicle, with ECW body EX11, which was exhibited in Bristol Omnibus livery on the Bristol Commercial Vehicles stand at the 1966 Earls Court Show. The filler below the driver's signalling window was for fuel, the tank being beneath the cab floor, while that at the rear corner was for the cooling system although it incorporated a front-mounted radiator. Note the high-level engine air intake in the rear dome. Although there was no glazing towards the rear offside of the lower deck, the internal engine cover extended only to waist height, the space above being available to carry passengers' luggage or parcels.

The installation of the Gardner 6LX engine is revealed in this view of the first prototype with the side cover removed and the hinged panel at the rear open.

impracticable due to the necessity of the long rear overhang to accommodate the engine, and there were proposals for both double- and single-deck versions.

In the event, however, the prototype chassis, numbered NX.001 and 002, delivered to ECW on 23rd and 29th June 1966, were both to be double-deckers measuring 33ft 1in long. The two bodies (EX10 and 11 respectively), of generally similar design and having seats for 80 passengers, were completed in time for the Commercial Motor Show which opened at Earls Court on 23rd September that year, thus making a strong showing for Bristol and ECW's first appearance there since 1948. The two vehicles were still at that stage the property of Bristol Commercial Vehicles but EX10, on the ECW stand, was in Central SMT maroon and cream, while EX11 on the BCV stand, was in Bristol Omnibus livery – in other words Tilling green and cream – details such as destination display being to the respective group standards.

By that time it had been decided to call the new model the VR (Vertical Rear-engine), the chassis being renumbered VRX.001 and 002, though the Central SMT fleet number BN331 which was derived from the original N classification was not altered. The 33ft model was briefly called VRS, though later this version became VRLS, but in the event no further examples were built.

The body design gave little external indication of the engine position, and internally there was simply a large box-shaped cover in the offside rear corner of the lower deck. The body had five main bays, with a slightly longer one at the rear, the outlines having an obvious affinity to the Lodekka forward-entrance designs, though the provision of the entrance ahead of the front axle and absence of an engine cover made it possible to use an almost unbroken profile, with two simple basically rectangular windscreen glasses. Both vehicles returned to ECW after the Show but official records show that they were re-delivered to the operating companies on 31st December 1966 and 24th January 1967, both acting as demonstrators for a time until purchased by Bristol Omnibus in May 1970, though VR development and that of ECW double-deck bodywork had followed a different course by then, as described in the next chapter.

(Top of page) The rear of the VR prototypes was very neatly executed, with little but the ventilating grille at the rear of the engine compartment to give a clue to its position. The front was to prove the aspect that changed least when the production version appeared a little over two years later, though the style of windscreen, with the panels separately glazed, was not repeated. These official views of HHW 933D with completed body EX11 are dated 14th September 1966; notes on the back of the prints refer to the chassis as being of type NS6G, chassis number NX.002 despite the Bristol VR nameplate – no doubt it had been so described at the time of arrival.

The same vehicle visited various Tilling group fleets and is seen here in service with Mansfield District not long after its appearance at the 1966 Show.

Single-deck developments

Although the prototype VR double-deckers attracted much attention around the time of the 1966 Show, there was no lack of activity in regard to single-deck developments. Also at Earls Court were two RELL buses, selected from the normal 1966 programme, which itself amounted to only 36 vehicles, most of which were 54-seat single-doorway buses, though three each for Crosville and United had 50 semi-coach seats. One of sixteen for West Yorkshire was selected for use as a demonstrator, being of interest as

the chassis had the Self-Changing Gears semi-automatic gearbox, a new option, though soon to become the usual choice and accepted standard. It had a two-door body (15970), basically to the standard saloon design with a centre exit added, and two pairs of seats deleted, reducing the capacity to 50. It had been delivered to the BCV works on 17th August 1966. Body 15959 from a batch for United was completed to a similar specification for display on the ECW stand at the Show, though this vehicle was returned to single-doorway specification by removing the exit door and increasing the seating capacity to 54 immediately

History was made when West Hartlepool Corporation began taking delivery of five Leyland Leopard L1 single-deckers in January 1967, the first vehicles with ECW bodywork to go to an operator outside the State-owned sector since 1950 (earlier deliveries to the Sheffield fleet qualifying within the latter because they were railway-owned). The body design was a shortened version of the style as had been built on the Bristol RELL. Seen here in service is No.37 (EEF 37D) with body 16052 – the bodies were in Batch 414, otherwise made up of the newly-introduced RESL. A low-set front grille was provided, though the radiator of the Leopard chassis was set back somewhat.

afterwards. Both vehicles had chassis to an interim specification, based on the original RE design thereafter known as Series 1, but with some Series II features.

The share exchange arrangement made with the Leyland group in 1965 as described in the last chapter opened the door to orders from operators outside the State-owned sector. The first to take advantage of this opportunity were two municipalities, West Hartlepool and Coventry, neither of which had ordered ECW bodywork previously. West Hartlepool Corporation's vehicles were five Leyland Leopard L1 models, a chassis type already known to ECW as the basis of Sheffield Joint Omnibus Committee vehicles of 1961, but this time with 42-seat bus bodywork (16049-53) of a design derived from that then being supplied to Tilling companies on Bristol RELL chassis. The bodies were suitably shortened and of 5.5-bay construction, with front entrance and centre exit, the latter occupying part of the fourth bay, only a short distance ahead of the rear wheels. They received D-suffix registration numbers appropriate to 1966 vehicles but were in fact delivered between 13th and 27th January 1967.

The Coventry Corporation order broke new ground in several different ways. It represented the return of Bristol chassis to the open market, the first examples of the short (16ft 2in wheelbase) RESL version of the RE bus chassis and the first examples of RE Series II chassis. The bodies (16080-85) were not unlike those for West Hartlepool in being of 5.5-bay form and in having the mildly rounded rear-end styling with centre emergency door of the early RE style. However, the overall appearance was very different, mainly because of a new almost flat-faced frontal design that was a first indication of ECW single-deck bus ideas over the next three years. This helped to give space for a wider entrance, with four-leaf folding doors, but the return to flat windscreen glass was also influenced by concern at the replacement cost of curved glass, which was quite widespread in the industry at the time. The Coventry vehicles comprised three 44-seat buses with single doorway and three 42-seat vehicles with centre exit, this being in the third bay, and roughly midway between front and rear axles. They were also delivered in January 1967 beginning on the 20th with the

Coventry almost achieved a dead-heat with West Hartlepool as the first non-State recipient of ECW bodywork under the new regime, its first example following the latter's a week later, but its buses were of wider significance as the first Bristol-ECW deliveries of this kind and also in showing how the RE range was about to develop. Most obvious was the squared-off front-end, partly a consequence of a desire to widen the entrance doorway somewhat from the narrow type fitted to earlier RE buses and partly a reaction against the replacement cost of curved windscreens. They were also the first examples of the shorter RESL model, and the first of the modified Series II version of the RE. Seen here soon after entering service is No. 518 (KHP 518E) with body 16082, one of the three single-door 44-seat examples.

The other three Coventry RESL buses were of two-doorway layout, the exit being almost equidistant between the axles. This view of No. 519 with body 16083 shows that the rear retained the curved outline used on previous RE designs as well as on the remainder of Batch 414, in which they were included. The chassis were of type RESL6G, this being RESL-1-104. The 'slice of cake' effect of the almost vertical front-end is also clearly shown.

last one going on the 31st.

During the following months, up to April 1967, further orders for buses on RESL chassis were fulfilled for several Tilling companies, plus a further municipality. These reverted to the bow-fronted style of the early RELL. The 'short' version of the model at this stage measured 31ft 9¼in

overall. Eastern Counties took fourteen, Red & White 21 and Southern Vectis four, all of single-door layout but South Shields Corporation's batch of five were two-doorway 45-seat buses. In effect, these were to an interim design, for the chassis were RE Series II but the bodies of the style associated with Series I.

The first Tilling-group deliveries of the RESL model, all RESL6G built in Batch 414, included four for Southern Vectis delivered in February 1967, this one, seen some years later in NBC corporate livery, being 809 (HDL 24E) with body 16384. These vehicles, and others for Eastern Counties and Red & White built in the same period, were of a transitional design, with Series II chassis but the bow-fronted body then about to be phased out. The chassis of these early vehicles was basically the same RESL1 type as the Coventry buses and the overall length 31ft 9in.

South Shields Corporation was another new customer for Bristol and ECW, taking five RESL6L, with Leyland engines, and having bodywork very similar to the contemporary Tilling standard but with two-door layout, seating 46 and painted in this operator's blue and cream livery. Here No.3 (ECU 203E) with body 16656 is seen near the depot soon after delivery in March 1967.

Another important step in the return of Bristol and ECW to the commercial market was the supply of five RELL6G buses to East Midland Motor Services Ltd in April 1967. This concern, a regular customer for ECW and its predecessors until 1939, was part of the BET group and these were the first deliveries to that combine since 1950. They were also the first deliveries of the RELL in Series II form, the vehicle shown, seen in Nottingham in 1970, being the first of the batch, 0511 (LAL 511E), with body 16664 on chassis RELL-3-102. The body design established what was to be the standard single-deck ECW outline until 1972, with front profile similar to the Coventry RESL batch but with the destination panel leaning forward slightly and a similarly upright rear end. The RELL Series II chassis, with set-back front axle, together with the squared-up body allowed the provision of a much wider front entrance with double folding doors.

What could be described as the complete definitive Series II version of the model appeared in April 1967. The RE range was becoming quite complex, Series II chassis being given serial numbers in accordance with a new system, for in addition to the descriptive type letters RESL, RELH etc, there was a series of five versions, each of which were allocated individual chassis numbers beginning at 101. Thus the Coventry buses had chassis numbers RESL-1-101 upwards, and the new Series II RELL version was RELL-3-101, that chassis, which had been displayed at the 1966 Show, being reserved for bodying as a demonstrator. The first examples to be delivered, however, were on the following five chassis, RELL-3-102 upwards, which received bodies 16664-68 and, in addition to being the first of a new type, were the first Bristol-ECW buses to be supplied to a BET company since 1950, going to East Midland Motor Services Ltd. This was especially significant, since BET was at that date still a private enterprise organisation completely free to buy whatever vehicles it chose. They were 49-seat single-door vehicles, also unusual among buses in having no opening side windows, ventilation being mainly dependent on the roof vents.

The new body outline was largely similar to the Coventry RESL buses at the front, with almost vertical profile and rather shallow flat-glass windscreens, though the destination panel now had a slight inclination forward. At the rear the previous rounded outline was replaced by vertical profile and the roof extended fore and aft to give a peaked effect at both ends of the vehicle.

An RELL Series II demonstrator, with body 16222, also conformed to the new style but was a two-door bus with 35 seats and space to carry 40 standing passengers, a form of vehicle in which there was much interest at the time. It was delivered on 27th May 1967, painted in a distinctive caramel and cream livery, breaking new ground as a Bristol Commercial Vehicles demonstrator as opposed to the previous situation of being in the Bristol operating company's or other Tilling group livery.

Production of RELL Series II saloons on a wider scale got under way that same month, continuing through the year and into early 1968. The 1967 programme included 183 such vehicles, the majority being 53-seat single-doorway buses for various Tilling companies. There were, however, seven two-door buses for Hartlepool Corporation (as what had previously been the West Hartlepool undertaking had become) and five for Luton Corporation as well as five of similar layout for the West Yorkshire company fleet, all of these having 48 seats with varying provision for standing passengers. Two for

The first RELL Series II chassis had appeared at the 1966 Commercial Motor Show, and was then sent to ECW to be bodied as a demonstrator, being returned to BCV in May 1967 with body 16222. It was a two-doorway vehicle, designed to carry 75 passengers, of which only 35 were seated, interest in vehicles of this type for urban service being quite high at the time. In its distinctive caramel and cream livery it was soon to be a familiar sight on such work and is seen here in the demonstration park at the 1968 Show at Earls Court. Numerically, this was the first of the revised-outline bodies, though the East Midland batch shown on the previous page were the first to be delivered, the previous month. In fact, regular production was getting under way, these vehicles being in Batch 418 together with other early RELL deliveries of the 1967 programme.

(Above) The overall shape of the RELL body as modified for Series II chassis became much more box-like. Crosville took three varieties, all on RELL6G chassis, in its 1967 programme allocation of nineteen, the vehicle shown above, ERG596 (NFM 596E), with body 16471, being the first of three with 50 coach seats (of which those over the front wheel arches were longitudinal), and painted in a reversed version of the Tilling green livery – there had been three similar vehicles using the previous type of body shell in the 1966 deliveries. Even with such a specification the weight came out at a modest 7tons 15cwt 2qr. They were delivered in June 1967.

At the other extreme, two of Crosville's buses were supplied with glass-fibre seats for only 30 passengers and standing room for 54, the interior of SRG8 (OFM 8E) with body 16475 being shown. These were intended for experimental use in Runcorn, though it was to be four years before the reserved-track Busway system was opened there in 1971. The view also show the light, almost clinical, internal finish typical of ECW bodies of the time. The remaining fourteen buses for Crosville were to standard 53-seat pattern. The whole 1967 RELL programme of 183 bodies was built in Batches 418-422 in April-December of that year and included 160 for Tilling fleets (16374-8/415-569).

The RELL was beginning to attract municipal orders, Hartlepool Corporation taking seven RELL6L with two-doorway 48-seat bodies (16712-8) built in Batch 420 and delivered in July-August 1967, the example shown being 43 (FEF 43E), with body 16716. In this case the front door was not as wide as now possible, permitting a full-length bay behind it. The unladen weight is shown as 7tons 7cwt 2qr, fairly typical for the type and underlining that this sturdy vehicle was among the lightest of comparable models. Luton Corporation, a new customer, took two batches of five generally similar buses with bodies 16659-63 and 16745-9, also in the 1967 programme.

There was a bewildering variety of body designs on RE chassis in the 1967 period, partly because of the changeover to the Series II chassis and partly because of the addition of the shorter variants. In addition, the RESL chassis production moved after only a few months to type RESL-5, with 6in longer front overhang and these received bodywork to the squared-up outline, 50 being built in the 1967 programme, including 37 for Tilling companies (16330-8/87-414) included in Batches 415 and 416 and delivered in June-November 1967. Most were single-doorway, but Thames Valley took eight of the two-door type in September-October, with seats for 38 and standing room for 27, the example shown being S333 (LJB 333F) with body 16389.

Again, variations of door position and width were evident on bodies based on chassis of the RESL-5 series, Newport Corporation favouring front entrance only, but with wider opening than Thames Valley had specified, for eight RESL6L delivered in September-October 1967 with bodies 16719-26. Seen here is 102 (JDW 302F) – note the array of quadruple headlamps and twin foglamps. Leicester's five examples (bodies 16750-4) delivered in the same months were the same 42-seat capacity but were two-door.

Crosville had seats for only 30, with standing space for 54, though most of that company's batch were single-door buses seating 53 or in some cases 50 with semi-coach seats, a version also found in some other fleets.

During much the same period, from June 1967, a further batch of RESL appeared with body to the same square-cut style. The RELL Series II chassis had an 18ft. 6in. wheelbase instead of the 19ft. of the original type, the difference being due to setting the front axle 6in. rearwards to give more space for a double-door front entrance. The corresponding version of the RESL, with chassis numbered RESL-5-101 upwards, also had the 6in. extra front overhang

as bodied but the 16ft 2in wheelbase did not alter, and thus this version of the type measured 32ft 3¼in overall. Some 50 such bodies were built, going to the Crosville, Thames Valley and United fleets plus two more municipalities, Newport and Leicester Corporations, which received eight and five respectively. There were various combinations of entrance layout and seating capacity, with the 46-seat single-door bus as the maximum seating version.

There was yet another RE variant, the RESH, to prove much the rarest, with only eleven built and only two of these, RESH-2-105 and 106, being bodied by ECW. Contrary to what might have been expected, these were

The rarest variant of the RE was the RESH, of which only two were bodied by ECW, and these to dual-purpose standard. Strangely, the bus body shell was used almost completely unaltered save that the floor was level, permitting the use of forward-facing seats throughout, the front section being raised as compared to that used on the lower-framed RESL chassis. They were for Midland General, though also bearing Mansfield District fleetnames, and on Gardner-engined RESH6G chassis. Possibly the strangest feature was the retention of the bus-like three-window rear end despite the absence of an emergency door in this position, it being on the offside, as seen in this view of 133 (SRB 66F), the first of the pair, with body 16570 – seating capacity was 43. Understandably, they were included with RESL buses in Batch 415, being delivered in September 1967.

not a shorter version of the RELH coach but effectively a dual-purpose derivative of the bus body, though with a uniformly higher internal floor level, permitting all the 43 semi-coach seats to be forward-facing. A full width row of five seats was provided at the rear, with a shallow luggage locker below and the emergency exit was thus on the offside, behind the rear wheels. However, most unusually, the three-window arrangement was retained at the rear. The two bodies (16570/1) were supplied to Midland General in September 1967 – Duple bodied the remaining RESH chassis as coaches. Although the two Midland General vehicles remained unique, the idea of building a bus outline body on a high-frame RE chassis and fitting coach seating was one to be taken up in later years as a

variation of the RELH. This complex series of developments expanded production of RE models with ECW bodywork of various types considerably – the total 1967 programme amounted to 337 vehicles, and that for 1968 to 401, compared to previous annual totals only just exceeding 100. They also exceeded the output of Lodekka models, admittedly winding down, but the RE was starting a spell of forming the major part of ECW's output. The 1967 RELH coach deliveries, completed early in the year, were to the standard Series I pattern, and the RELH-4 variant did not appear until the 1968 programme, the coach body style being virtually unchanged. The wheelbase length of the Series I chassis was 19ft while Series II coaches were on the 18ft 6in version of the chassis.

The 1967 programme RELH coach and express carriage deliveries, all made in the first six months of the year, were all on Series I chassis and introduced no design changes though there were the usual specification variations. Seen here in High Wycombe is one of three for Thames Valley, painted in the South Midland maroon and cream livery for the Oxford-London service, C422 (LJB 422E) with body 16580. It was one of the 43 bodies (16572-614) built in Batch 413 which were officially classified as 'express', basically on the basis of the folding entrance door, the largest number of the group being 25 with 43-seat capacity for United. The fifteen official 'coaches' (16615-8/23-33) were in Batch 412.

Obtaining an order for the RE complete with basically standard ECW body from Ribble, traditionally wedded to Leyland vehicles, was quite an event, even though ECW bodywork had been supplied in some quantity up to 1948. There were ten RELL6L with bodies 17218-27 for this company in the 1968 programme, delivered in March-May as part of Batch 430. By that date, Ribble, as part of the BET group's bus interests, had been sold to the Transport Holding Company, but the order had been placed before this had been agreed. They were to largely standard two-door form, with seats for 41 and space for 31 to stand but a noteworthy feature was the use of parallel-action doors at the centre exit, thus leaving the whole width clear and allowing two passengers to alight simultaneously – permission had recently been given to allow such doors to project beyond the vehicle width when open. The first vehicle, 221 (FRN 221F) is shown. A total of 272 bodies for the RELL were built in the 1968 programme in Batches 422, 430-4, 439 and 441 with deliveries through the year and up to March 1969. They included 202 for Tilling companies (16755-935 and 17137-50/63-9) plus a repeat order for seven for East Midland (16942-8), also from the BET group and in the same position as Ribble. Municipal RELL6L orders comprised six more for Hartlepool (16936-41) another 20 for Luton (17187-96/202-11), plus three for Leicester (17434-6), these latter being two-door 47-seat buses.

Although the Scottish Bus Group companies had been large-scale customers for double-deck bodies from ECW, single-deckers were more rare and the only examples on the RELL were twelve (17401-12) delivered in March-April 1968 to the Alexander (Fife) fleet, generally similar to most of those for Tilling companies with 53-seat capacity and, as usual for SBG, with Gardner engines. The destination and route number display, under a single quite wide but relatively shallow glass, was standard for many SBG single-deckers of the period. Seen here is FE27 (JXA 927F).

The 1968 RELH coaches were on Series II chassis, identifiable by the 6in-greater set-back of the front axle. The body design was not visibly altered in other respects except that the rearmost side window on the nearside was arranged to open as an emergency exit, a change that had first appeared on the later 1967 examples. There was the usual rather arbitrary 'coach' or 'express' split, with 43 classified as the former (17034-48/228-35) and 28 of the latter (17069-96), all in Batches 428-9 and delivered to Tilling fleets in the first half of the year. By that date, the Tilling companies in south west England were adopting a standardised livery layout for coaches, cream or white with a broad coloured waistband. The Bristol concern chose magenta for the latter and had revived the Greyhound name of a former subsidiary for its coaches. With suitable emblem and distinctive 'handwritten' lettering, the overall effect was very effective. Seen here is 2155 (NHW 312F) with 45-seat body 17079 – note that this was counted as a coach though having a folding door.

Possibly the most interesting of the 1968 output of RESL buses were the ten for Brighton Hove & District, that company's first single-deckers since a handful of Dennis Ace 20-seat buses entered service in the 'thirties and the first 'full-sized' single-deckers since Tilling began the Brighton operation in 1915. They were of two-door layout, seating 35 with standing room for 27, and were on RESL6G chassis with Gardner 6HLW engines, the first bus, 201 (PPM 201G) with body 17097 being shown. Although the livery was red and cream it made another break with tradition in not conforming to the usual Brighton layout, the window surrounds being red rather than cream. Despite the novelty, they soon became known locally as 'cattle trucks'.

There were 58 bodies on RESL chassis that year (17097-136/51-62/212-7), all built in Batches 435 and 436, delivered between July and November. Most were single-door buses for Tilling fleets on RESL6G chassis, Crosville taking 30, but South Shields took another six two-door RESL6L, this time, like the rest, with the 'squared-up' body on RESL-5 chassis.

Forming an interlude in the story of development of ECW bodywork on light Bristol chassis, the 20 'stop gap' bodies built on Bedford VAM chassis in late 1967 had, even so, a clear place in the evolution of design. The idea of combining an entrance position ahead of the front axle with a front-mounted engine was not new, but Bedford gained widespread acceptance for it in the 'sixties, though bus bodies on the VAM were quite rare. ECW's design, apart from the windscreen, had a general resemblance to the MW version, by then recently out of production, allowing surplus stocks of parts to be used up. Even so, quite a well-balanced appearance resulted and weight was very modest, at 4tons 12cwt 3qr on this example. Western National, with its steady demand for light buses, took twelve, and 710 (KDV 140F) with body 16649 is seen here – note the injunction to boarding passengers 'Pay Here' on the engine cover, partly visible through the entrance door.

The MW origins of the body design used for the Bedford VAM buses is very evident in this view of Eastern Counties SB663 (NAH 663F) with body 16637, which also shows the reversing light and sign. This was one of the minority on VAM14 chassis with Leyland O.400 engine, soon to become familiar in horizontal form in the LH.

New lightweight buses

Production of the Bristol SU lightweight chassis ceased in 1966, manufacture of the Albion EN250 engine having ended the previous year. The Bristol design team was very busy with the new VR and RE Series II but it was decided to introduce a new light model with a broader spread of size, partly because a demand had arisen from the Tilling group in particular for larger lightweight buses . This was influenced to some degree by the demise of the MW, and

also because Bristol, with its new commercial freedom, was interested in the lightweight coach market, in those days very large and mainly covered by Bedford and Ford. Several Tilling companies had purchased Bedford coaches in modest numbers for duties where heavier-duty vehicles were thought unsuitable, but that maker's VAM model introduced in 1965, had been chosen by both Hants & Dorset and Wilts & Dorset for bus duties.

ECW had not been involved in bodying these vehicles, mainly fitted with Duple coach or Willowbrook bus

The 30ft by 8ft body for the new Bristol LH underfloor-engined lightweight chassis had strong styling and structural similarities to the design for the RE Series II introduced a few months earlier, though with offside rear emergency door and single rectangular rear window. This view of the prototype, on Perkins-engined LH6P-type chassis number LHX.001 and with body EX12, was taken before delivery back to BCV, registered NHU 100F, in January 1968. It carried the maker's names as 'fleetname' and was painted in Tilling green and cream, using a modified layout that was to be characteristic of production LH buses, the body not having the waistband of the RE design. In January 1970, the vehicle was sold to Eastern Counties, becoming LH719 in that fleet.

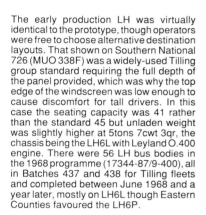

The early production LH was virtually identical to the prototype, though operators were free to choose alternative destination layouts. That shown on Southern National 726 (MUO 338F) was a widely-used Tilling group standard requiring the full depth of the panel provided, which was why the top edge of the windscreen was low enough to cause discomfort for tall drivers. In this case the seating capacity was 41 rather than the standard 45 but unladen weight was slightly higher at 5tons 7cwt 3qr, the chassis being the LH6L with Leyland O.400 engine. There were 56 LH bus bodies in the 1968 programme (17344-87/9-400), all in Batches 437 and 438 for Tilling fleets and completed between June 1968 and a year later, mostly on LH6L though Eastern Counties favoured the LH6P.

bodywork, the latter firm by then a Duple subsidiary, but in 1967 it was decided that ECW would body 20 Bedford VAM chassis, largely as a stop-gap until the new light Bristol became available. The VAM was a front-engined model but the front axle was set back so as to permit the entrance to be positioned ahead of it, passengers turning towards the rear immediately inside the door to pass the engine cover. The arrangement was not ideal when the driver was collecting fares, particularly as the noise level was quite high, even at idling speed.

For it, ECW built a batch of bodies (16634-53) derived from the MW design and of similar size, with seats for 41 passengers. The front end was quite different and more in keeping with the RE bus designs, but with a windscreen having its lower edges sloping downwards slightly from the centre. Below it, a very plain almost rectangular grille was provided for the radiator. Western National was the main recipient, with twelve, these being on the standard VAM5 chassis with Bedford's own 5.4-litre diesel engine. Four for West Yorkshire had VAM14 chassis, with the Leyland 400 engine of 6.54 litres then offered in certain Bedford chassis, and Eastern Counties had two of each type. They were delivered between September and November 1967.

Shortly before any of these were delivered, ECW received the first example of Bristol's new LH (Light Horizontal) chassis, on 19th August. This was of what had been conventional mid-underfloor-engined layout but constructed to a simple and light specification. There were to be three lengths, respectively LHS, LH and LHL, the first of these intended for bodywork about 26ft long and thus roughly comparable to the SUS in length, the 'plain' LH catering for lengths around 30ft and the LHL intended as a basis for a light 36ft (11-metre) coach.

Of these, ECW was to concentrate mainly on the LH, destined to be built in larger numbers than any of the earlier lightweight buses, though the LHS was also to be built in fair quantity, mainly in the mid-'seventies. The prototype, chassis number LHX.001, was of the LH6P type, with Perkins H6.354 5.8-litre horizontal engine, which continued to be an option until 1972 and favoured by a fair-sized minority of operating companies. The more usual choice was the LH6L, with Leyland O.400 6.54-litre engine in its horizontal form, much as had been fitted to later versions of the Tiger Cub model. The chassis incorporated various proprietary units, including a five-speed synchromesh gearbox made by Turner and similar to that in contemporary Bedford and Ford coach chassis.

There was quite a degree of variety in the modest initial LH body production run, In addition to the buses, there were six bodies in reversed livery and with 41 coach seats (17413-8) on LH6P chassis for Lincolnshire, maintaining a tradition of coachstyle lightweight Bristol-ECW models for this fleet that had begun with the SC. They were included in Batch 437 and delivered in July 1968, the first vehicle, 1651 (GVL 907F) being shown (left). In the same month Lincolnshire took the first of three of the shorter LHS6P buses built in Batch 438 of which the last arrived in October.
Hants & Dorset took a single LH6L, 828(NLJ 817G), in November 1968 with body 17352 which had the distinction of being of two-door layout, a feature which was in favour for that company's intake of light single-deckers, the seating becoming 38 but with standing room for up to 19 – the idea was followed up in later deliveries for this concern. The photograph (right) shows it in later years, by then renumbered 1521, with windscreen modified in similar fashion to the subsequent standard, as was applied to many of the early production examples.

The prototype body (EX12) was 30ft long and 8ft wide, with 45 seats, similar in outline to that used on RELL Series II models, but with its emergency door at the offside rear and a single almost rectangular rear window. The completed vehicle had an unladen weight of 5 tons 6 cwt and was delivered to BCV on 4th January 1968 for use as a demonstrator in a slightly different version of Tilling green livery, with cream window surrounds later adopted as standard for the type but with 'Bristol ECW' lettering.

Production began soon afterwards, the 1968 programme LH vehicles being mostly almost identical to the prototype. There were 62 of these, plus three for Lincolnshire of the shorter LHS type, these having four full-length bays rather than the 4.5 of the LH, the seating capacity being 35 in this case. The first to be delivered (17353) was for Southern National, on 11th May 1968 but production of this programme continued well into 1969. One LH, for Hants & Dorset, had a centre exit door, the seating capacity being reduced to 39 though the vehicle also accommodated up to 18 standing passengers, that company having used a similar arrangement for its Bedford VAM buses.

New owners

While all this development of ECW's products was occurring, immense change in the structure of the bus industry, on both operating and manufacturing sides, was afoot. During 1966 and 1967, the policy gradually took shape. Particular attention was paid to the major urban areas around big cities and it became clear that some form of local passenger transport authorities would be created. At the same time, moves were afoot to press the BET group to sell its bus-operating interests in Britain to the Transport Holding Company and thus allow a State-owned national operating concern to be formed. This latter was announced on 22nd November 1967 and although it did not take legal effect until 1st March 1968, the implications for both Bristol and ECW were immediately clear, in that the BET operating companies, running about 11,000 buses between them, would come into the same State-owned family. Even so, it is important to bear in mind the degree to which the RE in particular had impressed BET engineers and management. The delivery of ten RELL vehicles with

At the Commercial Motor Show in October 1968, a modified LH body was exhibited, with windscreen extended upwards, overcoming the problem of inadequate forward vision for tall drivers and, to general agreement, also improving the appearance – it was to act as prototype for later production from the 1969 programme. The vehicle was the final example in the 1968 programme batch of eight LH6P for Eastern Counties, LH 692 (RAH 692F), with body 17351.

ECW bodywork to Ribble, traditionally one of Leyland's most consistent customers, beginning in March 1968, just as the transfer to THC went through, was based on choice made before the deal.

Meanwhile a new Transport Bill was introduced, in December 1967, providing for the creation of the National Bus Company to take over and control the THC's bus subsidiaries in England and Wales – in effect the Tilling and BET bus groups. These interests included the shareholding, then 75 per cent, of Bristol and ECW. In Scotland, the Scottish Bus Group was to form part of a new Scottish Transport Group. New Passenger Transport Executives, controlled by Passenger Transport Authorities formed of representatives of local authorities, would take over existing municipal bus systems in Merseyside, the area around Manchester (known as South East Lancashire North East Cheshire, generally abbreviated to SELNEC), Tyneside and the West Midlands. This was passed, becoming the Transport Act 1968, receiving the Royal Assent on 25th October of that year. The National Bus Company was to become operational on 1st January 1969, though co-operation between the headquarters management teams of Tilling and BET bus groups, in the knowledge that the formation of NBC was a virtual certainty, had begun almost as soon as the agreement to the takeover of BET by THC had been announced. Even so, the companies from each group continued with their own purchasing agreements for new buses at first. Quite apart from existing orders placed by BET, which had not favoured as much standardisation between its operating subsidiaries as Tilling, it took some time before the two organisations' methods and structure could be unified.

While all this was going on, a series of mergers in the motor industry was in progress, some seemingly little related to bus manufacture but ultimately to produce as complete a change as had occurred on the operating side. One was the merger in December 1966 of the British Motor Corporation (which had been formed in 1952 and whose main business was the manufacture of Austin and Morris cars) with the much smaller Jaguar car concern. The former had virtually no bus involvement, but Jaguar had taken over both Daimler and Guy, in 1960 and 1961 respectively. The resulting British Motor Holdings group was short-lived, as in May 1968 it merged with the Leyland Motor Corporation to form the British Leyland Motor Corporation. At that stage, this was still a private-enterprise organisation, though the merger had the support of the Government.

As a result, almost the whole of the heavy-duty bus chassis manufacturing business came into, or was closely linked with, the new BLMC. For the time being, the 25 per cent Leyland shareholding in both Bristol and ECW passed to BLMC, though this was soon to increase, with wider consequences, as described in the next chapter.

Coventry Corporation Transport's order for eighteen bodies on Daimler Fleetline chassis played a key part in the sequence of development of ECW double-deck body design for rear-engined chassis. Numbered 16727-44, they were included in the 1967 programme, built in Batch 423, just before the final FLF models, and delivered in February-May 1968. The general affinity to the two VR prototypes built just over a year previously is obvious, yet there were two fundamental differences – the transverse rear engine position and consequent shorter rear overhang, and the full-height build. ECW approached the design in its usual 'Meccano set' way, by in effect lifting most of the body structure, and shortening it at the rear. Coventry's livery of the time, a pale cream and dark maroon, made a positive virtue of the broad band surrounding the bus at upper-deck floor level, and helped to produce a striking overall effect.

At the rear of the Coventry Fleetlines, the 'bustle'-style engine cover was as supplied by Daimler, and ECW followed the established convention for rear-engined double-deckers in building the rear of the upper deck to overhang this. The FLF-style foreshortened rearmost side window gave the requisite length and was thereby perpetuated into the next generation of design. The location of the stairs opposite the centre exit was neatly accommodated within the same bay. Coventry had established a system of pre-paid tickets and these vehicles were among the earliest British double-deckers designed from the start for driver-only operation. Another noteworthy feature was the provision for ventilation. with sliding vents for most of the lower deck windows and small hinged vents at the rear – upstairs, the familiar hinged vents at the front were omitted in favour of a ventilator in the front dome, and rotating cylinder fittings were provided in alternate side windows. Both this view and that on the previous page show No. 23 (KWK 23F), numerically the first of the batch in Coventry's fleet but with the second ECW body, 16728 – unusually for ECW, body numbers were not in sequence with fleet numbers, which was very often the case with bodies on non-Bristol chassis.

Coincidentally, a batch of vehicles was going through ECW's works which illustrated some of the effects of these changes, though by no means the largest so far as ECW was concerned. Coventry Corporation had followed up its initial order for single-deckers on Bristol RESL chassis by one for eighteen double-deck bodies. The chassis for these were to be Daimler Fleetline CRG6LX models – Daimler chassis, built in Coventry, had been favoured by the local municipal fleet for many years and the Fleetline had become the top-selling double-deck chassis in Britain, outstripping the Leyland Atlantean.

These bodies (16727-44) were also the first double-deck bodies supplied to a non-THC operator since the supply restrictions had been lifted. The ECW body structure as developed for the VR was adapted to the Fleetline chassis, there being two main differences. The Fleetline's transversely-mounted Gardner 6LX engine produced a shorter overhang than on the 1966 Bristol VR prototypes, this being accommodated by use of a very short rearmost window on the upper deck, in much the same manner as the FLF. The chassis was supplied with an external rear engine cover, giving the 'bustle' effect common to both the Atlantean and Fleetline models in standard form.

Although the Fleetline was capable of being built to low overall height, Coventry favoured full-height layout

and so the major part of the body structure was, in effect, lifted bodily as compared to the prototype VR buses and also the standard production version then in course of design and described in the next chapter. The driving position was at a similarly low level to the VR and so the windscreen design was similar, with a deeper band of between-decks panelling above it, a characteristic that was subsequently found on other later full-height rear-engined double-deck ECW bodies. The vehicles were designed from the start for one-person operation, with four-leaf front entrance and centre exit doors. The stairs were located opposite the exit, and seats for 72 passengers (45 up 27 down) were incorporated. The vehicles were in Coventry's cream and maroon livery of the time.

Delivery began in February and was completed in May, the month in which Daimler had become a BLMC group company. Hence ECW was linked in a cousin-like relationship with it, even though the link with Bristol remained far stronger in practical as well as financial terms. Although Coventry Corporation's bus undertaking was not at first affected by the provisions of the 1968 Transport Act, it passed to the West Midlands Passenger Transport Executive created by it as a result of local government reorganisation on 1st April 1974.

By chance rather than design, the entry into service of the first Bristol VRT models virtually coincided with the coming to life of the newly-created National Bus Company on 1st January 1969. Western National 1058 (OTA 292G), with body 17317, was one of ten for this fleet in the initial modest programme of 55 similar bodies (17264-318, built in Batches 427 and 440) on the VRTSL6G chassis. The first of WNOC's batch, 1050, with body 17309, had been delivered in December 1968, when the Tilling group was part of the Transport Holding Company; the next two, 1051/2, with bodies 17310/1, were the first two bodies to leave ECW for a subsidiary company of NBC, on 2nd January, and the rest, including the vehicle shown (on chassis VRT-SL-124), later that month.

The derivation of ECW's body design from the two VR prototypes of 1966 is clear, but the shortening at the rear related to the transverse engine position echoed the effect of the Coventry Fleetline design of a few months earlier shown on the opposite page, though the VRT eliminated the 'bustle' effect with the engine cover designed to merge neatly into the body outline. At that stage there was no attempt at an NBC corporate livery, ex-Tilling fleets continuing their traditional shades of red or, as in this case, green, and cream.

Of practical importance to operators was the degree of commonality to the FLF body, simplifying the stocking of spares, and repair work. The main side window bays and pans, (at 51½in centres) the upper-deck front windows, that unmistakable rearmost side window and the rear emergency window were all carried over, unchanged, from the FLF to the VRT in this original flat screen form. The windscreen glass was also common to the flat front RE bus in its shallow windscreen form. This 'Meccano set' approach accounts for the odd rearmost main bay of 54½in, doubtless considered acceptable in view of the standardisation of so much of the rest of the structure.

Chapter Nine: **Early days with NBC**

The transfer of most of the major bus operating companies in England and Wales, previously almost equally divided between the Tilling and BET groups, to the new National Bus Company took effect on 1st January 1969. Their brief spell together as subsidiaries of the Transport Holding Company had no visible effect on them so far as the general public was concerned, and in most respects this continued to be so during the first years of NBC. At that stage there was a deliberate policy of not publicising the group as such, putting the emphasis on the local companies, so diversities of livery and lettering continued, especially among the ex-BET fleets.

There was considerable activity aimed at achieving unity in methods, and in setting up a group programme for new vehicle deliveries, but it would not have been possible at that stage to achieve standardisation across the group, even if a standard had been agreed. The British Leyland factories were geared to produce a variety of types and indeed were hard pressed to meet the industry's orders

quite apart from the practical limitations on capacity at Bristol and ECW.

The VR in production

However, despite the variety of makes, models and bodybuilders, again particularly on the ex-BET side, the double-deck deliveries of ex-Tilling companies switched to the Bristol VR, complete with standardised ECW body, at almost exactly the beginning of the NBC era. This was coincidental, for the development of the production version had been continuing since the prototypes entered service early in 1967.

It had soon become clear that the main demand was for a vehicle nearer the traditional 30ft length than the longitudinal rear engine position used in the prototype allowed. Because of the limitation on overhang in relation to wheelbase, the minimum length possible for that layout was approximately 33ft. so a transverse-engined version of the chassis was produced, designated VRT, as first announced in July 1967. The previous layout continued to be offered but now called VRL, both types subdivided into short and long versions as well as 'high' and 'low' frames, at least in theory, for some variants offered were not built. Two wheelbase lengths were standardised, applying to both types, 16ft 2in and 18ft 6in, these giving overall lengths slightly over 30ft and 33ft respectively for the VRT but 33ft and 36ft for the VRL. The chassis was designed to suit 8ft 2½in wide bodywork.

In July 1968, the Government introduced a new bus grant scheme to encourage fleet modernisation and, in particular, the introduction of vehicles suitable for what was still officially described as one-man operation. To qualify, vehicles were required to conform to a series of specifications covering various types of single- and double-deck bus. The only double-deck designs included had transverse rear engines and were of 9.5 or 10 metre nominal overall length – in practice a range of dimensions near these figures was permitted – and the Bristol VRT was among the models which conformed. The VRL did not, but as will be seen it found application as a double-deck coach, for which bus grant was not available, as well as an export chassis.

The VRT model went into production without any prototypes of this variant being built. The Gardner 6LX or the very similar but updated 6LXB were the most usual power unit, and Self Changing Gears semi-automatic transmission was standard. The first public showing was

of a VRT-SL-6G chassis, destined for Eastern National, displayed at the Commercial Motor Show in October 1968. This was chassis VRT/SL/101, eventually receiving ECW body 17264. This version was set to become the most popular type of VRT, but the bodied VR at that Show was a prototype of the VRL version in coach form with Leyland 680 engine, type VRL-LH-6L, a prototype for W. C. Standerwick Ltd, Ribble's coaching subsidiary.

The exact date on which the order was placed for this remarkably advanced vehicle, particularly in regard to its bodywork, has not been established. However, it seems inescapable that discussions on the possibilities, at least, must have begun well before the sale of BET's bus interests to THC had been agreed in November 1967. The order for the body appeared in ECW's 1968 production programme issued on 19th January 1968 and the chassis was delivered to Lowestoft on 30th January 1968. The specification of the chassis would have had to be settled and at least the general layout of the body, completely new in form, agreed before work on even the chassis could begin.

This was one of the star vehicles on display at that Show, its striking appearance set off by a cream and maroon livery. Ribble and Standerwick had used double-deck coaches for many years , using a special version of Weymann-bodied Leyland Atlantean since 1959. The VRL coach prototype, body 17197, was 36ft long and 14ft high, overall, with seats for 60 passengers, of which 42 were on the upper deck and 18 below, the rear of the lower deck being devoted to luggage space. All seats faced forward and offered virtually unobstructed forward vision, the

Even by the standards of over a quarter of a century later, the lines of the double-deck coach body on Bristol VRL chassis built in time for display at the 1968 Commercial Motor Show can only be described as outstandingly clean and striking. Standerwick was the Ribble concern's coach subsidiary, and had been running the Lancashire-London express services with Leyland Atlantean 30ft-long double-deck coaches using the standard MCW highbridge body shell, quite well-appointed internally but of utilitarian outline externally, so the new ECW design, longer and lower as well as of more shapely lines, was even more impressive by comparison. The livery of cream and cherry red suited it well. After delivery and on the production vehicles which followed up to 1972, the front door was marked 'No entrance', passengers using the double doors ahead of the rear axle.

The head-on view of the first of the Standerwick double-deck coaches on Bristol VRL chassis, with body 17197, was just as impressive as that from the side in its neat detail design and smooth lines. This photograph is dated 16th September 1968, having been taken just after the vehicle was completed and before it travelled to Earls Court for the Show, at which it was a star exhibit. The chassis was number VRL-LH-102, the second production VRL, and the fleet number, 50S, followed a system used by Ribble at the time, in which vehicles in the Standerwick fleet had an S suffix, although this had been dropped when the production examples were built. The Chief Engineer of Ribble, Harry Tennant, played a major part in the development of these vehicles in conjunction with Bristol and ECW and took an understandable pride in the end result, which stood up well in terms of layout and appearance against the early ventures in double-deck coach design then occuring in Germany.

stairs being to the rear of the twin centre entrance and exit doors, though there was also an outward opening door at the front.

Curved glass was used for both the driver's windscreen and the front of the upper deck, in both cases with a slim centre division, and at the rear of the upper deck there were curved corner windows set in a manner rather like the RELH coach. The body had five main bays, though the rearmost window on the upper deck was similar to a full-length bay in visual effect. The vehicle was delivered after the Show, on 5th November 1968, soon beginning extensive tests to be followed by delivery of production batches in 1970-72, building up to a fleet of 30 vehicles.

The design of the production vehicles remained almost unchanged from that of the prototype. The fuel tank was repositioned to the nearside, and the rear access door to the luggage compartment at the rear of the lower deck was no longer glazed. The lower-deck emergency door was moved to a position just behind the offside front wheel, splitting one of the window bays and somewhat spoiling the tidy appearance of that side of the vehicle.

The 1970 order for eleven (18303-13) was delivered between December of that year and February 1971, followed by ten (18972-81) in August-November 1971 and the final eight (19847-54) between May and July 1972.

Meanwhile, work was in hand on the first VRT buses. The first to be delivered were 83-seat buses of the 33ft.-long VRT-LL variety for Scottish Omnibuses Ltd, which used the fleetname Eastern Scottish, (17319-43), delivered between 19th November and 21st December, 1968. The

Good forward vision was a feature of the seating arrangement in both decks of the VRL coaches for Standerwick, and in this and many other respects, they were directly comparable to the accepted double-deck coach standards of a quarter century later. The view of the upper deck shows the arrangement of the staircase, the top of which emerged at about two-thirds of the length from the front. In both decks overhead racks were provided for coats and light luggage and incorporating the Jet-vent outlets for the forced-air ventilation system. These views are of 51 (LRN 51J), the first of the production batch, with body 18303, completed in December 1970.

The most noticeable difference introduced on the production version of the VRL coaches was the relocation of the lowerdeck emergency door to a position just behind the front axle, giving a rather 'bitty' effect, with a succesion of odd-sized windows. The final coach of the last batch, 79 (PRN 79K), with body 19854 was painted in the newly-introduced corporate all-white National coach livery before delivery on 19th July 1972. The name 'Standerwick' was reduced to miniscule lettering on the upper deck directly over the front axle. The overall effect lost much of the stylish look of the original livery, but the whole batch were similarly repainted, passing to National Travel (North West) in 1974. By that date problems of unreliability with the transmission and a suspicion of instability when running at speed arose after an accident, even though the latter was not initiated by the coach, had put these vehicles under a cloud, but their contribution to the evolution of the double-deck coach remains clear.

The first Bristol VRT chassis to be bodied were also the only examples of the 33ft-long VRT-LL type to receive ECW bodywork. There were 25, built in Batch 426 and delivered in November-December 1968, for Scottish Omnibuses Ltd. The upper deck was very like that of the two VR prototypes of similar length built two years previously, but the lower deck differed both in providing for the tranverse engine position, and also because of the longer wheelbase, the rear axle being moved back, reducing the rear overhang. The seating capacity was 83, with 47 on the upper deck, and unladen weight was quite modest in relation to a vehicle of this size at 8tons 18cwt, as signwritten on the side of AA286 (LFS 286F) seen here before delivery,

first of the VRT-SL for various Tilling companies began to be delivered in December 1968, continuing until April 1969.

By the 31st December 1968, twelve VRT-SL buses had been delivered to Tilling companies:- Eastern National 3001 (with body 17265), Thames Valley 500 (17269), West Yorkshire VR1-7/9-10 (17276-82/4-5) and Western National 1050 (17309), these thus having the distinction of being the only examples for English companies to pre-date the activation of NBC.

Thus, effectively, the introduction of the VRT to fleets in England and Wales almost exactly coincided with the inauguration of NBC. The original plan had been that there were to be an initial run of 83 for ex-Tilling companies (17236-318) but the first 28 ordered by Bristol Omnibus were cancelled, that operator having decided upon a policy of using more single-deckers for urban routes, using the two-doorway RELL. The largest delivery was to West Yorkshire (34 vehicles), followed by Western National (10), Eastern National (5), United Counties (4) and Thames Valley (2). In practice, the Bristol Omnibus allocation was diverted to United (20 vehicles) and Brighton Hove & District (8, these being legally owned by Southdown, into which fleet BH&D had been incorporated, even though still run as a separate undertaking), given fresh body numbers as part of the 1969 programme. Two of the

Western National vehicles, with bodies 17310/1, were the first deliveries to a subsidiary of the newly-formed NBC, leaving the works on 2nd January 1969.

The standard ECW body for the VRT-SL had a general resemblance to those on the two 1966 prototype VR buses so far as the front and main side sections are concerned, with five full-length bays, each generally having windows with top sliding panels. The rear end was shorter, and thus an effect very similar to the FLF body was produced at the rear of the upper deck, with very short D-shaped window on each side. In a sense, this could be regarded as a spin-off from the general resemblance in terms of dimensions of the VRT to the Atlantean and Fleetline, since it had also been evident on the Coventry Fleetlines built earlier in 1968, as mentioned in the previous chapter. Although the chassis was supplied complete with engine cover, this differed from those of the Leyland Atlantean and Daimler Fleetline in being designed to be incorporated into the rear panels of the body, with an internal shelf rather than the 'bustle' effect. A single window above it lined up with that in the emergency exit at the rear of the upper deck and the overall effect was much neater than had been achieved by competitive makes. The lower deck emergency exit was moved to the offside, just behind the rear axle, and there were other minor revisions to the design, such as the use of a windscreen with slim centre dividing strip instead of two completely separate panels. The overall length at this stage was 30ft 3in and the height 13ft 8in, this being the low-height bus grant standard.

The VRT-LL version was generally similar, but with an extra half-bay on the lower deck, this having the emergency exit on the offside, and relatively long upper-deck rearmost side windows. In this respect they resembled the 1966 prototype, the main part of the body structure being almost the same. As had been the case on the Lodekka buses supplied to the same fleet, opening windows were provided only in alternate bays. As it turned out, this batch of vehicles was to be the only delivery of ECW bodywork on the VRT-LL chassis, although the latter was specified by some operators who chose other makes of bodywork.

Also delivered in November and December 1968 were further double-deck bodies for municipal operators, this time Leyland Atlantean of which ten PDR1A/1 were supplied to Leicester (17177-86) and four PDR1/1 to Ipswich (17198-201). These were of 74-seat front-entrance layout, based on the same full-height body shell with overall height of approximately 14ft 6in, this being the full-height bus grant standard, similar to the Coventry Fleetlines supplied earlier in the year but lacking the centre-exit doorway and having the stairs in the position usual on rear-engined buses of this layout, immediately behind the driver. There were several minor differences between the two operators' specifications, notably in regard to opening windows. A delivery of seven Daimler Fleetline CRG6LX to West Bromwich (17170-6) made in April-

Just as the first bodies on Bristol VRT chassis were being built, ECW fulfilled two municipal orders for normal-height bodies on Leyland Atlantean chassis. Ipswich Corporation, though an East Anglian local authority, had not hitherto chosen ECW bodywork, for many years favouring AEC chassis and Park Royal bodywork, though East Lancs had secured some body orders. In 1968, a complete break was made, with four PDR1/1 with 14ft 6in-high bodies based on much the same structure as the Coventry Fleetlines, but with single doorway and stairs behind the driver. This view of the first of the batch shows the separately-glazed windscreen panels, a feature reminiscent of the 1966 VR prototypes.

The ten Atlantean buses for Leicester were basically similar to the Ipswich examples, but incorporated variations in detail, such as the omission of the hinged vents above the front upper-deck windows, and what had become the standard form of windscreen, with slim central dividing strip, though both incorporated the ventilator in the front dome as chsen by Coventry. The Leicester livery was not unlike that of Coventry in colours, though much simpler in form of application. This view shows the marked difference in height of the windscreen to that of the driver's and other lower-deck side windows on these vehicles, conveying how most of the structure was lifted by comparison with the standard 13ft 8in-high VRT.

The air of change pervading the industry in 1968-9 is conveyed by the story of this bus. The chassis was the second VRTSL, number 102, and originally was to have been one of 20 for Bristol Omnibus, but that company decided to adopt the RE in 'standee' form for the expansion of its one-man-operated services, and eight of the batch were switched to Brighton Hove & District. Its body, one of the first 40 VRTSL bodies built in Batch 427, was at first numbered 17236, and would have been the lowest-numbered VRT body, was renumbered 17751 and transferred to the 1969 programme before delivery in December 1968.

The vehicle is seen when ready to leave, with fleet number 93, fleetname and legal lettering for BH&D, and in that undertaking's style of red & cream livery. However, it had been decided that as the two operating companies in the Brighton area no longer belonged to different groups, BH&D would be merged with Southdown on the same date, 1st January 1969, as

NBC came into operation. So the batch received Brighton registration numbers rather than East Sussex, as had been appropriate to the BH&D's Hove headquarters, 93 becoming OCD 762G, and the legal lettering was altered to show Southdown's name, though the batch retained BH&D livery and fleetname, which continued until 1971. This view shows the original form of engine cover for the VRT, almost devoid of any form of grille, apart from two small rectangular openings below the rear window.

The 1969 VRT body programme amounted to 157, of which 88 (numbered 17751-838) were for NBC companies, all on VRTSL6G chassis as was to remain standard practice until 1974. Apart from the special case of the BH&D/Southdown vehicles illustrated above, they were for companies that had been in the Tilling group, though historically Midland General had come into that fold via the nationalisation of the electricity industry in 1948, and still indicated its Balfour Beatty origins in its attractive blue and cream livery. Seen here is 317 (BNU 681G) with body 17783 – note the Harrington-bodied Barton coach passing in the opposite direction.

May 1969 were closer to the standard VRT body shell as supplied to ex-Tilling fleets, as they were of low-height type, though a slightly recessed windscreen as well as the bustle rear-end gave a different appearance. These remained in West Bromwich ownership for only a few months, passing to West Midlands Passenger Transport Executive when it took over all municipal buses in its area on 1st October 1969.

The 1969 and 1970 programmes generally continued the pattern established by the new Bristol chassis and ECW body designs introduced in the previous year or two, with only minor changes in design, for the most part. The upsurge of interest in orders for ECW bodywork on other than Bristol chassis died down in 1969, though the one order of this type in that year's programme was noteworthy in being for four single-deck bus bodies on the rear-engined AEC Swift chassis for Lowestoft Corporation.

The local municipality's fleet was one of the smallest in the country, with about 20 buses, so its orders were modest, ECW having last been favoured for the 1947 batch of Regent II buses. The Swift bodies (18060-3), were 45-seat two-door saloons based on the RELL design, but with minor changes, most notably the lack of a front grille (the Swift having its radiator at the rear offside) and the use of a single rear window.

A change in design applicable to both LH and RE bus bodies was deepening the windscreen. The original LH version was particularly shallow and the 1968 Show example, for Eastern Counties, had differed from that year's standard in having the top edge raised to line up with that of the side windows. That alteration was adopted as standard for the 1969 programme, amounting to some 128 LH and twelve LHS, all for ex-Tilling companies and far larger in numbers than for previous lightweight types. A

A change of policy caused the 'express' version of bodywork on the Bristol RELH chassis to become based on the bus body shell, much as used on the RELL chassis, from the 1969 programme, instead of being almost identical to the coach version, as hitherto. With polished wheel trims and a coach-style livery, an appropriately functional design for medium-distance express work was produced. United Counties had a long history of favouring equivalent versions of previous models, and its 284 (TBD 284G) with body 17734 was the last of eight RELH6G delivered in May-June 1969 – this operator had an increased demand for such vehicles as a consequence of taking over the former Birch Bros service from Kings Cross to Rushden. There were thirteen bodies in all of this type in the 1969 programme (17722-34), all built in Batch 456, the balance of five going to Bristol Omnibus. The higher chassis provided the basis for a level floor line, in much the same way as had been produced with the two RESH coaches built for Midland General in 1967 and shown on page 28. In this case there were coach seats for 49 passengers, all facing forward. At the rear, a single rectangular rear window was provided, the emergency door being on the offside, though there was also an emergency window at the nearside rear.

This view also shows the taller windscreen adopted for all RE bus-outline bodies from the 1969 programme. This was similar to the alteration made on the LH, but as the base of the screen, appreciably lower on the RE version, remained unaltered the effect created was more marked than on the similarly modified LH.

corresponding change was applied to the RE bus body shell that year, giving a more striking effect as the drop in waist level at the front was greater on this type. The Lowestoft Swifts had this style of screen, standardising on it for repeat orders in 1971 for four more and a final two in 1973, although the RE bus design had moved on again in this respect meanwhile.

The RE was climbing towards its peak in terms of ECW body production in this period. Output of RELL bodies in the 1969 programme was 305, the shorter RESL going through a period of falling interest, adding 27. However, similar in terms of being of bus outline, though with single rear window, and emergency door on the offside, near the rear, were thirteen bodies to an express design with coach seating and based on the RELH chassis. This was a change of policy from the previous practice of making the express body a derivative of the coach version. There were also 54 RELH coaches, of the now-familiar design virtually

Bodywork for the Bristol RELL had become ECW's main product, and the 1969 programme total of 305 of this type was built in Batches 441-6, 451 and 458 and delivered in a period up to March 1970. They included 238 ordered by ex-Tilling companies (17505-714, plus 18064-91, the latter a reflection of Bristol Omnibus's switch to single-deckers). Typical of the single-door examples, mostly seating 53 as in this case, was Eastern Counties RL707 (VAH 707H) with body 17580, seen in service in this view, – it was one of nine similar buses. The foregoing all incorporated the revised windscreen and shallower front dome (the latter altering in the same way as the LH, the two models being similar in this area) for which a 1968-programme body for Crosville, 16810, built in February 1969, had been the prototype – it was that operator's SRG71 (XFM 71G).

Lowestoft Corporation remained faithful to AEC chassis, thus introducing ECW to the Swift rear-engined model, though the 45-seat two-door body was closely related to the contemporary RE design. This view of No. 1 (YRT 895H) with body 18060 shows the absence of front grille, due to the rear-mounted radiator of this model, for which the grille is just visible at the extreme rear of the offside, with emergency door also occupying part of that bay. As was quite often the case with small orders, these bodies were not batched. The chassis were of the 2MP2R type with AH505 engine. The Lowestoft livery was chocolate and cream.

Two-door bodywork had grown in favour, and of the 1969 programme RELL output, some 172 were of this type, including 30 for Ribble (17437-66) and all 37 of those intended for municipalities (17715-21 for Hartlepool, 18102-21 for Leicester and 18127-36 ordered by Luton, though after that undertaking was sold to United Counties they were delivered to the latter). However, the remaining 115 were for ex-Tilling fleets, among which five for Midland General, including 137 (DRB 304H) with body 17637 is seen here. As well as the unusual livery and the provision of full destination display at the rear, these had two-leaf centre exit doors rather than the more usual four-leaf type. This resulted in a doorway some 6in narrower than standard, albeit within the standard bay. Similar vehicles went to Mansfield District, Bristol Omnibus Co, Hants & Dorset and Crosville at least.

The RESL was going through a period of decline after its quite promising start, only 27 being bodied (17839-65) in the 1969 programme, all in Batch 447 and delivered in May-June of that year. All were on the RESL-5 chassis and incorporated the modified front-end as on the RELL version. The largest group, fifteen for Bristol Omnibus, were also of interest in being on RESL6L chassis – Leyland engines were becoming less of a rarity in former Tilling companies. The first of the batch, 500 (THU 346G) with body 17839 is seen here, looking distinctive with scroll-style fleetname and rear wheel disc.

At first, the Scottish Bus Group was an enthusiastic buyer of the VRT, following up its initial 1968 order for 25 VRTLL6G by taking 69 VRTSL6G (with bodies 18001-59/92-101) out of the 1969 programme total of 157 bodied by ECW. Among them were 20 for Central SMT, including BN373 (NGM 173G) with body 18017 seen here in Motherwell in June 1970, a little under a year after delivery. An early modification was to fit a cooling fan to the engine and grilles on the sides of the engine compartment, even though the radiator was at the front. There were more fundamental problems, however, mainly with the transmission, leading to a remarkable series of exchanges, in which all the SBG's VRT buses were swapped for FLF-type Lodekkas from former Tilling fleets, mostly in 1973-4, though Alexander (Midland)'s fifteen, the last VRT Series I buses, went after only just over a year's service, in 1971.

unaltered since 1963. Thus the RE formed the basis of over half ECW's output, the RELL alone outnumbering that year's VRT figure of 157 (all on VRTSL6G chassis) by nearly two to one.

The emphasis on single-deckers and consequent fall in double-deck demand within NBC fleets was even stronger, for 69 of the 1969 output of bodies on VRT chassis went to Scottish Bus Group companies, the largest number, 39, going to Western SMT, together with 20 for Central SMT and ten for Scottish Omnibuses to join the latter's 25 VRT-LL. This Scottish enthusiasm for the new model was short-lived, and only fifteen more of the type went to an SBG subsidiary, (18824-38) being built for Alexander (Midland) as part of the 1970 programme, delivered in January-February of that year – they were also to be the last of what became known as the Series I version of the model to be bodied by ECW. The Scottish companies had taken only twelve ECW-bodied RE models, these being RELL buses for Alexander (Fife) supplied in 1968. Thus the Bristol-ECW combination fell out of favour north of the border, though the RE chassis was favoured for Alexander-bodied

coaches and ECW bodywork, basically very like the standard low-height VR pattern, was chosen for many of the Daimler Fleetline chassis which were favoured for much of the group's double-deck needs through the 'seventies. The 1970 programme included 81 ECW examples, mostly with 77-seat capacity, the largest batch being 35 for Central SMT.

Thus the 1970 output of ECW-bodied Bristol VRT models was only 82, of which a mere 67 (body numbers 18181-247) were for NBC companies and, at first, ordered for ex-Tilling fleets. However, ten which had been intended for Brighton Hove & District were delivered in green and cream livery to the main Southdown fleet, while three at first allocated to Southern Vectis were diverted to City of Oxford Motor Services Ltd, a former BET company which thereby became a new user of Bristol-ECW vehicles. These three vehicles, with bodies 18207-9, were also of interest in having the first VRT Series II chassis (VRT/SL-2-101 to 103) also used for the rest of this batch as well as being the first buses to be ordered via NBC, the first two being delivered on 11th April 1970.

The Scottish Bus Group had been including some Daimler Fleetline double-deckers in its new vehicle intake since 1965, but from July 1970 deliveries began of the combination of this chassis with ECW bodywork. Clearly the disillusion with the VRT did not extend to the body, which was very largely as on that chassis, taking advantage of the capability of the Fleetline as a basis for low-height bodywork. The rear end accommodated the usual 'bustle' type of Fleetline engine cover, the lower build giving the illusion of making it seem larger than with a normal-height body. There were some 81 in the 1970 programme (bodies 18248-302/798-823), built in Batches 462 and 478, delivery continuing until June 1971. Alexander (Midland) MRF97 (UMS 97J), with body 18807, was among the first to be delivered, in the summer of 1970. The unladen weight of 9tons 1cwt 3qr was about 7cwt more than the VRT.

The Bristol VRT, meanwhile, had graduated to its Series II phase, of which 67 were bodied in the 1970 programme. The grilles at the sides of the engine compartment were now standard, a modification applied retrospectively to all Series I models, and sets of louvres were also added in the body sides above them. The vehicle shown, the City of Oxford company's 901 (OFC 901H) with body 18207 was one of the first three buses ordered via NBC and also has chassis number VRT-SL-2-101, the first Series II VRT – it still survives as an open-topper. They were finished in that concern's distinctive crimson and duck-egg green livery, which by then had been slightly simplified from its earlier form, eliminating the two-tone red effect. They had been diverted from a Southern Vectis order.

The VRT Series II chassis incorporated various modifications in the light of experience, among them being a revised engine cover, with only the centre section of the rear panel opening in the manner shown. The original 1968 design had the entire outer face hinged so that the complete engine and gearbox assembly was exposed, but this made it more prone to minor damage and consequent difficulty in closing properly. This view of Oxford 901 also shows how the cover was designed to fit snugly over the Gardner 6LX or 6LXB engine, as well as the unmistakable ECW look of the rear of the body. The 1970 programme VRT body production was built in Batches 460, which included the final Series I buses built for Alexander (Midland) completed in January-February 1970 as well as the first Series II buses delivered from April, and 461, deliveries being completed by December.

Among the modifications incorporated in the Series II VRT, though also found on some earlier examples, was the provision of an engine-driven fan within the engine compartment, in addition to the electrically-driven fan forming part of the front-mounted radiator, and accordingly there were grilles on each side of the vehicle at the rear. The body, although still at that stage virtually unchanged, was now quoted in some published material as 30ft 6½in length rather than the previous 30ft 3in, but careful measurement of actual vehicles indicates that there was no change at that point, and the longer figure may have anticipated the later changes to the BET type of windscreen, not adopted for production until two year's later.

When NBC was formed, the position of Bristol & ECW as its major suppliers seemed assured, with the ex-Tilling companies firmly committed not merely by their position with the majority shareholding which had passed to NBC but woven into the organisation, with over 30 years of close liaison with operating companies through the Tilling group which seemed almost certain to be expanded. What was more, the Bristol RE in particular had won the respect of the BET engineers and several of its companies were set to adopt the model even if the takeover had not occurred. NBC was indeed to continue as the main user of Bristol and ECW products, but not in the way most observers expected.

The Leyland influence grows

In July 1969, it was announced that agreement had been reached between British Leyland and NBC to the effect that the former's shareholding in Bristol Commercial Vehicles and ECW would be increased from 25 per cent to 50 per cent. Also announced at that time, and closely related, was the formation of the Leyland National Co Ltd, set up as a joint venture by BL and NBC to produce integral-construction single-deck buses at a new factory to be built at Workington in Cumberland. These plans were formalised with effect from 1st January 1970, when Bus Manufacturers (Holdings) Ltd was set up with equal BL and NBC shares and took over the entire capital of BCV, ECW and the new Leyland National company.

Significantly, a Leyland nominee was appointed as Chairman and in many respects BCV and ECW had been brought into the BLMC empire. It had been made clear from the start that the Leyland National was to be built in large numbers, using many of the techniques of the mass-production car industry, largely replacing the entire range of the BL group's single-deck bus models. The NBC was by far the largest purchaser of such vehicles in Britain and the supply of its needs by the new factory was an essential part of making the whole project an economic proposition.

This history is not intended to judge the merits or shortcomings of the Leyland National, but its introduction signalled the forthcoming demise of the Bristol RE and hence the ECW body for that model. Indeed, it significantly altered the structure of the manufacturing industry in relation to full-sized single-deckers in general, causing widespread cuts in production. At ECW, there was to be a change of emphasis, for double-deck production was to be expanded and the role of the LH bus also tended to grow in importance, with coaches also figuring in the output from time to time.

However, all this took time to develop. Prototypes of the Leyland National were built in 1969-70, and the example at the 1970 Commercial Motor Show was virtually in production form, but deliveries to operators did not begin until 1972, initially on a modest scale, though growing rapidly later that year. The story of the Leyland National and the Workington factory is told in *Beyond Reality: Leyland Bus – the twilight years*; by Doug Jack, published by Venture Publications Ltd.

Up to 1966, the RE had been better known as a coach than a bus, and the visual success of the standard body for the RELH during a period of rapidly changing tastes can be judged by the fact that the original production design of October 1963 remained almost completely unaltered until the last example of this style left the factory on 1st May 1970. There were 54 in the 1969 programme (17467-504/735-50), all built on the Series II RELH-4 chassis in Batch 455 and delivered by April of that year, including Southern National 1458 (OTA 630G) with body 17488 seen here – it was in Royal Blue livery but not one of those bearing the latter as fleetname – there were seventeen for this company and Western National, the two companies being administered as one unit. The Gardner 6HLX continued to be the standard power unit, giving an average 13.5mpg and giving a normal 300,000-mile life between unit changes for Southern/Western National. A final 44 (18137-80) were built in Batch 459 in the 1970 programme, and again the Southern/Western National fleet was the largest recipient, taking 22, though the last to be delivered, on 1st May, was one of five for United, 1285 (BHN 585H) with body 18163.

Swan song for the RE

Although it became clear that the future of the Bristol RE was limited from the first announcement of the Leyland National in mid-1969, its output, and in particular that of the RELL complete with ECW bodywork, continued to rise. The ECW body output figures for the RELL in the 1969, 1970 and 1971 programmes were respectively 305, 348 and 441, only falling back to 125 in 1972. The shorter RESL bus figures for the same four years were 27, 9, 161 and 14. When it is remembered that in this period the RELH express body was based on the RELL outline and added respective figures of 13, 23, 29 and 44, it becomes clear that bus-outline body production was at a high level, with figures of 345 for 1969, 380 for 1970, a remarkable 631 for 1971 and then 183 for 1972.

Demand for single-deck buses was high during this period from the operating industry as a whole, but Bristol and ECW reached an exceptional peak of production volume and market share with the RE in 1971. There seems every reason to believe this level of success would have continued for much longer had not the Leyland National venture intervened.

The basic design continued unchanged until the spring of 1970, after the first 40 of that year's programme output of the RELL had been built, when the deep flat-glass windscreen gave way to a new front-end style, using the curved-glass windscreen favoured by BET for its standard designs since 1963. This was not just a visual acknowledgement of the 'marriage' of BET and Tilling, nor even mainly an endeavour to improve appearance, but was influenced largely by the reduction in the problem of

The 1970 RELL programme began with the 'tall-screen' version of the flat-fronted design introduced the previous year, of which 40 were built (18338-46/94-405/54-62/537-43/610-12), all produced in Batch 468 and delivered between February and May of that year the fragmented numbers being because they were parts of larger orders for various fleets. The nine for Eastern Counties were on RELL6G chassis, and including RLE865 (WPW 865H) with body 18458 seen here, were in reversed livery and had semi-coach seats for 50 passengers. The fleet prefix indicates that they were regarded as 'express' by the operator, but ECW classified them simply as stage carriage.

Another major change in design for the standard ECW body for RELL and related models first appeared in April 1970, when the BET type of curved windscreen was adopted for this type, gradually spreading across all standard ECW bus-outline bodies. To avoid reducing the entrance door width, the front of the body was extended to accommodate the bowed contours and an increase of length to 36ft 5in resulted. In addition, the layout of the floor was altered, replacing the previous two-step entry to the front platform and gently ramped gangway with adjacent seats on plinths. Instead, a third step immediately behind the platform was used to give access to a floor which was virtually flat over the mid part of its length.

Some 308 bodies were built to this specification in Batches 469-476, the numbers filling in the blanks left between the final flat-front deliveries quoted at the foot of the opposite page to complete the run of numbers 18314-661 making up the total of 348 RELL bodies in the 1970 programme, though deliveries were not completed until September 1971. There were 136 two-door examples of the BET screen version, of which 61 were for the various fleets of Bristol Omnibus, including the example shown, C1180 (YAE 443J) with body 18361, which was exhibited at the 1970 Commercial Motor Show. The cream and green livery distinguished buses equipped for operation without conductor. The seating capacity was 44, and the vehicle incorporated an 'electronic eye', housed in the aperture in the roof above the first nearside window, the narrow fin on the top of the roof nearby housing a radio aerial, both part of the equipment for a control system for Bristol City services. These buses were on Leyland-engined chassis, but the Gardner was chosen elsewhere, save for three of West Yorkshire's delivery. Most were for ex-Tilling fleets, but also included 23 for West Riding, a former independent that had sold out to THC in 1968, and a further seven for Hartlepool Corporation.

The RESL also received the revised front-end, but was yet again the subject of other dimensional changes, this time affecting the whole body structure. The chassis was now of type RESL-8, with 16ft 6in wheelbase and the body length increased to 33ft 9in, some 1ft 5.75in more than the previous version. The body structure now had 54in pillar centres rather than 51in, which eliminated the need for two shorter bays at the rear. Only nine such bodies (18662-70) were built in the 1970 programme, all in Batch 477 and delivered in August-September, though they could be counted as precursors of the peak year of RESL output that followed. The vehicle shown was the first of three for Southdown, number 600 (TCD 600J) with body 18662, though the only one in that operator's livery, the others being for the Brighton Hove & District section.

internal reflections at night which the BET design gave. In order to accommodate it without affecting the entrance width, the overall length was increased from the precise 11-metre figure (36ft 1in) to 36ft 5in, and special dispensation from the new bus grant specification was obtained to allow this. Most examples continued to go to ex-Tilling fleets, with single-doorway versions slightly in the majority – seating capacity of 53 being typical in such cases – though dual-doorway versions were supplied to quite a number of fleets. Bristol Omnibus received 61 (plus nine of the previous outline) of such buses for its various

ECW's output of bodywork for the Bristol RE reached its peak in the 1971 programme, with some 631 examples, all of bus-outline. Even though deliveries were not completed until November of 1972, the rate of output of around 400 per annum made it the largest-scale output of a standardised single-decker in Britain at the time. The RELL 1971 programme figure was 441, built in Batches 484-494 and 507, of which 423 (bodies 18982-19158/63-408) were standard examples for NBC companies, though these now included more of the ex-BET companies, an example being the 33 for Northern General Transport and its subsidiaries. There was also some variety in specification, though one of the most popular variants was the 53-seat single-door version, represented (above left) by Cumberland 289 (ARM 389J) with body 19128, delivered in April 1971 and the first of fourteen on RELL6L chassis for that fleet. Also widely favoured was the 44-seat two-door version also illustrated being East Midland's O551 (GVO 551K) with body 19182, dating from December 1971 – it was one of fifteen on RELL6G chassis which were licensed to carry up to 23 standing passengers. In addition, there was also a further batch of seven for Hartlepool Corporation (19409-19), also two-door but seating 46, and two replacement bodies, 19677 for United Counties, and 19846 for West Yorkshire, both replacing 1968 originals.

constituent fleets, favouring 44-seat capacity, though there were other versions, some with specific provision for a proportion of standing passengers.

The RESL bus and RELH express versions also received the BET screen from the 1970 deliveries, though the small total of nine RESL, all delivered in the late summer of that year, also differed in a change of wheelbase, increasing by 4in to 16ft 6in, on the RESL.8 type chassis, the overall length of the bodied vehicles going up by a greater proportion from 32ft 3¼in. to 33ft 9in The body design was altered quite extensively to achieve this, with wider pillar spacing.

Three two-door buses went to Southdown (two for the Brighton Hove & District section) and six single-door buses for Bristol.

The 1971 RELL and RESL programme was notable mainly for its size, which led to a reversion to delays in completion, deliveries continuing right through 1972, but in general continued as in 1970 so far as design was concerned. The increase in numbers was largely related to a much broader spread of deliveries within NBC, which now included many more of the ex-BET companies – although other makes of chassis and bodywork were still being purchased, the ECW-bodied RE, and generally the

RELL, had been established as NBC's standard single-decker, even if only briefly. However, there was also a repeat order for seven RELL from Hartlepool Corporation, plus ten RESL for Merseyside PTE, these latter vehicles being a diverted order originally intended for Potteries Motor Traction.

A noteworthy non-standard order was one for nine RELL single-door buses for the North Western Road Car Co Ltd completed in April 1971 (19668-76). They had a special low-profile bow-shaped roof contour to enable them to pass through a low bridge at Dunham Woodhouses under the Bridgewater Canal on routes linking Altrincham to Warrington and Lymm. These vehicles replaced ten Bedford VAL twin-steer six-wheelers with Strachans bodywork of similar roof design dating from 1964. There were also two instances of new RELL bodies being built to replace damaged originals, the first instances of this type for several years, in both cases on 1968 chassis, one being for United Counties and the other for West Yorkshire, all of these being included in the production batches for that year.

The 1972 programme was the last to include RELL buses for NBC subsidiaries, although deliveries did not

Among the most unusual-looking ECW bodies of this period were the nine on RELL6L chassis with special roof contour for North Western. The shape was dictated by that of a low bridge under the Bridgewater Canal and had first been seen on Bedford VAL buses with Strachans bodywork which the RE batch replaced. No.375 (SJA 375J) with body 19670, is seen in company with one of its predecessors in October 1971, when six months old – three months later the batch passed with part of North Western's fleet to Crosville, following the break-up of the former company's activities as a result of the SELNEC PTE take-over of routes running within its area. The interior of the same vehicle shows the effect from within, the normal parcel racks being omitted, as well as the internal seating layout, with luggage carrier at the nearside front – note the window mounted low in the emergency door to aid reversing. The roof structure proved weaker than the standard form, and the vehicles had relatively short lives.

The express body for RELH chassis continued in the bus-outline form basically as introduced in 1969, but had received the BET windscreen from the 1970 programme, in which 23 such bodies (18763-85) had been built in Batch 464 and delivered in May-July. They had narrower entrance doors than those of other years. The 1971 programme deliveries were made earlier in the year, between February and April and amounted to 29 examples (19567-95) in Batch 499. They included East Midland C292 (EVO 292J) with body 19580, one of a pair for that fleet, seen in Nottingham in June 1971. It seated 49, like most of those mentioned, though Lincolnshire's four of 1970 were 47-seat vehicles. The largest single order in these two years was twelve for United in 1971, though United Counties took nine in each year.

The RESL also had its peak year in 1971, with 161 in the programme, built in Batches 495-498 and delivered between March 1971 and November 1972. Clearly the extra length put the type into a category with wider appeal, with passenger capacities of up to 67 with standing passengers and yet more manoeuvrable than the RELL. Body numbers 19416-566 originally had all been intended for NBC subsidiaries but the first ten out of an order for 26 for Potteries Motor Traction were diverted to meet an urgent order from Merseyside PTE (19486-95), these being made up by an added ten (19679-88) for PMT, itself one of the new users of ECW products brought via the formation of NBC.

Another of these was Aldershot & District Traction Co Ltd, also an ex-BET company, which ordered 20 RESL with two-door bodywork seating 40 and with standing space for 20. This was a colourful period so far as ECW output was concerned, and A&D's distinctive two-tone green and cream suited the design well, as conveyed by this view of 644 (YHO 635J) with body 19544, one of the first dozen, delivered in May-September 1971. From 1st January 1972, A&D became merged with Thames Valley Traction Co Ltd to form The Thames Valley & Aldershot Omnibus Co Ltd, using the fleetname Alder Valley and the last eight went to that fleet, which at first adopted a dark red livery before giving way to NBC poppy red.

begin until November and were not completed until almost a year later. The front panel was modified, now being in one section from windscreen level downwards, easily detachable for repair, eliminating the 9½in fixed valence at the bottom used hitherto. It was 2in shallower at the bottom, the foglamps being moved up slightly to straddle the decorative strip. In other respects, the design remained unchanged. This did not apply to that year's small RESL batch, completed some months earlier. After that, ECW's small-scale production of RE bus bodies was basically for municipal operators, as explained in the next chapter.

The original production RELH coach design of 1963 had continued virtually unaltered until 1970, appearing for the last time in that year's programme. Output was never very large, the largest total in a yearly programme being the 54 of 1969, but the vehicles offered a high standard of comfort and refinement to passengers, as well as being popular with most drivers.

The RELH proved to be the last version of the RE to remain in production for NBC. A new coach design was to appear on some of these chassis, as described in the next chapter, but the express version, with body based on the

During the spring of 1972, preliminary work on NBC's new corporate image was in hand, much of the early application to vehicles being carried out at ECW under the supervision of Norman Wilson, who was responsible for it as design consultant to NBC. This RELL for Midland General, with body 19203 built as part of the 1971 programme in Batch 492 and delivered in May 1972, was in a short-lived dark blue and white version of the corporate style which was not adopted as standard.

The small 1972 RESL programme of fourteen bodies was very largely a spillover from that of the previous year. The largest buyer was Aberdare Urban District Council with seven single-doorway 44-seat examples (19792-8) on RESL6L chassis, of which No. 36 (LTG 36L) is seen here. They were in an all-maroon livery, with only the cream glazing rubber as relief – it was being phased out at that time in favour of grey, to better suit the NBC corporate livery. Three more similar bodies (19799-801). but with 47-seat capacity on RELH6G chassis were for another south Wales municipality, Gelligaer, all being delivered in August-September 1972. The balance of four, the last for an NBC fleet, were for Keighley-West Yorkshire, delivered a little earlier, in April-May 1972, though they had later body numbers 20243-6. All were built in Batch 507, which somewhat unusually also included a batch of RELL, seven examples (19780-6) for Hartlepool in the 1972 programme and delivered during July-August of that year.

The 1972 programme included the final production run of 113 RELL bodies for NBC fleets (20130-242) built in Batches 508-510, which incorporated a modified design of front panel, detachable as had been standard for many years but now extending down to include what had hitherto been a separate valance and slightly shallower in depth. It is thought that there had been plans for a 'Series III' RELL, with revised pillar spacing, as for the RESL, but the advent of the Leyland National stopped further development. Most were single-doorway buses, but five of Western National's order for ten RELL6G, delivered in February-April 1973, were of the two-door type with 48-seat capacity for Devon General, by then run as part of the WN concern. The NBC corporate livery had become firmly established, and 225 (ATA 225L) with body 20207 was in poppy red. A noteworthy feature was the provision of wheel discs at both front and rear, these being in grey as also laid down for the corporate style – vulnerable to minor damage and generally discarded quite rapidly. The unladen weight is quoted as 7tons 15cwt 2qr, slightly more than early RELL types but still well below the Leyland Nationals then coming into service and, especially with the Gardner engine, these vehicles gave much better fuel economy than their successors.

The interior of Western National 2763 (ATA 763L) with body 20212, one of the five for this fleet that were of single-doorway 53-seat type, delivered in July 1973, conveys the look of the typical interior of the type towards the end of production, rather plain in terms of finish, and with the type of parcel racks, a little reminiscent of railway practice, that were typical of the period. The gangway, step-free once the front platform had been negotiated, is noteworthy. The 1972 programme total of 125 bodies for RELL also included the seven for Hartlepool mentioned above as well as five (19787-91) for Colchester Corporation included in Batch 510 and delivered in April-May 1973.

The 1972 programme construction of the RELH with express body, delivered in March-July of that year, retained the same design as the 1970-71 batches illustrated on page 49 – there were 44 (19802-45) built in Batch 504 and delivered, all in 'pre-corporate' liveries, between March and July 1972 – they retained the 1971-style front panel. The 1973 programme vehicles, of which there were 43 (20331-73) in Batch 522, delivered between March and October of that year, were in the NBC 'local coach' style, red or green below the waist and white above, as shown by United Counties 216 (KRP 216L) with body 20371, seen here at Victoria Coach Station, London. The revised front panel with foglamps at the level of the decorative strip was incorporated in this Batch.

The final year for the RELH express body was 1974, when 37 were built (21402-38) in Batch 540, delivered in July-November. The design was unchanged but the use of the all-white National coach livery for some, seen here on Eastern Counties RLE742 (GCL 344N) with body 21430, underlined the degree to which these vehicles offered good standards of comfort, certainly for medium-distance journeys. Two other vehicles of the same batch were the last new RE vehicles for an NBC fleet.

RELL shell but with higher floor line internally and coach seating remained in favour, acquiring the BET-style windscreen from 1970 and going on until 1974. In the early years no corresponding version of the Leyland National was available and hence this RE variant continued. The 1973 programme included 43 examples, with revisions to the front panel, as on the 1972 buses, and other minor revisions of exterior lighting equipment – of these, 20 were for United. The final batch, included in the 1974 programme, consisted of 37 examples (21402-38), divided among seven NBC companies, ranging from ten for United down to one for Jones of Aberbeeg, a former independent which had decided to sell out to NBC but which had continued as a separate business under Red & White management. The last RELH Express bodies to be delivered were Eastern Counties RLE 746 and 747 with bodies 21423 and 21426, supplied on 22nd November 1974. They were also the last new RE models for NBC subsidiaries.

The choice of ECW to body the AEC Sabre rear-engined coach exhibited on the AEC stand at the 1970 Commercial Motor Show came as quite a surprise, for hitherto ECW's relationship with the British Leyland Motor Corporation had been rather muted in terms of public display. By that date, the increase in BLMC shareholding to 50 per cent had come into effect, and the association with a promising-seeming new model raised the possibility of ECW coach bodywork finding a broader market than hitherto.

The vehicle was taller in overall proportions than then usual, disguising its 12-metre length but the overall shape was in line with contemporary thought among the leading British coach designers. This was partly due to the use of front and rear screens of the type used in Plaxton's epoch-making Panorama Elite design of 1968, and the combination of large side windows with marked 'tumble-home' gave a similar overall effect, even if the detail trim did not have quite the same self-assurance. This view of body 18786 shows it just prior to delivery from Lowestoft on 11th September 1970.

Chapter Ten: **'Double-deckers and lightweights'**

As already indicated, the arrival on the scene of the Leyland National altered the balance of much of the British bus bodybuilding industry, not least Eastern Coach Works and its range of products. The winding down, under Leyland influence, of the production of bodywork for the well-regarded Bristol RE threatened to remove nearly 75% of its output as it stood in 1971.

The obvious move was for ECW to build more double-deckers, and this did occur from the early 'seventies, largely as Bristol VRT output increased, though also on Daimler Fleetline and Leyland Atlantean chassis, NBC adding orders for both the latter types, generally for ex-BET companies, to the 'mainstream' VRT contracts. However, the volume of NBC demand for double-deckers, inevitably the main basis for such expansion, was not at first as great as the lost output of the RE single-decker for this sector had been, and it was not until the mid and, especially, the late 'seventies that this began to take off more dramatically.

The other main plank in the raft of alternative products was the Bristol LH lightweight single-decker, and the advent of the Leyland National, both heavier and more sophisticated than earlier generations of single-decker used by major company fleets, left a broader opening for a simpler model with lower day-to-day running costs.

A coaching excursion

It might have been expected that coach body manufacture would be another line adopted more strongly by ECW in the 'seventies, for the firm had built many fine vehicles in this category over the years. In the event this proved to be so only to a very limited extent, though beginning quite dramatically, and in a way which seemed to hold fresh promise.

Just before the formation of BLMC in 1968, AEC had developed a new V8 diesel engine which was announced as the British Leyland 800-series. It was of 12.1-litre capacity, giving 247 bhp and intended largely for goods vehicle use but a new coach chassis, called the Sabre, with this powerful engine mounted at the rear appeared in left-hand-drive form at the 1968 Commercial Motor Show.

The front and rear views show how the Plaxton-type screen glasses helped to give an illusion of the Sabre coach having curved sides. Neither AEC nor ECW badges were fitted – this was the era when the British Leyland 'L' was all-pervading. The small 'letter-box' opening between the headlamps was an air intake for the heating and demisting system. The V8 engine – literally an Achilles heel for the whole project, due to inadequate development – dictated a high-set rear seat and hence the high floor level.

The use of the same glazing and similar outlines at front and rear is clearly evident in this view. The radiator was at the offside rear, as was standard for AEC's rear-engined single-deckers, and louvres in the engine cover indicate the power unit's location. This was ECW's first 12-metre coach.

Mid-underfloor luggage accommodation was provided, extending under the chassis frame but rather cramped by it – the technique of cutting the frame as was later to become standard practice on DAF and other coaches had not then been developed. The front hatch housed the spare wheel.

The interior incorporated overhead racks inset from the side windows to avoid impeding passengers' view and incorporating the Jet-vent forced-air system outlets.

Little more was heard until the 1970 Show, when a right-hand example with an ECW body (18786) to a completely new design was displayed on the AEC stand. It was of 12-metre length (ECW's first example), but seated a modest total for a vehicle of this size of 46 passengers in individually reclining seats.

The vehicle broke new ground in several respects. One, quite significant in its implications, was the use of ECW bodywork on a demonstration vehicle for British Leyland, especially a seemingly promising one and a clear sign of the firm being regarded as part of the Leyland family. At that date the policy of playing down individual non-Leyland make names was also beginning to take effect and the coach displayed only the group's corporate L symbol, rather than the AEC badge that might have been expected.

In terms of design, there was a distinct echo in the overall outline of a new body design that had been introduced by Plaxton at the 1968 Show and indeed the windscreen glazing was common to that Panorama Elite model. However, ECW did not adopt the curved-glass side windows which were the main new feature of the Elite, even though the 'tumble-home' effect of inclined side windows was stronger than usual and gave an impression quite similar in the overall look of the coach from a distance.

The vehicle was quite high-built, partly because the rearmost seat needed to be mounted high to clear the engine, but also no doubt to give adequate luggage space in the side lockers under the floor in the absence of a boot at the rear. In consequence it did not look as long as other 12-metre coaches, then just beginning to gain limited favour although the maximum legal length had been increased from 11 metres in September 1967.

It is interesting to note that the display lettering on the window near the entrance read 'Eastern Coach Works –

aluminium alloy body', the latter having been normal for ECW for over 20 years but perhaps mentioned here to draw a distinction from Plaxton's design, which was of composite construction, using wood framing with metal reinforcement at that date. Duple was to introduce what almost amounted to an Elite look-alike in 1972 which was metal-framed, but ECW was justified in its touch of oneupmanship in 1970.

As it turned out, the Sabre was never put into production, the V8 engine proving troublesome to develop to give satisfactory reliability and causing the project to be dropped despite its obvious promise – BLMC was beginning to face a severe financial crisis. The prototype coach was sold off to Best Coaches of London W.5., registered CBU 636J. There can be little doubt that the collapse of this project also tended to delay plans for the adoption of the body design, also promising though it was.

A production coach based on the prototype body designed for the AEC Sabre appeared, but not until the 1972 season. This was for the Bristol RELH chassis and not so high-built as the Sabre, though comparable to most coaches entering service in major fleets at the time. It began as a true 11-metre design, but it was found that seat spacing at a 49-seat capacity using ECW's traditional and very comfortable wood-framed coach seat was too tight, though legal. A version with 11.23-metre length solved this, the extra length being achieved by 'thickening' the rearmost pillar.

The layout of the RE chassis, with gearbox ahead of the rear axle, allowed provision of a small boot at the rear, behind the engine, though again side lockers were the main location for luggage. A slightly bolder front peak allowed room for a larger destination display.

The overall result was an attractive vehicle and, with hindsight, at first thought it seems rather surprising that it was not adopted for wider marketing, including perhaps

Derived from the Sabre body in terms of styling was the design introduced for the Bristol RELH, though the end result differed in several respects, perhaps most notably the lower build, closer to ECW's original design for the RELH. There were 57 in the 1972 programme built in Batches 505 and 506 and delivered in June-November of that year. Some were in 'pre-corporate' liveries, among them City of Oxford Motor Services Ltd No.71 (GBW 71L) with body 19878, one of three RELH6G with 11-metre body for this fleet, seen in the style with dual Oxford-South Midland fleetname – South Midland had begun as an Oxford-based fleet but had come under Thames Valley control in the Tilling era, before coming under the COMS wing as part of NBC. Also taking the 11-metre type of this body were Crosville (10), Northern General (14), Alder Valley (3) and Trent (4).

sales to independent operators. However the imminent arrival into large-scale production of the Leyland National was undermining the future continuity of output of RE chassis of any type, doubtless discouraging any ambitious marketing plan.

In the event, 57 were produced in the 1972 programme (bodies 19855-911), all for NBC subsidiaries and largely on the RELH6L chassis with Leyland engine though a minority took the Gardner version. Delivery began with one for Crosville on 16th June 1972, continuing until November, the largest single batch being one of fourteen for Northern General Transport. Seating capacity varied from 42 to 49 according to the type of duty for which they were intended – entrance doors in some cases were of two-piece 'glider' type and in others the single type pivoted so as to swing largely inwards, as used on the Sabre. The earlier deliveries were in individual company liveries but the later ones were painted from new in the all-white NBC corporate coach livery.

In 1973, this body design was adapted to Leyland Leopard PSU3B/4R mid-engined chassis for a batch of ten bodies (20321-30) ordered by the SELNEC (South East Lancashire, North East Cheshire) Passenger Transport Executive then operating in the Manchester area, delivered between March and June of that year.

No deliveries of ECW coach bodies to NBC were made in 1973, but the 1974 programme included 28 more examples (21439-66) on the RELH chassis for five NBC fleets, supplied in April-June, Crosville being the largest recipient, with a further nine to add to its previous ten. These proved to be the last ECW coach bodies to be built on Bristol chassis.

Two repeat orders for operation in and around Manchester were supplied to the Greater Manchester PTE, as the former SELNEC undertaking had become, these being for two further batches of six vehicles each, with bodies 21499-504 and 21555-60, almost identical to their predecessors, delivered almost without break in March-September 1975. ECW's coach bodybuilding activities then ceased until 1981/2.

The further 28 coaches built in Batch 539 on Bristol RELH4 chassis in 1974 were all of the 11.23-metre type. They were generally similar to the 1972 examples though the polished mouldings were simplified in accordance with NBC requirements. Seen here is Crosville CRL306 (SFM 306M) with body 21452, one of the nine vehicles supplied to that fleet – these were officially classed as dual-purpose, with the wide 'bus grant' entrance, along with three for Oxford and six for Red & White, though the eight for Trent also had similar doors. Two ordered by Eastern National but operated by National Travel (South East) had the single pivoted door, their duties not making them eligible for grant – they were on RELH6G chassis, the others being RELH6L.

Further deliveries of Leopard coaches were made to Greater Manchester PTE, which was the successor to the SELNEC undertaking. There were two orders, each of six vehicles, the first, on PSU3B/4R chassis belonging to the 1974 programme and built in Batch 557 and the second, on PSU3C/4R, in the 1975 one and in Batch 565, though delivered almost continuously during 1975. These were all of the 11.23-metre type, seating 49, and were more plainly finished than the SELNEC batch, the livery having altered to all-orange save for the roof and the side mouldings simplified to suit – 83 (HNE 643N) with body 21501 of the earlier batch is shown. Some structural failures of the rear boot framing were experienced, but these were repaired by GMT without reference to ECW – significantly in view of the subsequent B51 story. Seven of these coaches were rebodied by Duple in 1981/2.

Slow growth in double-deckers

In 1971, RE single-decker output was at its peak and the production programme for that year included a relatively modest total of 129 Bristol VRT models (bodies 18843-971), delivered between March of that year and 16 months later, plus one replacement body (19678) completed in July 1971 for a Western SMT VRT of which the original body had been damaged beyond repair. Of the new vehicles, 106 were as built in the 1970 programme, with single

doorway, 39 seats upstairs and 31 down, though noteworthy as including the first of the type for Ribble, East Midland and Devon General, all ex-BET companies.

The balance of the 1971 programme VRT models, with bodies 18949-71, were of two-door layout, noteworthy in retaining the lowheight construction, rare in two-door double-deckers of other makes. The 70-seat capacity was retained by including an extra row of seats upstairs, bringing the upper-deck total to 43, thus allowing the lower-deck total to drop to 27 to accommodate the extra

After a period of emphasis on single-deckers for its city services, Bristol Omnibus made a modest return to double-deckers with eight VRT but they broke new ground in being of two-door layout – the first, C5002 (EHU 361K) with body 18964, being seen when ready for delivery in December 1971. Maintaining the standard 70-seat capacity on a low-height bus of this form was only achieved by a complex lower-deck layout, in which only ten seats of the 27 faced forward at floor level, the remainder being raised by 9in, twelve being longitudinal over the wheel arches plus five at the rear. These vehicles, and fifteen similar buses for Southdown of which delivery began the following month, were built in Batch 482, which also included 23 standard single-door VRT, the remainder of the 1971 programme output of this type being in Batches 480 and 481.

The first production deliveries of ECW double-deck bodies with the BET type of windscreen were, appropriately, made to former BET companies by then part of NBC. They appeared on Daimler Fleetline buses ordered by concerns which were already users of that model, though the choice of ECW bodywork on that chassis and also the Leyland Atlantean was an indication of a stage in NBC's vehicle ordering methods in which some continuity of previous practice was accepted but now as part of a co-ordinated policy. Trent Motor Traction Co Ltd took nineteen examples on CRG6 chassis with 77-seat capacity, of which 561 (OCH 561L) with body 19375 is seen looking resplendent in red and white livery in Derby bus station in August 1972, the month after it was delivered. The body was basically the normal-height design as introduced for municipalities but, in addition to the windscreen alteration, it had now been recognised that the cab side window should be aligned with the windscreen. These 'ex-BET' orders totalling 69 bodies were all built in Batches 502 and 503 and although in the 1971 programme were all delivered in 1972, while 20 lowbridge Fleetlines for Scottish Omnibuses in Batch 520 did not leave ECW until 1973.

Northern General Transport Ltd was, at that stage, still running parts of its activities via subsidiaries, and thus the Tyneside Omnibus Co was the recipient, on Fleetline CRL6 chassis, of five of the 23 two-door bodies ordered by NGT, the vehicle shown being 92L (ETY 92L) with body 19706, though yet to receive its registration plate when seen before delivery in August 1972. Tyneside, in earlier days the Tyneside Tramways and Tramroads Co, had been an ECW customer, for eight Leyland Titan TD5 double-deckers, in 1938 but not in the intervening years. The livery was green and cream but the fleet was absorbed by NGT from 1976.

door. The staircase was moved opposite the centre exit door, becoming of forward-ascending type. The first built, in December 1971, was for Bristol Omnibus Co Ltd, which took eight for use on Bristol Joint Services, and subsequently placed a series of repeat orders for similar buses. Southdown also received 15.

Body designs for the Daimler Fleetline and Leyland Atlantean had been introduced by ECW to meet the demand from municipal operators standardising on those chassis. Several of the ex-BET companies within NBC also had favoured these models, and the 1971 programme included 56 bodies on Fleetline (19691-746) and 13 on Atlantean (19747-59) for such fleets, all being delivered between May and November 1972, establishing a pattern that was to continue alongside the VRT production through the decade. The basic body design was based on those of earlier examples on these chassis, of what by then was being described as 9.5-metre (approximately 31ft) full-height form, though a new feature was the BET-type curved-glass windscreen, at that stage already adopted as

standard on ECW single-deck buses and now being adopted on double-deckers.

The largest uniform batch of this initial delivery comprised nineteen Fleetline buses on CRG6 chassis with Gardner engines and 77-seat capacity for Trent, though 74-seat capacity was chosen for Southdown's fifteen CRL6 buses with Leyland engines and Yorkshire Woollen District's twelve CRG6. Northern General Transport split its order between ten Fleetline CRL6 and thirteen Atlantean PDR1A/1 Special chassis, the latter being a transitional model having some features of the forthcoming much improved AN68 type. Both versions had two-door 72-seat bodywork and, in the manner then still common with that company, many were actually distributed to subsidiary companies – the Fleetlines split five apiece between Tyneside Omnibus and NGT itself, while the Atlanteans went to Gateshead.

An order for 20 lowheight bodies (19760-79) on Daimler Fleetline chassis for Scottish Omnibuses retained the flat-glass windscreen despite the fact that they were not

What was to prove the most familiar general form of VRT first appeared at the Commercial Motor Show in September 1972, when Southern Vectis 630 (XDL 377L) with body 20026 on chassis VRTSL2-301 was displayed. It had the curved BET-type windscreen and to maintain the 9.5-metre length the entrance door was moved rearwards slightly, a change that also applied to the other double-deck body types. It was also in the then new NBC corporate livery, in this case green and white. The body was the first to be completed in Batch 514, general production of the 1972 programme VRT bodies continuing in Batches 515-519 (of which Batch 516 were of 13ft 5in height) until August 1973. With the new windscreen the actual length became 30ft 6½in, the figure wrongly quoted in 1970. The confusion may have been caused by the existence of a 'mockup' styling dummy.

delivered until February-April 1973, and indeed this continued for some years as a difference applicable to Scottish examples of the type.

The BET windscreen was introduced on the VRT body for the 1972 programme, together with a modified grille design. The 9.5-metre nominal length was retained, and the entrance doorway was moved slightly rearwards, causing the pillar behind it to become narrower. Also at that point, the VRT body officially became available in three alternative overall heights, although most continued to be built to the 13ft 8in figure which was the bus grant lowheight standard, in all probability on the strength of the VRT's position even in 1968, when it was only in the design stage, as NBC's future standard double-decker. Some operators required a lower-built vehicle because of low bridges or other restrictions, and a 13ft 5in version was introduced, the 3in drop being achieved partly by reducing the lower saloon height. As the windscreen was not altered, the cream band above it, already slimmed considerably by the adoption of the BET screen on the 13ft 8in version, disappeared entirely at this point, there being

only a single line of beading. The lower-deck gangway was lowered to maintain internal headroom and about half the reduction was gained by reducing the camber of the road springs on the chassis.

Conversely, the 'normal height' (14ft 6in) version, which as it turned out was not produced until mid-1975 (1974 programme), had an almost full-depth cream band at this point, the lower-deck windows, and indeed the body structure as a whole, being lifted to give more internal headroom. Seating capacity began to vary more, even though 70 at first remained the usual figure, with some operators specifying 74 or 77.

The main 1972 programme VRT batch (19912-20129) was intended for NBC companies but two further individual orders were also included, one (20315) being the first ECW-bodied VRT for an independent operator, Hutchings & Cornelius Services, of South Petherton, Somerset. The other (20846) was for the Dept of the Environment, used for its Driving Establishment fleet, at first at Harmondsworth and then Cardington, though sold about five years ago to Rapson's of Alness, with whom it is still in service.

Briefly, some vehicles were delivered in traditional colours but with fleetnames to the NBC corporate standard. Among them was East Yorkshire's first order for Bristol buses, though that concern had been a customer for Lowestoft-built bodywork since 1932. They comprised eight VRT with the new-standard body, painted in traditional indigo blue, though with white relief rather than the hitherto-usual primrose. Seen here is 927 (DKH 927L) with body 19983, delivered in December 1972 and placed in service the following month – it was repainted poppy red, by then East Yorkshire's standard, in 1975.

The first sale of an ECW-bodied Bristol VRT to an independent operator was that of this vehicle to Hutchings & Cornelius Services of South Petherton, Somerset. The vehicle, RYA 700L had standard 13ft 8in-high 70-seat body 20315 on a VRTSL6G chassis and was delivered in June 1973, having been built in Batch 317. The same operator had already received body 20316, a 43-seat single-decker on a Bristol LH chassis six months previously. Both vehicles had been ordered by Vincents of Yeovil, an associate company which acted as dealer.

The break-up of North Western Road Car Co Ltd led to 25 VRT buses that had been ordered by that operator being delivered to SELNEC PTE which had taken over most of NWRCC's services. The transfer process was one of setting up a new company, SELNEC Cheshire Bus Co Ltd and accordingly 404 (AJA 404L) with body 20005 bears this name as legal owner and the ex-North Western address of Charles Street, Stockport, in its official portrait before leaving Lowestoft – the fleetname 'Cheshire' was in accordance with SELNEC's divisional practice at the time. Apart from the orange and white livery, the vehicles seated 75 and were fitted with SELNEC's three-box front destination display, inherited from Manchester Corporation practice, though an industrial dispute prevented the 'via' box from being used for some time after they entered service. They were built in Batches 517-9 and delivered between January and August 1973.

Delivery of the programme began in September 1972 with the supply of Southern Vectis 630 (XDL 377L), with body 20026 painted in the newly introduced NBC corporate livery, green in this case, and to be exhibited at the Commercial Motor Show, though some vehicles were delivered later in 'traditional' colours. The first 13ft 5in examples, nine for City of Oxford (these being two-door 68-seat buses), sixteen for Maidstone & District and thirteen for Yorkshire Traction, all included in the above series, were delivered between January and April 1973.

A batch of 25 generally standard 13ft 8in single-door buses ordered by North Western Road Car Co Ltd was diverted to SELNEC PTE, which had taken over the bulk of North Western's services in one of a series of settlements, markedly different in outcome, between the four PTEs that had been formed in major urban areas in 1969-70 and the local NBC operators. A subsidiary company SELNEC (Cheshire) Bus Co Ltd was formed to take over the ex-North Western operations and these vehicles were delivered to it, painted in the white and orange SELNEC livery and with the latter's standard three-box destination display,

though ironically a trade union dispute precluded its full use.

The 1972 programme included only two double-deck bodies on other than VRT chassis, these (20319-20) being on Daimler Fleetline CRL6 models ordered by Harper Bros, of Heath Hayes, Staffordshire, an independent operator whose fleet was expanding due to success in serving new housing areas and running a through service into Birmingham. The bodywork was largely to the design as built for Scottish Bus Group, with flat-glass windscreen and the two vehicles were delivered in the pale green livery of this operator in April 1973. A year later, Midland Red took over the Harper Bros business and two more bodies (21473-4) for Fleetlines, this time on CRG6 chassis, that were on order from the 1973 programme were delivered directly to Midland Red in October/November 1975.

Double-deck output was rising, and nearly half (46%, to be precise) of ECW's 1973 production programme comprised bodywork on the Bristol VRT chassis – with those on Fleetline chassis the ratio rose to over 60%. In terms of types of body, the pattern was much as the

Harper Bros of Heath Hayes was an independent operator who showed that it was possible to expand a relatively small bus operation in the climate of the 'seventies, despite the proximity of both Midland Red, which was the largest subsidiary of NBC, and the even larger West Midlands PTE. ECW bodywork was chosen for a pair of Daimler Fleetlines. No. 34 (TRE 949L) with body 20320 being seen in Birmingham. They had flat-glass windscreens which doubtless simplified their manufacture in Batch 520 alongside the last of 20 basically similar buses (bodies 19760-79) built for Scottish Omnibuses Ltd. This illustrates how the Batch number system is often a better guide to when and what was built by ECW than other factors – the SOL buses were in the 1971 programme and the Harper pair in that for 1972, but all were built in the spring of 1973.

previous year, with the 269 VRT bodies (20463-711 and 20792-811) split between 212 of 13ft 8in height and 57 of the 13ft 5in type, new users of the latter being the PMT and United Counties fleets. Deliveries began in September 1973 and ran through to the early months of 1975. Most were for NBC fleets, generally with single doorway, but the 20792-811 batch of 20 buses were for the Cardiff municipal fleet, a once-only purchase, though VRT chassis with other bodywork were later bought by that undertaking. The 74-seat capacity was now more common, though a minority still favoured 70.

A new development at this period was the Series 3 version of the VRT, which brought in an encapsulated engine compartment designed to reduce noise emission, resulting in the repositioning of the engine ventilation grilles to upper-deck waist level – there was also a slight deepening of the radiator grille in the front panel. The prototype chassis, VRT-SL3-101, also introduced a new option, the Leyland 500-series 8.2-litre turbocharged engine, at that stage called the 510, the vertical equivalent of the unit used in the Leyland National – all Series 1 and 2 versions had Gardner 6LX or 6LXB units. It was given priority treatment, and although having body number 21086 included in the 1974 programme, was completed

Representative of much of the 1973 programme VRT output were 20 basically standard 13ft 8in-high buses for the City of Cardiff fleet, of which 587 (PKG 587M) with body 20793 is seen ready for delivery – they were built in their own Batch 532 and delivered between December 1973 and March 1974. By that time there was wider consciousness of a desire to preserve the Welsh language and thus the fleetname appeared in this form on the offside. They largely conformed to the standard design as being built on later VRT Series 2 chassis, the 1973 programme examples were in Batches 526-9 and 536, while 530 and 531 were of the 13ft 5in type – production was running about a year late, only a minority of these being built in the programme year and the last not until early 1975.

The Series 3 version of the VRT was largely a response to proposed legislation on vehicle noise, the principle being that having a closed engine compartment with vents for both radiator and ventilation removed from its cover help to reduce noise emission. The idea of moving them to upper-deck level may well have come from earlier work on the Cave-Brown-Cave heating and ventilating system, though this time the grilles were at the rear, and not symmetrical – that on the nearside being on the corner. The prototype, on chassis VRT-SL3-101 which was also the first with a Leyland 510 engine, seen here with body 21086 but without any identity lettering, was Western National 1078 (ODV 78M) delivered in January 1974. A noteworthy change was the adoption of the standard 51½in bay width for the rearmost lower-deck side window in place of the previous 56in at this point. The longer bay was retained in the corresponding position on the upper-deck, the difference being made up by introducing a 4½in panel behind the lower-deck side windows. This vehicle also has the earlier Mark 3 upper engine cover: – a change was made to accept standard advertising posters.

The second VRT Series 3 was Northern General Transport's 165N (HUP 441N) – that company was applying the registration suffix letter also to fleet numbers at the time – with body 20539, which was exhibited at the Commercial Motor Show that year. It was one of a batch of five two-door 70-seat 13ft 8in-high buses on Gardner-engined chassis for this fleet, the others being Series 2 models and all in the 1973 programme, two built in Batch 526 being supplied in December 1973 and the rest, including this one, in Batch 529 in September 1974. This view shows the position of the grille on the offside rear of the upper-deck, just in front of the corner panel rather than on it as applied on the nearside.

and delivered to Western National as its 1078 (ODV 78M) on 11th January 1974, when the majority of 1973 programme deliveries of VRT buses were yet to be delivered. This was a clear indication of how the delivery of vehicles was again running well behind the programme date.

All but thirteen of the 1973 programme VRT models were of the series 2 type, the exceptions being Series 3. One example, Northern 165N, with the second chassis of this type, VRT-SL3-102, a VRTSL6G, with Gardner engine, having body 20539, was chosen for display at the 1974 Commercial Motor Show, it being one of five with two-door bodywork, though the others of the order were Series 2 buses. The other twelve early Series 3 buses, not delivered until April-July 1975, had Leyland 510 engines, being split equally between Hants & Dorset and Southdown.

Some of the 1973 programme Daimler Fleetline deliveries introduced a new and unfamiliar outline, causing considerable surprise, for ECW double-deck bodywork ever since 1946 had shown not only firm standardisation of design regardless of customer but a continuity of style

which meant that the outline of the basic VRT body showed distinct resemblances to previous styles which could be traced right back to the original early postwar design used on Bristol K-type chassis. The order in question, for 55 two-doorway 70-seat bodies (20737-91) of 14ft 6in height on CRG6 chassis, was placed by Sheffield Corporation, but before it could be fulfilled that undertaking was absorbed by the South Yorkshire Passenger Transport Executive, which was one of two PTEs formed as a consequence of the local government changes which took effect on 1st April 1974. Delivery was spread from September 1974 to May 1975. One additional similar bus with body 21498 was built and delivered in March 1975 as a replacement for a vehicle destroyed by fire.

The outline was intended to resemble that of a batch built by East Lancashire Coachbuilders supplied a few months previously. They incorporated projecting peaks at the front and rear domes and a generally more upright-looking outline than ECW's standard. Not only East Lancs but some other bodybuilders and operators were tending to favour such an appearance. In fact, the basic body structure

Sheffield Corporation had received various versions of peaked outline double-decker from different bodybuilders, so when an order was given for ECW to build 55 bodies on Daimler Fleetline chassis, the largest single municipal contract it had received, broad conformity in appearance to the operator's other vehicles of the period was a feature, one very rarely found on ECW double-deck bodywork over the years. By the time they were delivered in 1974-5, the customer had become South Yorkshire PTE. The shape of the peak on front and rear domes closely resembled the East Lancashire version, with ridge following the roof cross-section, and this alone altered the appearance quite dramatically, though the overall profile was more upright, partly due to the deep vee-form windscreen. Yet the body structure was basically the standard ECW full-height of the period. The first of the batch, 788 (CWE 788N) with body 20737 is seen before delivery.

This view of South Yorkshire 788 shows the rear peak and squared-up rear quarters. Also evident is the thickness of the driver's offside windscreen pillar, largely due to the retention of a rectangular outline for the cab side window in conjunction with a flat-glass sloping windscreen – it was to lead to a modification. Batch 533 covered the order for 55 bodies (2073791) but similar body 21498 for an additional new Fleetline to replace a fire victim was in Batch 537, along with the six Colchester Atlanteans being built at much the same time.

Colchester Borough Council took one batch of six Leyland Atlantean AN68/1R buses which had bodies 21467-72 to the same basic design, though of single-door layout, as the South Yorkshire Fleetlines, being delivered in February-March 1975. The windscreen pillars were rejected as unsatisfactory by the local Certifying Officer and the small quarter glass seen here added, leading to a similar modification on the balance of the South Yorkshire order going through the shops at the time and then retrospectively to the earlier SYPTE buses. It seems to have been more of a token alteration than a practical one, as the driver has to rise from his seat to peer through the offside one.

was not as extensively altered as might be thought from the much changed outline. After a few months, complaints from drivers of obstructed vision led to the inclusion of small windows in the rather wide windscreen side pillar assemblies.

The South Yorkshire style remained non-standard, though it was repeated in single-doorway 74-seat form on a batch of six Leyland Atlantean AN68 buses with bodies 21467-72 for Colchester Borough Council which went through the workshops during the same period though part of the 1974 programme – they too received the windscreen pillar windows after a few months.

The final delivery of Scottish Omnibuses Fleetlines to the flat-screen 13ft 8in design with 75-seat capacity took place in July-October 1975 when 25 (body numbers 20712-36) on CRG6 chassis were supplied as part of the 1973 programme, although a further two (21483/97) had

been supplied in November 1974 on similar chassis dating from 1971, of which the original bodies, also by ECW, had become fire casualties.

The 1974 programme was noteworthy for the inclusion of 14ft 6in high bodywork on Bristol VRT chassis for the first time, though the quantity was modest, at 21 out of the total of 344 bodies (20908-21251) on this model, and all were for one operator, Maidstone & District (bodies 21108-28). They were of 77-seat single-door layout and were delivered between June and August 1975. The bulk, as previously, were 13ft 8in high, of which there were 265,

Scottish Omnibuses Ltd continued to take the flat-windscreen style of standard ECW body on its Fleetlines until 1975, DD694 (KSX 694N) of the final batch, with body 20714, being seen here in Edinburgh in 1980. The original green and cream livery had received white upper-deck panels as part of an advertising display.

and the balance of 58 were 13ft 5in, the latter including some for Cumberland and Alder Valley as well as other operators which had received earlier examples. Seven 70-seat vehicles (20976-8 for Hants & Dorset and 21248-51 for Alder Valley), were painted in coach livery and had dual-purpose seats even though ECW records include no mention of non-standard seats in these cases. Delivery spread from January 1975 to June 1976, and the chassis included both Series 2 and Series 3 versions, batches for individual operators often including some of both types in the usual manner to give equitable delivery – normally a different registration series marked the switch of chassis type. The Series 3 chassis included both Gardner and Leyland-powered versions.

In addition to the Colchester Atlantean buses mentioned above, the 1974 programme also included ten Daimler Fleetline CRG6 for Thamesdown Borough Council, a new customer for ECW and one of the municipal fleets which took new names in a somewhat confusing way after the

1974 local government changes, the town in question being far better known as Swindon. The body design was the contemporary 14ft 6in standard in single-door 74-seat form, and the batch (20848-57) were delivered between December 1975 and March 1976 – subsequently further similar vehicles were to build up to a fleet of 35.

Heyday of the LH

While this gradual expansion of double-deck output had been evolving, ECW's efforts on single-deckers were becoming more concentrated on the Bristol LH, though the yearly programme figures for this model in 1970-2 actually showed a decline from its initial peak in 1969. This was during the period when the RE was rising to its 'swan song' period before being cut back under the Leyland National influence.

The 1970 programme LH output, delivered between February of that year and January 1971, consisted of 92

The 1970 programme was the last in which the flat screen remained standard for the Bristol LH body. The model had switched to 8ft 2½in-wide form as standard during the 1969 programme, in which 50 such buses were built in Batch 450 and delivered from November 1969 to March 1970, the removable front panel being revised with a more elaborate moulding around the headlamps as well as becoming shallower and no longer including the foglamps. The 1970 total of 92 of the type were built in Batches 465-467. United Counties was not a major user of the smaller Bristol-ECW models, but 404 (XBD 404J) with body 18743 was one of nine LH6L with 45-seat capacity supplied in September-October 1970. This now emphasises the 7ft 6in width of the chassis design.

bodies (18671-762), all single-doorway vehicles and all but one having the deeper flat windscreen as standardised a year earlier, mainly of 45-seat capacity but some with 43 seats, including a version for Hants & Dorset and Wilts & Dorset which allowed for up to 12 standing passengers. Six for Lincolnshire had coach seats for 41 and were painted in coach livery, though having the standard bus shell. The exception was body 18673, one of a batch of seventeen on the Perkins-engined LH6P chassis for Cumberland, which had the BET curved windscreen and was exhibited at the 1970 Show.

The 1971 programme deliveries had the BET screen as standard, and also introduced a slightly higher radiator grille position. This time, 72 were built for NBC fleets (19596-667), delivery spreading from June 1971 to October 1972. Two more (19689-90) went to independent operators for the first time as examples of this model with ECW bodywork, though the LH range was by then quite well

established as the basis for coach bodywork of other makes. The recipients were Hutchings & Cornelius Services, of South Petherton, and Dan Jones, of Abergwili, Carmarthen, both being delivered on 23rd December 1971, almost as if they were Christmas presents! Once again, one appeared at the 1972 Show, this being the last of a batch of fifteen for Eastern Counties, with body 19631, and this time the grille design itself was modified, as also applied to the VRT at the time, with five sets of three slim horizontal bars, again adopted for subsequent production.

The 1972 total of 69 LH buses (bodies 20247-314/6) was more standardised, all seating 43 (though the fourteen for Hants & Dorset again provided for 12 standing passengers) and on LH6L chassis, henceforth standard. The unbroken run of numbers were for NBC fleets, supplied between December 1972 and September 1973, noteworthy for the 50 supplied to United, a company

The BET windscreen had appeared on the 1970 Show LH but did not appear in production until deliveries began of the 1971 programme in June of that year. The front-end of the body had to be reshaped to accommodate it, with a slightly narrower grille and there were minor revisions to the positioning of sidelamps. The 74 examples were built in Batches 500 and 501, production running on a modest scale to the autumn of 1972. The example shown ready for delivery in September of that year was the last of twelve for Lincolnshire, 1022 (RVL 251L) with body 19613, in the Tilling-style green and cream livery soon to be superseded.

The Bristol LH in NBC corporate style, as exemplified by United 1521 (PHN 521L) with body 20265, the first of some 50 examples for this fleet, accounting for much of ECW's 1972 programme of 69 bodies for this chassis, built in Batches 511 and 512 – all were of the LH6L type, by then standard. It was delivered in December 1972, both United and other deliveries continuing until September 1973. United had favoured succeeding types of standard 'heavy-duty' Bristol-ECW single-deckers even for rural area services since the late 'thirties, showing no interest in models such as the SC, and the adoption of the LH on quite a large scale was a significant departure. They were replacing LS or MW models of 30ft by 8ft dimensions for which the LH was seen as a closer match than the Leyland National. Weight of the LH had crept up from the 5tons 6cwt of the prototype, partly due to the extra width, that of this example being 5tons 13cwt 3qr, but was still half a ton lower than a typical LS5G, the differences in design approach being very evident in the axles, for example.

On the other hand, London Transport's country bus department had run fleets of small buses since the 'thirties, and thus the 23 Bristol LHS models with ECW bodies built for London Country Bus Services Ltd, the NBC subsidiary set up to take over its activities from 1st January 1970, was a revival of an old tradition. They were comparable in length with earlier bonneted types yet seated 35, as many as 'full-sized' single-deckers of the pre-1950 period, thanks to their underfloor-engined layout. The first of the batch, BL1 (RPH 101L) with body 20440 is seen before delivery in June 1973. They formed part of that year's programme and were built in Batch 523, supply being completed in October. The standard LH was represented by 66 examples in Batches 524 and 525 delivered between October 1973 and March 1974.

which had hitherto not favoured lightweight buses, but which was building a large LH fleet mainly for rural services. The exception (20316), among the earliest deliveries, was another example for Hutchings & Cornelius, ordered via its dealer associate Vincents of Yeovil, the intervening number being a VRT as mentioned above.

The 1973 LH programme (for once completed within the year, between March and October) showed a modest increase if the 66 LH buses, all repeat orders for NBC fleets (20374-439), were taken together with 23 of the shorter LHS buses with 35-seat capacity for London Country Bus Services (20440-62) and one unique example of an LHS finished as a 29-seat coach (20847). This last was for A. Timpson & Sons Ltd, one of the less well-known NBC subsidiaries, about to disappear into National Travel, and could perhaps be more fairly described as of dual-purpose character, with coach seats in a bus shell, even if finished with more brightwork and in National white livery. The LHS had not figured in ECW production since the 1969 programme, though about to grow slightly in output and ultimately outlasting the LH itself.

One other body, 20847, also built in Batch 523 had more elements of coach specification than any other produced by ECW on the LH series of chassis. It was also based on the LHS and the body shell was as used for the LCBS buses in the same b atch, but in addition to the provision of coach seats for 29 passengers, ventilation was improved by two lift-up roof hatches and additional sliding windows, the internal bulkhead was removed and a single smaller destination box provided. Externally, polished trim and the National white coach livery added to the effect. It was for A. Timpson & Sons Ltd, of Catford, an old-established coach operator that had been jointly owned by BET and the THC and thus found itself within NBC. The vehicle is seen with the registration PLU 618L before delivery in July 1973, but it was re-registered THX 618M before entering service. It was to remain unique, though the LHS was quite often used as a basis for coach bodywork of other makes.

The Ford R1014 was a front-engined chassis chosen as a basis for 50 of NBC's requirements for light single-deckers in the 1973 programme. The bodywork built for it, all in Batch 538, was based on the design used for the LH but extended at the rear by adding an extra bay, this being logical on a chassis with engine weight ahead of the front axle. The chassis were not available when ECW was ready to build the bodies so, very unusually for ECW, they were built almost to completion and stored until the chassis arrived. One of the 25 for Hants & Dorset (20883-907) is seen (left), glazed, with seats, many of the fittings and even some of the lettering, mounted on blocks in the factory yard.

The view (right) of Alder Valley 705 ((TRD 705M) with body 20859 shows the long rear overhang of the version of the LH body applied to the Ford R1014 chassis – it is easy to understand how the unofficial designation 'LHF' was coined. The end result was more satisfactory from a passenger's point of view than might have been expected, the turbo-charging of Ford's 5.8-litre engine and its low mounting helping to mitigate the noise level associated with a front-mounted engine in a vehicle without a full-height bulkhead.

However, a further 50 bodies (20858-907) to a design so close to that of the LH as to be described within the ECW works as 'LHF' were also included in the 1973 programme, thus bringing the total of this family of bodywork to 140. These were for Ford R1014 chassis. A front-engined model basically rather similar to the Bedford VAM in having the engine ahead of the set-back front axle. The length was 10 metres and seating capacity 45. These were the only Ford vehicles to be bodied by ECW, the order being split, 25 each going to Alder Valley (the amalgamation of Thames Valley and Aldershot & District) and 25 to Hants & Dorset. Unusually, most if not all were built before arrival of the chassis, being stored on blocks in the yard, delivery of the completed vehicles being spread between May and October 1974.

This was a period when single-deck output at ECW was undergoing major change, influenced by the Leyland National, by then in full production. Although there had been some success in export markets for that vehicle, there was resistance in some countries where importation of

Although output of bus bodies on RE chassis for NBC had ended with the 1972 programme, it continued on a smaller scale for municipal operators for three further programmes. In 1973, the RESL6G in RESL-8 form with single-door ECW bodywork (20822-8) was chosen by Welsh municipalities. Gelligaear UDC took three 44-seat examples and Merthyr Tydfil Corporation four seating 47, all also taking up to 20 standing passengers and being delivered in October-November 1973. The Merthyr buses had the first ECW bodies for this fleet after a 28-year gap, but were the only examples of the type taken – 190 (NHB 190M) with body 20827 being seen below.

Colchester Corporation took ten Bristol RELL6L with 53-seat ECW bodies 20812-21 in the 1973 programme. They were built in two sets, the first five in Batch 510 along with some of the last of the final 1972 programme vehicles for NBC companies and delivered in April-May 1973. The second five were in Batch 535, along with other municipal 1973 programme single-deckers, these being delivered in December, among them the final vehicle, 23 (OWC 723M) with body 20821. Another purchaser was Hartlepool Corporation, adding five more to its fleet of two-door RELL6L buses with bodies 20841-5, these too being in Batch 535 but delivered in July-September 1973. An internal difference from NBC practice applying to many ECW bodies on RE chassis for municipalities was the inclusion of straight ceiling cove panels, but this did not apply to Colchester which took the curved style.

The AEC Swift had continued to figure in ECW's output in small numbers. Lowestoft Corporation had continued to take the flat-windscreen style of body as shown on page 43 on its examples, the final two, identical to the previous two batches of four each (bodies 20317-8) being included in the 1972 programme, unbatched, though delivered in January 1973. Later that year, the municipality of Great Yarmouth, Lowestoft's neighbouring town, 10 miles northwards along the coast of East Anglia, turned to ECW to body twelve AEC Swift 3MP2R buses. These were two-door 43-seat buses largely to contemporary standard RELL pattern, with BET-type windscreen, though incorporating the differences in emergency exit position and other minor changes to suit the Swift chassis. They were 20829-40, included in Batch 535 and delivered in September-November 1973. No. 82 (WEX 682M) with body 20830 is seen here. Great Yarmouth subsequently purchased the two 1972 Swift-ECW buses from the Lowestoft fleet when that municipal undertaking ceased operation in 1977.

The 1974 programme included fourteen bus bodies for RE chassis, all built in Batch 546, all delivered between October and January 1975, and all but one for local authority fleets. Hartlepool took seven more (21490-6) of its usual two-door RELL6L and one replacement body (21505) was supplied to Eastern National for an H-registered RELH6G. There were six single-door bodies (21475-80) on RESL-8 chassis, three with Leyland engines for Cynon Valley District Council (the post-1974 name for the former Aberdare undertaking), and three with Gardner engines for Rhymney Valley District Council (which combined the former Bedwas & Machen, Caerphilly and Gelligaer UDC fleets). The vehicle shown is Rhymney Valley No. 58 (GTX 361N) with body 21478.

The final year for the ECW-bodied RE was 1975, when 28 were built, all in Batch 563 and delivered between April and July. There were a final five RELL6L for Hartlepool (21529-33), to that undertaking's usual 46-seat two-door style. The remaining 23 were of RESL-8 type, with single-door bodies 21506-28, in order comprising five on RESL6G chassis for Thamesdown, the remainder all being RESL6L comprising three more for Cynon Valley, five for Fylde Borough (formerly Lytham St Annes), and a repeat order for ten for Merseyside PTE. Fylde was thus a new customer right at the end of the model's availability, its No. 40 (HRN 107N) with body 21517 being shown.

The Leyland C27 prototype, complete with ECW body EX13, was curious hybrid in both appearance and construction. The underframe as delivered to ECW in July 1973 was akin to the floor assembly of a Leyland National complete with its running gear, front end assembly and much of the rear – more of the latter was built into the aluminium-framed body, which was based on a version of the contemporary RELL. The roof line was lower than the National and the vehicle lacked the roof pod housing the latter's heating and ventilating unit. The wider windows and even pillar spacing was reminiscent of the body designed for RESL-8 chassis and it seem possible that what might have been intended as the structure for a planned Series 3 version of the RELL was used. The paint scheme may have been intended to disguise the unusually broad rear corner pillars – note also the use of C2701 as a spurious fleet number, rather reminiscent of a Bristol Omnibus 'City' vehicle, though clearly intended to convey that it was the first of its type – in the event it remained unique. After delivery to Leyland in February 1974, it was eventually sold to a private owner for use as a caravan.

products which could be made or assembled locally was politically unacceptable. Although some Nationals were exported 'completely knocked down' (CKD), even then the local content was considered too limited. A further compromise was developed, in which a National underframe, complete with front and rear end assemblies and given the designation C27, was fitted with an ECW body using more traditional methods, although the National's Avdelok rivet system was adopted for ease of reassembly. The prototype body was given the number EX13 by ECW. The underframe arrived in Lowestoft on 4th July 1973 but the completed vehicle did not make the return trip until 20th February 1974. In the event, it remained unique, and although a production 'chassis' version of the National was developed under the designation B21, none received ECW bodywork. This model was sometimes called the Lion and it is slightly ironical to recall that its frame was largely based on the RE.

Thus the main focus of ECW single-deck production in the mid-'seventies remained with the LH. The 1974 programme for a total of 129 LH buses, delivered between April 1974 and just over a year later, was mainly one of repeat orders for vehicles of unchanged design, there being 120 for NBC fleets (21252-371), with some 50 for Hants & Dorset and 45 for United as the main deliveries. The largest of the remainder were six (21484-9) that had been ordered by Wigan Corporation, which would have been a new customer, but whose bus undertaking had become part of Greater Manchester PTE as a consequence of the local government changes of April 1974, just before they were delivered. The flat-glass windscreen had been specified, and thus the appearance reverted virtually to the 1970 style. The remainder comprised two more for Dan Jones (21481-2), and one (21567) for Davies Bros., of Pencader. A further batch of 30 LHS (21372-401) supplied in late 1974 were for London Country, this time of 7ft 6in

Six LH buses ordered by Wigan Corporation were delivered to the newly-formed Greater Manchester PTE in April-May 1974 – this photograph of 1321 with body 21485 before delivery shows it painted but only partially lettered, with the 2 Devonshire Street North, Manchester address but no fleetname or operator's title, no doubt during the period when the replacement for the former SELNEC name was still being considered. It also shows the registration number as XVU 389M but the final version was BNE 764N. The front-end reverted to the 1970 style, a flat-glass windscreen having been specified.

Another batch of LHS for London Country was notable in being of 7ft 6in width, and produced yet another variation of front panel, with combined sidelights and flashers above the headlamps. The vehicle shown, BN43 (XPD 143N) with body 21391, was chosen for display at the 1974 Commercial Motor Show.

Hants & Dorset had a succession of buses of various types over the years which were modified so as to be able to negotiate the ramps on and off the Sandbanks ferry. Some of the 50 LH buses for this fleet in the 1974 programme, including 3532 (ORU 532M) with body 21324 shown here, were supplied as shown, with the front skirt cut back – hardly an improvement visually.

width to suit operation on narrow lanes in rural areas – one was at the 1974 Show.

ECW's peak programme year for the LH series was 1975, with a total of 251 LH and 28 LHS bodies produced. Of the latter, supplied between June 1975 and May 1976, only eight (21568-75) were of the hitherto usual LHS 35-seat form for NBC fleets, in this case 7ft 6in wide, and of these, only four, for Southern Vectis, could be counted as standard products. A similar number for East Kent had a low roof line to keep the height down to 9ft 8in. The remaining 20 were of reduced 24ft length, with short rear overhang, and were described at the time as 'midibuses'. West Yorkshire PTE took twelve (21576-87) and the Cardiff municipal fleet two (21983-4), these seating 27. London Transport was the customer for the other six (21749-54), these, designated BS and needed urgently, being almost standard, including the five-speed synchromesh gearboxes, though seating 26. They were delivered in June-July 1975. A further eleven for LT (22039-49) ordered with less haste and included in the

1976 programme, had four-speed gearboxes and were delivered in September-October 1976.

There were 155 LH for NBC fleets (21594-748) delivered from July of that year to February 1976, but the most noteworthy order was some 95 for London Transport (21856-950), of which deliveries ran from the latter month to May 1977. These, classified BL by the operator, were purchased to replace the remaining vehicles from the RF class of AEC Regal IV buses of 1952-3, and noteworthy in being of 7ft 6in width, like those buses, though contrasting greatly in general character and being about 2 tons lighter. However, these did have Self-Changing Gears transmission to meet London requirements and seating capacity was 39 rather than the usual 43, the body incorporating many minor non-standard features, though based on the familiar outline

There was also one standard body (21755) built to the order of the dealer, Arlington Motor Co Ltd, for ABC Taxis (J. Lambley) Ltd, which used the fleetname Blue Saloon.

Variations on the LH family grew apace in the 1975 programme. A minor one, yet with quite a marked effect on appearance, was the flatter roof shape and consequent shallow destination box, adopted to reduce the overall height of four LHS buses for East Kent Road Car Co Ltd. They were 7ft 6in wide and otherwise generally standard, being built among a collection of LH/LHS variants in Batch 558 and delivered in July 1975. Seen here in Station Road, Ashford, in September 1979 is 1561 (GFN 561N).

(Above) United continued with its large-scale additions of LH buses to its fleet, the 1975 programme including a further 40, bringing the total to 185 since 1968. Among them was 1682 (NGR 682P) with body 21630, built in Batch 562 and delivered early in 1976. It is seen here in August 1981 in the cobbled town square of Richmond, North Yorkshire, at the centre of an area typical of the rural parts of the company's territory in which these vehicles had become a common sight – it was for duties in such areas that the LH was primarily intended. Also visible is United 4293, an RELH with dual-purpose ECW body, and in the background is Trinity Church.

(Centre) The 1975 programme output of 155 LH buses for NBC fleets received bodies 21594-748, all of 43-seat capacity, built in Batches 558-562 and delivered between June 1975 and February 1976. This view shows Western National Omnibus Co Ltd 114 (KTT 44P) with 21661, one of eight out of a batch of 20 for that company which were allocated to what had become the Devon General section of the WNOC fleet, the old Devon General Omnibus & Touring Co Ltd having been made dormant. The white waist band was seen as an unnecessary cost by NBC's hierarchy, with a price of £70 being established! Crosville demonstrated that the use of self-adhesive vynil reduced this to £7 with the same visual benefits.

(Lower) This view of the interior of the same vehicle conveys the typical LH interior of the period, very similar to the RE bus in details and finish, though with floor at a level set by the mid-underfloor engine and gearbox, the access traps for which can be seen in the gangway. The overall effect was perhaps a little austere by comparison with some earlier generations of ECW bodywork but was intended to be durable and easily cleaned.

71

In the mid 'seventies, the LH family of buses began to be used increasingly for urban duties of one kind or another. One was in a version even shorter than the standard LHS to produce an early venture in the midibus class. Among them were two for the City of Cardiff fleet, of which the first, 104 (LUH 104P) with body 21983, is seen in these views when ready for delivery in May 1976. The seating capacity was 27, using high-backed seats so as to permit use for private hire parties. The reduction in length of roundly 2ft 3in was made by shortening the rear overhang, the rearmost bay being reduced in length and, on the offside, occupied entirely by an emergency door, itself quite narrow.

London Transport took delivery of both LH and LHS models in 1975 and 1976, all 7ft 6in wide. The LHS, classified BS, were midibuses of similar general appearance to the Cardiff vehicles shown above, replacing Ford Transit minibuses and to near-standard mechanical design, though the bodywork incorporated LT destination boxes and other minor differences from ECW standard. The LH buses incorporated fluid flywheels and what were recorded as Bristol/SCG direct-acting epicyclic gearboxes but were in fact standard Leyland-built GB350 units, there being no need for special casings in this application; there was also power-assisted steering and automatic brake adjusters. The bodies (21856-950 built in Batches 567-9) incorporated a side destination box as well as at front and rear - the last three, for a Hillingdon Borough Council service, also had an offside box. Other significant details included a revised entrance to give shallower steps and modified handrails. The example shown when new was BL30 (KJD 430P) with body 21885.

At the other end of the scale in terms of operator type was ABC Taxis, trading as 'Blue Saloon', of Guildford, to whom this standard LH, KPB 881P, with body 21755, was supplied. It was included in Batch 559 and delivered in September 1975.

Chapter Eleven: **Volume for the VRT**

The 1975 programme included a modest total of 105 bodies on VRT chassis, and while this may have been related to the peak output of LH single-deckers, it seems that an attempt was once again being made to get production a little nearer the programme year, for the overall trend was upwards. Noteworthy was an order for five for Lincoln

These examples of body production on Bristol VRT chassis from the 1975 programme allow comparison of the three alternative heights available on this model. The City of Lincoln was a new customer for ECW, though Bristol RELL chassis with Alexander Y-type bus bodies were already in service. An initial five VRTSL-3 chassis with Gardner 6LX engines and bodies 21550-4 were delivered in September-December 1975. These were of 14ft 6in height, and had been built in Batch 556, following on from the first 21 examples of this height built for Maidstone & District in the previous year's programme and illustrated on page 64. This nearside view of 21 (LFE21P) with body 21550 shows how the raising of what was very largely the standard body structure meant that the top of the entrance doors, remaining at standard level with the front platform and windscreen assembly, was below the level of the lower-deck side windows. Lincoln specified a shallower destination aperture than standard. The only other VRT buses of this height in the 1975 programme were seven more for M&D (21849-55), built in Batch 575, delivered in September 1976.

The 13ft 8in 'lowheight' version of the VRT body continued to be standard, outnumbering the alternatives – in the 1975 programme, there were 77 of them (21756-832) out of the 100 built for NBC fleets. This series of numbers began with six VRTSL-3 with Leyland 501 engines for Crosville, including DVL290 (RLG 290P) with body 21759 seen here. They were built in Batch 573 and delivered in July 1976. In later years a few, though not this bus, were fitted with Gardner 6LX engines, as was common practice with 501-powered examples. Other bodies of this height were built in Batch 574, including ten two-door buses for Bristol Omnibus.

The 13ft 5in 'lowest-height' version of the body was readily identified by the way the white between-decks band did not continue over the windscreen as was the case with the 13ft 8in version, albeit reduced to a slim depth. The reduction of height was achieved partly by reducing that of the lower deck by use of a sunken gangway, and partly by use of road springs of reduced camber. City of Oxford Motor Services was one of the regular customers because of a low bridge, and 452 (TBW 452P) with body 21835 was one of three for that fleet in the 1975 programme, which included sixteen such bodies (21833-48) for five NBC fleets, all delivered in May-June 1976.

Corporation, another new customer, these being of the 14ft 6in-high type, with single doorway and 77-seat capacity. There were 100 for NBC companies, of which sixteen of the 13ft 5in version were delivered in May-June 1976 and 77 of the standard 13ft 8in type went out to operators between June and September 1976, while another seven of the 14ft 6in version went to Maidstone & District in November of that year. A new NBC standard was the use of one glazed panel to cover the front route number and destination displays and, from about mid-1976, the 'Double N' motif now appeared in blue and red on a square white background.

The 1975 programme included nearly as many non-Bristol double-deckers, there being 97, all to 14ft 6in height, including the second ten Fleetlines (21540-9) for Thamesdown, supplied in March-April 1977, these being on the Leyland-built FE30AGR, though substantially to the previous similar Gardner-engined specification. The remaining 87 were all Atlantean AN68/1R, and Colchester received six (21534-9) in May-June 1976, these being to standard ECW outline, unlike their predecessors. The remainder were for NBC fleets, Northern General Transport

receiving 27 of the two-door type (21951-77) seating 72 in November-December 1975. Some were in a yellow livery to conform with an agreement with Tyne & Wear PTE, though executed at that stage in NBC style. They bore Gateshead fleetnames though owned by NGT, the separate Gateshead subsidiary being on the point of being wound up at the end of that year. The remaining 54 (21985-2038) were supplied during February-July 1976 to Ribble (32), East Kent (15), Trent (four) and Midland General (three), all but the last, which was now under Trent control and about to be swallowed by that company, being former BET companies.

The 1976 programme was limited in total numbers as a catching-up exercise, but out of the total of 351 bodies included, some 273, or 78%, were double-deckers on VRT chassis, all of established designs with no significant alterations. As usual, the 13ft 8in version was the most numerous, with 184 (bodies 22095-278) delivered between September of that year and January 1977, most going to the usual broad spread of NBC operators and being single-door 74-seat buses, though Bristol Omnibus had 24 two-door 70-seat versions including two allocated to

Among the most surprising deliveries from the 1976 programme were fifteen 14ft 6in bodies on VRT chassis for London Country, which had favoured the Leyland Atlantean, mainly with Park Royal bodywork, for its double-deck needs since its formation. They were on VRT/SL3/501 chassis and delivered in March-May 1977. The first of the batch, BT1 (PPH 461R) with body 22058 is seen here in service from Grays garage – London Country still followed London Transport practice and the GY garage plate is evident in this view. They were very unpopular, the whole batch being sold to Bristol Omnibus in the latter part of 1980 – several subsequently received Gardner 6LXB engines in place of the Leyland 501. The demand for this tall version of the VRT broadened for a time, the 1976 programme including 43 for NBC fleets, including the LCBS examples, plus a second, and final, five for Lincoln, all built in Batches 575 and 583.

A direct comparison between the 14ft 6in and 13ft 8in versions of the body for VRT chassis is made by this view of two vehicles, both built with 501 engines, in the East Yorkshire fleet, taken in Bridlington in September 1981. It also conveys how production continued to almost unaltered specifications in terms of detail design. The standard lowheight bus on the right, 967 (SKH 967R) with body 22153, was one of the total of 184 of this type, 22095-278, built in Batches 576-579 in the 1976 programme, in this case delivered early in 1977. On the left, 508 (JKH 508V), with body 23755, was one of 35 of the 'normal-height' type (23748-82) built in Batch 619 in the 1979 programme and delivered in October-November of that year. East Yorkshire had lost its individuality in terms of livery, becoming just another NBC poppy red fleet.

Cheltenham & District. Another notable customer for this type included in the above was Great Yarmouth Borough, which took eight – its first double-deck bodies from this works since 1931. Two more (body numbers 22269/70) had been ordered by Waveney Borough Council, the successor to Lowestoft Corporation, but they were delivered to Eastern Counties in November 1976, which took over the Waveney operations early in December. However, 22270 returned to Bristol for test purposes and was not redelivered to Eastern Counties until the following July, receiving an S suffix registration when entering service in August 1977. There were 41 of the 13ft 5in type (22279-319) completed between October 1976 and March 1977, again for regular users.

The 14ft 6in type deliveries included 43 for NBC fleets (22052-94), delivered between September 1976 and May 1977, of which perhaps the most noteworthy were fifteen for London Country Bus Services, the successor to London Transport's country department, which previously had favoured Leyland Atlantean double-deckers with other makes of bodywork – they were given the type letters BT. Other recipients included Maidstone & District and Northern General, with eleven each, and six for East Kent. In addition there were five more (21978-82) for Lincoln, delivered in September-October 1976. The only non-

Bristol vehicles in that year's programme were a further ten Atlanteans for Colchester (22320-9) supplied in April-May 1977.

For four years from 1977, the output of ECW bodywork on the VRT chassis rose to unprecedented heights, with successive programme totals of 452, 550, 469 and 506. There were also batches on Fleetline and Atlantean chassis, in smaller numbers though the 1979 programme included 59 and 74 of these respectively, bringing the double-deck total to 602, a figure only exceeded in the exceptional circumstances of 1948, when the aftermath of war created huge demand. Even more remarkably, the actual ECW deliveries in succeeding calendar years, as recorded by Paul Heels in an analysis carried out for The Omnibus Magazine put ECW in first place among British builders of double-deck bodywork with successive figures for 1978-80 of 525, 524 and 606. This was partly a consequence of normal replacement programmes, with large numbers of older double-deckers which could not be operated without conductors being withdrawn from service, but was also influenced by studies carried out by NBC from 1977 under the name Market Analysis Project (MAP) which resulted in a policy of more intensive use of double-deck buses on suitable routes and a consequent need for more such vehicles. On the other hand, the revisions to

A convertible open-top version of the VRT was added to the options for the 1977 programme, 50 examples (22388-437) being built in Batches 586 and 596 and delivered between July 1977 and February 1978. The design was based on the standard 13ft 8in body and similar in principle to the Lodekka version, though the upper-deck windows are believed to have remained at standard depth. Thus the actual overall height was evidently increased by about 2in because of the strengthening rail built into the removable portion at the join. This view of Hants & Dorset 3375 (UFX 856S, though the registration plate had yet to be fitted) with body 22309 shows the effect on the upper-deck waist and the small lifting eyes built into the roof at positions above the axles.

Southdown took a two-door version for ten of its 30 VRT open-top buses, 598 (TNJ 998S) with body 22398 being seen in service with roof removed and the safety rails with windscreen added. The smaller view show the upper-deck of one of these vehicles, which were fitted with a periscope and mirror mounted centrally at the front to allow the driver a view of the upper deck, as required by a local Certifying Officer.

plans increased the number of instances where vehicles were diverted from the concern placing the original order – NBC subsidiarries were increasingly being governed from headquarters.

These big output figures were based overwhelmingly on well-tried designs, and no doubt the sheer familiarity made it easier for the work-force at Lowestoft to attain them. There were minor changes, and one area of concern was the provision of adequate ventilation, on which a dialogue took place between ECW and NBC headquarters during 1977-78, the outcome of which was the introduction of larger hopper windows on some operators' vehicles, as can be seen from the illustrations.

The 1977 programme included 452 bodies on Bristol VRT chassis (22385-836) completed between April 1977 and March 1978, all but three for NBC fleets. Apart from 48 of the 13ft 5in version, these were to the familiar 13ft 8in height – there were no 14ft 6in versions in this programme. There were some variations within the latter, but 313 were single-door buses to uniform design, apart from minor details, and these included the three for a non-NBC fleet, the United Kingdom Atomic Energy Commission, for staff transport from its Harwell premises – hitherto, it had favoured AEC buses, either ex-London Transport or Park Royal-bodied Regent V.

There were some 313 single-door 13ft 8in bodies for VRT chassis in the 1977 programme, distributed to NBC companies covering virtually the whole of England and Wales, including the Isle of Wight, where Southern Vectis 664 (ODL 664R) with body 22626 is seen here, typical of ECW's standard double-deck output of the period. It was one of eleven based on Gardner 6LXB-powered chassis for that fleet, being built in Batch 587 and delivered in April 1977, bodies of this type in general in that year's programme being built in Batches 587-594 and 598.

Of the rest, 41 were of two-door form, but the remaining 50 were convertible open-toppers, a familiar body type over the years for ECW, albeit produced in small numbers, but these were the only VRT examples. Southdown was the largest recipient with 30 (of which ten were two-door), but others went to Western National/Devon General (eleven), Hants & Dorset (six) and South Wales (three). The design followed the usual pattern, with minimal alteration to appearance to allow the detachable roof and window structure to be lifted as a unit and to fit snugly when in place.

The only other double-deckers in the 1977 programme were a further six Atlantean buses for Colchester (22837-42), delivered in April-June 1978.

The 1978 programme was similarly dominated by orders for standard types, with the VRT total rising to its peak figure of 550, deliveries beginning in March and continuing to June 1979. The main body number series ran from 22921 to 23458 but a final dozen numbers 23667-78 covered two more buses for UKAEA and ten for Burnley & Pendle Joint Transport, the latter's only ECW order, though the undertaking's predecessor, Burnley, Colne & Nelson Joint Committee, had taken one ECW body on a Leyland TD5 in 1938. These were all standard 13ft 8in buses, forming part of the total of 443 of this height, most for NBC fleets and largely 74-seat single-door buses, though 38 were two-door 70-seat versions split between the Southdown, Bristol and Oxford fleets. There were also three with 70 coach seats for A. Mayne & Son Ltd, of Droylsden, Manchester, an independent operator which had survived rather against the odds with urban services within a PTE area and which was to blossom in the deregulated atmosphere of later years. There were also four more for Great Yarmouth.

This time there were only three of the 13ft 5in version, for Cumberland, but 104 were of the 14ft 6in height, the first time the 'tall' VRT became so widespread a choice. In addition to a further fifteen for Maidstone & District, Northern General Transport took 55, Ribble 23 and East

Yorkshire eleven, all of these being single-doorway 74-seat buses.

The Fleetline, now Leyland-built, also came back into the picture in the 1978 programme, with 34 (23463-82/95-608) on the Gardner-engined FE30AGR chassis, of which 24, delivered in October-November 1978, were for the Scottish Bus Group, which came back to the Fleetline-ECW combination after a three-year gap, though this time the 13ft 8in bodies adopted the BET windscreen. They were divided between Scottish Omnibuses (ten), Alexander (Northern) (eight), and, for the first time, Highland Omnibuses (six). The balance of ten were delivered to

The 14ft 6in body for VRT chassis reached its peak of demand in the 1978 programme, with a total of 104 (bodies 22924-38/49-55/783055/308-11) – there were to have been 132 but changes to orders reduced the figure and account for the fragmented runs of numbers. They were built in Batches 607 to 609 and completed between April 1978 and June 1979 - it is noteworthy that Batch 607 also included six Atlanteans (1977 programme) for Colchester and Batch 608 ten Fleetlines for Thamesdown, underlining the commonality of this body between chassis types. The largest delivery of 'tall' VRT buses was of 55 for Northern General Transport, all on Leyland 501-powered chassis, of which 3383 (EUP 383S) with body 22981 is seen just before delivery, which was spread over a year from May 1978.

In the later 'seventies ECW was firmly within the nationalised sector because of its links to both NBC and BLMC, yet building bodywork for independent operators was an activity which grew in that period, even if still on a small scale. A. Mayne & Son Ltd of Droylsden, Manchester, was a rarity among such concerns in continuing to run urban bus services in an area where municipal and then PTE dominance was all but complete. AEC buses, often with Park Royal bodywork, had been favoured since the 'thirties but three Bristol VRT chassis with Gardner 6LXB engines and basically standard 13ft 8in bodies, though with coach seats for 70 passengers, were included in the 1978 programme and delivered between April and July of that year – a noteworthy feature of the chassis was the inclusion of automatic transmission. The first, VJA 665S, with body 23452, is seen being inspected before delivery. Some 411 bodies of this standard 13ft 8in pattern for VRT chassis were built in the 1978 programme in Batches 598-606, 611 and 613, delivered between March of that year and June 1979.

Scottish Omnibuses Ltd had added no new double-deckers to its fleet in 1976 or 1977, but reverted to the pattern of taking 13ft 8in ECW bodywork on Fleetline chassis for its 1978 requirements, The chassis by this date was Leyland-built and thus of type FE30AGR. The body specification was similar to earlier batches in its provision of opening windows in alternate bays and the 'hexagon' destination box, but this time the BET windscreen was accepted. The first, DD852 (GSG 852T) with body 23463 is seen just before delivery with the rest in October 1978. They were built alongside VRT bodies of the same height in Batch 603, as were eight for Alexander (Northern) and six for Highland Omnibuses.

Thamesdown slightly earlier, these being normal-height buses similar to previous batches.

The pattern of large-scale output of standardised types continued in the 1979-80 programmes. That for 1979 for VRT chassis, all delivered in a 13-month period beginning in June of that year, included 410 of the 13ft 8in type, including two for UKAEA (23552-3), a replacement for a six-months-old body of a West Yorkshire vehicle damaged beyond repair (23663), and the usual wide-ranging supply of standard examples for NBC fleets (23783-855/66-4199). the gap of ten in that series being 13ft 5in buses for National Welsh which were originally to have been standard height. Out of Alder Valley's delivery of 22, six had coach seats for 66 passengers and were in a mainly white livery.

There were 22 of the 13ft 5in type for NBC fleets – thirteen for Cumberland (23625-37) as well as the ten for National Welsh plus 35 of the 14ft 6in type (23748-82) mostly for previous users of the type, though East Midland was a new user with eight diverted from Northern General. One further 13ft 5in bus (with body 24206) was delivered to Leyland Nederland BV, though its intended purpose is not clear – it was later sold to Sijthoff Pers newspaper group in Rijswijk for use as a mobile office and hospitality unit.

Also in the 1979 programme were 133 double-deck bodies on Atlantean or Fleetline chassis. Of these, 54 were Fleetline FE30AGR for SBG fleets which received low-height bodies similar to those of the previous year, and were delivered between May and November 1979. Bodies 23554-98 were for Scottish Omnibuses (25) and Alexander Midland (20), while 23616-24 were nine for Highland. In addition, there were the final five 14ft 6in buses on similar chassis for Thamesdown (24200-9), supplied in January-February 1980. Of the 74 Atlantean AN68/1R which received 14ft 6in bodywork and were delivered from March 1979 to just under a year later, 69 were for NBC fleets (23679-747), all ex-BET companies which, even after more than a decade, tended to have different vehicle policies to their ex-Tilling counterparts. In addition to 30 for Northern General and 20 for Ribble, there were twelve for Yorkshire Woollen District and seven for Yorkshire Traction, the latter two both users of Lowestoft-built bodywork on Leyland chassis since the factory was run by Eastern Counties in the early 'thirties. The balance of five (23649-53) formed a repeat order for Colchester.

The 1980 programme was the last of the really 'big' ones for the VRT and the closely related version for the Atlantean or Fleetline, for the process of superseding all three models by a new generation double-decker was well in hand, as described in the next chapter. This time 506, all low-height, were built on VRT chassis between May 1980 and April 1981, another sign of change being the types of engines fitted. Although the Gardner, usually the 6LXB but in a few cases the slightly more powerful 6LXC, was the most common, and there were still some sizeable batches of the Leyland 501, this was being phased out along with its horizontal counterpart in the Leyland National, though a strike at Gardner's led to more 501-type examples being built and the Leyland 680 making its appearance in batches for Bristol Omnibus and Southdown.

The 1979 programme included some 410 of the 13ft 8in version of the VRT, largely as built in previous years, though the wider hopper window used in alternate bays was now a common feature. Alder Valley had inherited the tradition of taking successive types of Bristol-ECW double-decker with dual-purpose specification, mainly to suit its Reading-London services, from Thames Valley, and six VRT/SL-3/6LXB models were included in this programme, being built in Batch 625 and delivered between January and April 1980 - 983 ((CJH 123V) with body 24156 being seen here at Guildford, awaiting passengers for Winchester in April 1982. They had coach seating for 66 passengers and the largely white livery with red band shown. The 13ft 8in bodies in that year's programme as a whole were built in Batches 621-630 between June 1979 and July 1980.

The 13ft 5in version of the body continued to be built in small numbers – Cumberland 425 (FAO 425V) with body 23633 was one of thirteen VRT/SL3/6LXB for this fleet in the 1979 programme, delivered in January-February 1980 after being built in Batch 620, along with the others of this height. The small grille in the upper-deck side of the foremost panel was for an extra cab heater which became standard on lowheight VRT models at this time.

This view outside ECW's finishing shop in the summer of 1979 shows the rear of Ribble 1471 (TRN 471V) with body 23714, one of 20 Leyland Atlantean AN68/1R with 14ft 6in bodywork, alongside Scottish Omnibuses DD60 (OSG 60V) with body 23559, one of 25 Leyland Fleetline FE30AGR with 13ft 8in bodywork. It shows the body height comparison particularly clearly, as well as the similarity in outline of the engine covers of the two chassis types, even though differing in grilles etc.

Another comparison, this time involving two Ribble vehicles both with 14ft 6in ECW bodies – on the left, 1465 (TRN 465V), a VRT/SL3/501 with body 23782, and on the right, 1480 (TRN 480V), an Atlantean AN68/1R with body 23723. The latter, with rear-mounted radiator, has only three louvres acting as intakes for the demister system rather than the grille needed for the VRT radiator. The AN68's higher driving position is not matched by any alteration in windscreen or wiper position, but some similar buses for Yorkshire (Woollen District) and Northern General were modified in response to driver complaint, the screen being repositioned about 2in upwards. A similar modification became standard on new vehicles, almost at the end of production – see page 81.

The 1980 programme was second only to that for 1978 in numbers of bodies on VRT chassis and the total of 506 was entirely of lowheight versions, of which 478 were 13ft 8in, the peak for this type, though it was to be the last of the 'big' output years. They were built in Batches 631-634 and 636-644 and delivery spread from May 1980 to July 1981, though most had been completed by April – there was strong pressure to get vehicles out because of the tapering-off of new bus grant. This example, 212 (JAK 212W) with body 24404 in the Mansfield District fleet, by then part of East Midland, was typical, being one of four on 6LXB-powered chassis built in Batch 638 and delivered in October-November 1980 – it is seen in service in August 1981. Such vehicles remain a familiar sight in much of England and Wales 14 years later, and seem likely to continue so for some time in present circumstances. Note the revised suite of side/head lights now employed.

A final four of the sixteen VRTs for Great Yarmouth (23459-62) had been held over from the previous year's programme, but the main run of numbers (24207-705) was for NBC fleets, apart from the first two, which were further vehicles of the coach-seated type for A. Mayne & Sons. Another independent, already well-known but to expand considerably in later deregulated years, was Stevensons of Uttoxeter Ltd, which took one vehicle, with body 24720. There were also two instances of new bodies for vehicles of which the originals had been destroyed by fire after only a few months in service – United taking body 24720 and Hants & Dorset 24760. As usual most were 13ft 8in and single-door, with 74 seats, but Oxford had eighteen of two-door 70-seat form and, among those based on the standard shell, United had five with 70 coach seats while Eastern National still favoured this capacity in bus form. Of the 13ft 5in version, 20 were supplied to National Welsh and eight to Cumberland.

All the 42 bodies of 14ft 6in height in the 1980 programme were on Atlantean chassis, the final three (23654-6) of 30 for Colchester being completed in July of that year. These were AN68/1R chassis but the last of this type to be bodied by ECW were 30 for Ribble and eight for Trent (24722-59) delivered between November and January 1981. The final body of this pattern (24761) was built on a development chassis originally dating from 1975 and having a Leyland 690 engine (a turbocharged version of the 680), which caused the designation to be AN69/1R. It had a similar type of rear-end design to that used on the 'quiet' Fleetline chassis, also fitted with the Leyland 690

The Great Yarmouth municipality could be regarded as a 'local' customer for ECW, though it had been no more than an intermittent one over the years until the 'seventies. There had been eight VRT buses in the 1976 programme and four in that for 1978 but the last four were carried over from the 1979 to the 1980 programme, built in Batch 642 and delivered in February 1981, among them being 24 (PVG 24W) with body 23459, being seen here.

Stevenson's of Uttoxeter was another instance of an independent surviving through the years when publicly-owned buses dominated the scene. It purchased two VRT models with 6LXB engines and basically standard 13ft 8in bodies, this being the first, 50 (PFA 50W) with body 24720 having coach seats for 70 passengers, built in Batch 642 and delivered in November 1980. A repeat order in the 1981 programme and delivered as Stevenson's 49 (UVT 49X) in October of that year, with body 25065, proved to be an historic vehicle, having the last VRT chassis.

The final production examples of ECW bodywork for Atlantean chassis comprised 38 examples on AN68/1R chassis, all built in Batch 646 and delivered between November 1980 and February 1981. The problem of appropriate windscreen height for the high driving position Atlantean was rather belatedly addressed, this and the cab side window being raised about 3in, causing the white between-decks band to be noticeably slimmed in this area. Trent 577 (LRB 577W) with body 24752, the first of this company's eight vehicles of this type, is seen in late NBC days – the double N symbol had been omitted in the run-up to privatisation.

The balance of 30 vehicles again with the modified windscreen level went to Ribble, the example shown, the last of the order, 1515 (FBV 515W) with body 24751, also had a special electronic indicator display, with small route number aperture and shallow destination unit.

engines and generally known by their Leyland project number B20, supplied to London Transport in 1976-8. The ECW body was modified slightly to accommodate this and also the lower driving position of earlier Atlantean models, the latter causing the windscreen to remain at the earlier standard level, rather than being raised as was so on the final production models. The completed vehicle was supplied to J. Fishwick & Sons Ltd, the independent operator based in Leyland town which sometimes co-operated with Leyland in running test vehicles where operational experience was needed. One further Atlantean was also bodied for Fishwick but, in terms of bodywork, that belongs to the next generation and is described in the next chapter.

Possibly the strangest-looking rear end of any ECW-bodied vehicle was that of the solitary Leyland Atlantean AN69/1R, though the design of the Leyland-supplied part was readily recognisable by anyone familiar with the 'quiet' B20 Fleetlines in London Transport's fleet. It had been a Leyland development chassis but was sold to J. Fishwick & Sons and received the last 14ft 6in body of this style, 24761, virtually standard in specification and not having the raised windscreen modification of the others built in Batch 646 – it was delivered as Fishwick 23 (GRN 895W) on 13th February 1981. The lower view shows it in the operator's yard in November 1983.

The two-door lowheight body had remained a minority choice, almost unknown in Britain outside the ECW design for VRT chassis. Oxford took the last five, built in the 1981 programme in Batch 649 and delivered in June of that year, the first, 511 (PFC 511W) with body 24943 being seen in service.

The final VRT programme was that for 1981, much smaller than for the previous four years because of the beginning of production of the new design for the Olympian. There were 187, all 13ft 8in high, built between April and October of that year, the main group being 185 for the last deliveries of new VRT chassis, all with the Gardner 6LXB engine, for NBC which received bodies 24763-947. All but five were single-door 74-seat buses. The exceptions were 24943-7 for Oxford, which were two-door 70-seat examples. They were quite broadly distributed among the operating companies though there were extensive re-allocations in the manner becoming common. There was also a replacement body (24762) for South Wales fitted on a 1976 chassis.

One further body (25065), with 70-seat capacity, was a repeat order for Stevensons of Uttoxeter, a historic bus,

as it had the last VRT chassis, Series 3/3101, again with the Gardner 6LXB engine. It was delivered as No. 49 (registered UVT 49X) on 20th October 1981, but the last all-new example delivered was, rather appropriately, an Eastern Counties bus, VR 294 (VEX 294X) with body 24942 from the NBC batch, which was delivered on the 26th October. Fittingly, it was allocated to Lowestoft depot, remaining there ever since, right up to the time of writing.

Rather ironically, the last two examples of the VRT-style ECW body on new chassis (25066-7) were Fleetlines, which left the factory just over three weeks later. They were for South Notts Bus Co Ltd of Gotham, near Nottingham, an associate of the large independent concern, Barton Transport, and hitherto tending to favour Leyland chassis and Northern Counties bodywork. These were the last Fleetline chassis built, FE30ALR models with Leyland 680 engines, and received standard 13ft 8in bodies much as delivered to the Scottish Bus Group, with 75-seat capacity. They were delivered on 19th November 1981, numbered 116-7 (SCH 116-7X).

The very last bodies of this type were two standard 13ft 8in replacements (25400-1), both delivered on 18th April 1983, based on VRT chassis for South Wales and East Kent.

The LH in decline

There was quite a sharp drop in the numbers of Bristol LH and LHS buses being supplied to NBC fleets from the 1976 programme, which in combined total amounted to 68, less than a quarter of the previous year's peak figure of 279. There was no recovery in subsequent years and although the figures varied the general trend was downwards, towards vanishing point.

There were two specific reasons for this, and while there seems to have been an element of marking time in 1976-7, the drastic cuts in the 1978 programme indicate quite an abrupt change of policy. By then, the NBC's

It seems very fitting that the last new ECW-bodied Bristol VRT should have been delivered to Eastern Counties Omnibus Co, the company in whose direct charge the Lowestoft works had been when the connection with Bristol as an associated company had begun half a century earlier, in 1931, though it had been a couple of years later before the first Bristol-ECOC buses had emerged. The 1981 programme bodies for VRT chassis were built in Batches 648-50 and 654, ending with Eastern Counties VR294 (VEX 294 X) with body 24942 which left the factory on 26th October, but again appropriately, it did not travel far, operating from Lowestoft depot ever since, as seen here, almost as if a mobile museum to that era.

The buses with the last VRT-style ECW bodies on new chassis were also the last Fleetline chassis to be built, hardly the link-up that might have been predicted for either. They were a pair of FE30ALR models for South Notts Bus Co Ltd, and were built to 13ft 8in height and thus basically similar to the combination as built for Scottish Bus Group fleets – however the alternate opening windows were of the large hopper type. No. 116 (yet to receive registration plate SCH 116X), with body 25066, is seen awaiting delivery – it was noteworthy that these vehicles carried Daimler badges though officially Leyland chassis. The two vehicles were the only ones in Batch 658 and marked the end of an era when they left the works on 19th November 1981.

Market Analysis Project studies that increased the demand for double-deckers were also reducing that for types of bus, specifically the LH, that were used on the less profitable rural routes, which were being cut back to meet profitability targets. In addition, NBC had introduced a system of whole-life costing which revealed that the apparent savings in initial cost and direct running costs from operating lightweight buses were more than counterbalanced from heavier repair and overhaul costs in later years.

The first buses in this category to be completed in the 1976 programme were of the LHS type, the balance of eleven (22039-49) of the midibus version for London Transport mentioned in the last chapter being joined by two of standard length but 7ft 6in width for Trent (22050-1), the second of which appeared at the 1976 Commercial Motor Show. All were delivered in September-November of that year.

The 1976 programme LH buses did not leave the factory until February-August 1977, there being 55 to the

standard design (22330-84), distributed among nine fleets, with Bristol Omnibus as the main recipient, though Trent, not a fleet associated with lightweight buses, figured with six in addition to the two LHS. There had been a considerable number of cancellations and reallocations, Crosville having ordered 22 which in the event went to five other fleets, including four of Trent's six of this type. To meet new emergency exit requirements, provision was made on both models for the rearmost window on the nearside to open.

The 1977 programme, produced between August of that year and May 1978, could be counted as virtually a repeat of 1976 in terms of numbers, though distributed differently. At first 63 LH had been ordered, and some simply reallocated, notably 30 for Crosville which were sent instead to Bristol (21) and Western National (nine), but only two of six for East Yorkshire were built and taken by United, leaving a gap in the programme batch as actually built (22843-82/7-905), though two more of these numbers were later filled by LHS buses. The fourteen LHS

Bodywork for the Bristol LH continued in production through the late 'seventies, but in much reduced numbers, with successive figures in the 1976-79 programmes of 55 (built in Batches 5812), 59 (Batches 582, 595 and 597), 38 (Batch 612) and 42 (Batches 614-5). Cancellations and diversions became commonplace following NBC's decision to cut its intake of light single-deckers. Western National, traditionally a user of buses in this class, received nine LH6L with standard 43-seat bodies diverted from Crosville in the 1977 programme, including 1625 (VDV 125S) with body 22865 seen here – it was built in Batch 595. The last ECW body on LH chassis was delivered in April 1980.

models bodied (22907-20) were a further batch of 7ft 6in-wide buses for London Country, though it is noteworthy that the chassis were called in from various dealers who had them in stock in the hope of orders, no doubt anticipated as being for coaches.

Much more dramatic cuts curtailed the 1978 programme, for initially 179 body numbers for LH buses for NBC fleets were allocated (23483-661) but in the event only 37 were built (23483-94/599-607/38-48/57-61). Delivery was spread from May 1978 to April 1979, the recipients being Bristol, Lincolnshire, United and Western National fleets, the last-mentioned for Devon General. One order from an independent operator was also fulfilled, one LH with body 23662 going to ABC Taxis, Guildford in April 1979.

Production of the standard-length LH chassis ceased during 1979, though the shorter LHS continued to figure in ECW's programmes until 1981. The programme as planned provided for 43 LH buses of standard 8ft 2½in wide design, with 43-seat capacity, to be built as 23509-51, split between three for United and the rest to Bristol Omnibus. In the event, these two fleets remained the recipients but United's share was increased to nine, 23509-11, as planned, plus 23532-5 and 23549-50, these last two being replacement bodies for those of two 1975 LH buses of this operator damaged beyond economic repair in a fire at Durham garage on 22nd July 1979. Bristol received 33 LH bodies (23512-31/6-48), all on new chassis, the number 23551 not being taken up. The last of the Bristol batch, 466 (AFB 597V) with body 23548, was the last LH to be delivered from ECW, on 24th April 1980.

The LHS bodies in the 1979 programme were all 7ft 6in wide, of 7.85 metre length and delivered in the last three months of the year. Western National received eight (23608-15), and two (22883-4 – numbers originally allocated to cancelled East Yorkshire LH buses from the 1977 programme) were supplied to Northampton Borough

Transport, the only ECW bodies for that operator. These all seated 35, but a single vehicle, with body 24205, built for M. Taylor, trading as Westerbus, of Dundonnell, Ross & Cromarty, in the far north-west of Scotland, and had semi-coach seating for 27. It was the only ECW-bodied LH or LHS supplied north of the border.

The 1980 LHS output comprised only fourteen vehicles with bodies 24706-19, all delivered in the latter part of that year, but there was a surprising degree of variety. National Welsh received six of 24ft midibus length and 27-seat capacity for use on new services in the Rhondda and Cynon valleys. Three of these were actually the subject of a 1979 contract but included in the 1980 programme as they were not built until November of the latter year. The remaining eight were all to a slightly modified 'standard' 8-metre (26ft 5¾in) length, producing a slightly wider emergency exit door. Three were for the Devon General section of Western National, with 35 seats, as applied to a pair for Ribble, that company's only LH-series vehicles, purchased for a service linking villages in the Ribble valley that had been started with hired vehicles in 1978. They carried the name 'Betty's bus' after Mrs Betty Gray, the regular driver. The remaining three were for Southern Vectis and had semi-coach seats for 31 passengers – they were in the 'local coach' dual-purpose livery.

The end of the LHS came in the 1981 programme, when the last three examples (25062-4) were bodied in July of that year, these being further buses for National Welsh to midibus length and the same specification as the previous six. As well as bringing the story of the LH family of bodywork to a close, it marked the end of ECW's manufacture of bodies for small buses. They had formed no more than a minority part of the factory's output, but the LH types had become a familiar part of the landscape, particularly in rural areas in many parts of England and Wales.

In its final years, the emphasis for the LH design swung to the short LHS form, largely for NBC fleets but with some notable exceptions. Perhaps the most remarkable was this vehicle, the only example of an LH or LHS with ECW body built for service in Scotland. It was for the Westerbus business, proprietor M. Taylor of Dundonnell, Ross-shire and was registered WST 79V, having body 27205 with coach seating for 27. Its operating area is about 200 miles north of that for any similar bus.

Almost at the end of production, in the 1980 programme, the 'standard' LHS was increased slightly in rear overhang. Three examples were built as part of Batch 645 with semi-coach seats for Southern Vectis and painted in the dual-purpose green and white livery, being delivered in October-November 1980. The vehicle shown, 203, was originally DP3 (KDL 203W) with body 24716. These vehicles had similar brightwork to the Timpsons LHS 'coach' shown on page 61 though retaining more bus features.

While production of bodywork for the VRT was at its height, work was in hand on the next generation. This view of body EX14 taking shape on the first B45 prototype chassis was taken early in September 1979 – the chassis had arrived at Lowestoft in April, but progress had been quite slow, doubtless because of the extent to which many aspects of the design were laid down by Leyland headquarters and closely related to that of the equivalent Titan integral-construction model, already in production, mainly for London Transport, at Park Royal. That same month, it was decided that the Park Royal works would be closed, and the possibility of Titan construction moving to ECW soon became a firm proposal, even though not destined to succeed, thereby putting a cloud over ECW's future as a whole. In a more immediate way the dilution of ECW influence in the structural design of the body for the Olympian deleted some features which had proved themselves over three decades.

Chapter Twelve: **Into the Olympian era**

From soon after British Leyland had been formed in 1968, bringing the Leyland Atlantean and Daimler Fleetline into the control of the same manufacturing group, the idea of a new double-deck bus design to take over eventually from them had been in mind, the Bristol VRT also coming into the picture in due course. Fate was to delay the achievement of that goal in several ways, and ECW played a key role in the story, contributing to a highly successful product but also, sadly, in a way that ultimately helped to lead to its own demise.

A new double-deck design was given the code B15 in Leyland's series for bus projects and by 1973 discussions were being held with London Transport and the Passenger Transport Executives in particular. At that stage, the emphasis was on a design primarily for city routes, it having been realised that the Leyland National was not going to attract large orders from these sources. It was not expected at that stage that NBC would require large numbers of double-deckers and it was thought that the VRT would continue to meet most of its needs for some time, though the new project was being followed with interest by NBC and in due course a small order was placed, as mentioned later.

London Transport continued to think highly of its Routemaster vehicles, and favoured their key features – integral construction, independent front suspension and power-hydraulic brakes – so these were incorporated in the B15 design. Prototypes were built by Park Royal Vehicles Ltd at its premises on the western outskirts of London and an initial launch was made in 1975, but progress was slow and it was not until a second launch in 1977 that the name Titan was given to the new project.

London Transport ordered 250 Titans and various other orders were taken but further troubles meant that the first production bus for London was not completed until August 1978. By that time labour relations at Park Royal had soured, following abortive plans to move production of the model to the AEC works at Southall, about 5 miles from Park Royal. That plan was abandoned and then came the announcement in October 1978 that the AEC works was to close. Both concerns were experiencing difficulties arising from the strong demand for skilled engineers locally, notably from the growing need for maintenance workers for the various airlines operating from Heathrow. This had the effect of forcing up wage rates which were already higher than elsewhere within the Leyland group.

Titan production struggled on at Park Royal against a background of dispute centred on whether semi-skilled staff could be recruited to replace some of those who had left when it seemed that the Titan job would go to AEC. There was a sluggish output for London Transport plus small numbers of vehicles for the Greater Manchester and West Midlands PTE fleets, but other orders, including that for five for Maidstone & District on behalf of NBC, were cancelled. This was partly because it had become clear that there was growing interest, especially from NBC, in a further Leyland project, B45, to build a double-decker chassis having some of the characteristics of the Titan, but deferring more to the requirements of operators outside the major cities.

By that date, NBC had become more interested in double-decker development as a result of the MAP studies coming out in favour of the wider use of large-capacity buses. The need to find a successor to the Bristol VRT, particularly in the 13ft 8in height form used so widely by its subsidiaries, in addition to the Atlantean and Fleetline, had become more urgent. Another factor was the demand for a vehicle which could be bodied by 'outside' concerns, notably in Scotland, where support for local industry, in specific terms, Alexander, was strong.

Thus the B45 was designed to meet these demands. It had a separate chassis, itself designed to give maximum flexibilty in offering alternative lengths to suit not only home market but also export needs. The form of the frame, with sections running over the wheelarches, was visually a little reminiscent of the rear section of the Lodekka FLF. The overall concept was new, however, in its combination of front, centre and rear portions in combination with a perimeter frame to give the length options with minimum disruption to the mechanical design and a strong structure when tied to a suitably designed body. It is fair to point out that a principle akin to this had been embodied in the VR as originally conceived, and indeed there is evidence of NBC/BCV influence in the chassis, just as with ECW in the body, despite the Leyland headquarters overall control.

The engine installation, providing for a choice of Gardner 6LXB or a new Leyland engine, the TL11, derived from the O.680, with the general layout of the mechanical units at the rear, including the hydraulically-operated Hydracyclic version of what was in principle the familiar Self-Changing Gears epicyclic gearbox, was derived from that of the Titan. Air suspension was standard, but instead of independent front suspension there was a rigid front axle so designed to allow the low floor line essential to a lowheight vehicle.

The first prototype chassis B45-01, was delivered to ECW on 24th April 1979, and construction of a body for it (EX14) put in hand. Meanwhile the second chassis, B45-02, had arrived in July, and body construction on this was also in progress when what seemed a promising opportunity for major expansion at ECW arose. The situation at Park Royal, with trade union rejection of management proposals in July 1979, reached crisis point, and it was decided in September that the Park Royal works would be closed in June 1980. A special redundancy deal was conditional on completion of the remainder of the 250 buses for London Transport; a 'miraculous' improvement in output levels was achieved, and the last vehicle left ahead of schedule in May 1980.

Meanwhile, it was known that further substantial London orders for the Titan were due to follow and plans to add 2,000 new double-deckers to the LT fleet were to be split between the Titan and the competitive MCW Metrobus. It seemed logical to propose that ECW should take over much of this work, especially as the Titan and Olympian were related designs, with quite close affinities in both body and mechanical features, even though differing as described above, but it was not to be.

The B45 project went ahead, however, and was to prove highly successful. The first body, which was supplied as a prototype for development use, lacking seats but otherwise complete, was of front-entrance and centre-exit layout. It was delivered back to Leyland on 9th October 1979, and differed from subsequent bodies on this chassis in having a complete VRT-style cab front, though the rest of the body showed clear affinities to the Titan design, with a more square-cut outline. Even so, there were obvious differences, the lower build than that of the Titan being accommodated by using equal-depth side windows in both decks, while, at the rear, the centrally-placed lower-deck rear window, flush with the rear panel, and the general form of the engine compartment cover was reminiscent of VRT rather than than Titan practice, though more square-cut at the corners.

The second prototype, B45-02, which received ECW body EX15, was nearer to the production version as

Failure to resolve the problem of the pay differential for craftsmen led to the project to build the Titan at ECW being dropped, and undermined the future of the company, ultimately contributing to its closure seven years later. A Park Royal-built London Transport Titan T160 (CUL 160V), visiting to assist evaluation of the project, is seen in company with a VRT outside the famous doors on 1st February 1980, when the proposal was still in the balance – the crucial meeting came four days later. The subsequent ECW story might have been very different had the model found a home here.

The first prototype B45, with ECW body EX14, had clear visual affinities both to the Titan, in the overall shape and in particular that of the upper deck, and the VRT, most obviously in the cab front assembly, though the latter was a little uncomfortably out of character with the rest of the design. In building to the same 13ft 8in overall height as the standard VRT, there was a need to reduce the depth of the lower deck and it was logical to replace the deep side windows used at this level in the Titan by the size used in the upper deck of that model. This view shows it shortly before delivery from Lowestoft to Leyland on October 1979 – it was retained as a test vehicle until June 1983 when it was sold to Stevensons of Uttoxeter, rebuilt to single-door and registered Q246 FVT, entering service in January 1985..

There were further echoes of ECW's design for the VRT at the rear, perhaps most obviously the asymmetrical grilles in the upper deck sited in almost exactly the same positions, though the nearside one was on the rear face of the panelling rather than on the corner, partly because the body followed the Titan's more square-cut lines with only a small-radius curve at the corner. It is also noteworthy that, despite the two-doorway layout, the staircase was immediately behind the driver instead of being opposite the centre exit, as had been standard on VRT-generation bodies. Another noteworthy feature was the use of full-length hopper vents for the alternate opening windows, a feature that had been discussed between NBC and ECW for production a couple of years or so previously.

adopted for NBC deliveries, as well as being the first vehicle revealed to the public. It was delivered, initially back to Leyland, on 12th February 1980, but was handed over to Ribble as its number 2100 on 25th July it being used at the press launch of the model, at which its name was revealed to be Olympian. This had a single-doorway body, the seating capacity being 77, arranged 45 in the upper deck and 32 below, and this was to be the general standard for production bodies for NBC subsidiaries.

It also differed from the first prototype in having a new style of cab front, nearer to the Titan prodction standard and conforming more happily to the overall style of the vehicle. Appearance is always a matter of taste, but many observers seemed to agree that the Olympian with 13ft 8in ECW body, which was to prove the most typical style for the model, was a better-proportioned and neater vehicle than the Titan. On this particular vehicle, the white band at between decks level was not carried round the front, there being a single beading strip over the windscreen, rather like the 13ft 5in VRT, but later bodies had an

The second B45 prototype, with body EX15, came very close to the production Olympian complete with standard ECW low-height body, with the revised cab front, styled in a similar way to that of the Titan, though with grille shaped to suit the radiator mounted immediately behind it. The overall effect was now of a well-proportioned and homogenous design, though more angular than the traditional ECW styles. At this stage, the between-decks white band of the standard NBC livery did not extend over the windscreen, ending abruptly on each side, one of the few items to be modified for production. It is seen in January 1980, standing near the original office building dating back to 1920, at the entrance to the premises in Eastern Way. It was lettered for service with Ribble, but was initially delivered to Leyland in February, not going to Ribble until July, thereupon becoming 2100 in that fleet, registered DBV 100W. Though originally the London number UHV 995V was allocated.

The offside rear view was virtually unchanged from that of the first prototype, this view with engine access doors closed revealing the similarity to the standard VRT in the proportions of the engine compartment cover and the shallow window above. Minor details such as the sundry rear grilles were subject to a series of subsequent changes, during the type's production run. One item which was to alter from the next prototype was the rear registration panel, which was in Titan style on this vehicle.

arrangement nearer that of the VRT in 13ft 8in form at this point.

A third prototype body (EX16) was built by ECW for the 1980 Show, being built on chassis B45-04, and completed by 30th September 1980. It was generally similar to the Ribble vehicle but was for W. Alexander & Sons (Midland) Ltd, by then using the fleetname Midland Scottish, and differed in minor details such as the 'hexagonal' destination glass outline so characteristic of SBG vehicles. It entered service with Midland Scottish as MRO1 in February 1981, but four months later was transferred to the Alexander (Northern) fleet, becoming NLO1 – it had been decided within SBG that this operator would be building up a fleet of Olympian buses.

Other prototype Olympian chassis were being bodied by Alexander and Northern Counties, these having Leyland TL11 engines, as were to be fitted to further ECW-bodied prototypes to be described later, but all three of the above-mentioned buses had the Gardner 6LXB unit, as was to be usual on most ECW production examples, especially for NBC fleets.

Bristol Commercial Vehicles had been involved in the design and building of the B45 prototypes, under guidelines from Leyland Bus headquarters, so it was logical that production of the chassis, now with ON type prefix, was set up at the Bristol Commercial Vehicles works, being designed to fill the gap left by the cessation of VRT manufacture, and it is interesting to note that some vehicles were registered as being of Bristol make, a fact which is liable to lead to some statistical confusion. The period of Olympian assembly by Bristol was to last for approximately three years.

The first production chassis, ON1, of type ONLXB/1R, as was to be standard for most examples supplied to

The third prototype body for the B45 chassis was EX16, completed by late September 1980 in time to be displayed on Leyland's stand at the Motor Show that year. By then, the model had been given the Olympian name and this example was for the Scottish Bus Group – there were further B45 prototype chassis on other bodybuilders' stands. In essentials, this body was very like EX15 for Ribble, with 77-seat capacity, but as well as having the characteristic SBG style of destination box, there was a reversion to the position for the rear registration number over the rear lower-saloon window that had been standard on VRT bodies (the unit used in a lower position on the two earlier prototypes being similar to that on the Titan), plus minor revisions to front and rear light clusters. It was in a rather attractive version of the traditional blue and cream of Alexander (Midland) to which fleet it was delivered as MRO1 (OMS 910W) in February 1981, only to be passed on to Alexander (Northern) in June.

NBC subsidiaries, was fitted with a body of very similar design to EX15 and at first allocated the number EX17. Basically, it was the 'standard-setting' body, and was given the production number 24948 before delivery to Ribble on 24th March 1981, where it took the fleet number 2101 immediately following the previous year's prototype. It was the first of a batch of 23 for that fleet, though going out 2½ months before the flow of normal production bodies of the same design in the 1981 programme began to leave the factory. Briefly, there was a period when both the last VRT and the first production Olympian bodies were to be seen under construction at the same time within the works.

There were 94 to the same 13ft 8in single-door specification for NBC fleets including the renumbered EX17 (24948-25041), other recipients of this first programme series being United Counties (20), Northern General (40), East Midland (five), Yorkshire Traction (three) and Eastern National (three). They were delivered in a period running up to February 1982. In addition five largely similar buses but with 78-seat capacity and on ONTL11/1R chassis were completed in December 1981 for Strathclyde PTE (25052-6), a new customer for ECW, and one with no background of association with the company as the only fleet it took over on creation (originally as Greater Glasgow PTE) was Glasgow Corporation, never an ECW customer. A noteworthy feature was the use of flat-glass windscreens set in a slight vee-formation, an option that was to be quite widely favoured for PTE and export orders.

As production of bodywork for the Olympian got under way, there was a brief period during the summer and autumn of 1981 when examples of this design and its predecessor were to be seen together at ECW. This scene in the works yard in September of that year, shows East Kent 7676 (CJJ676W) with body 24909, the first of ten VRT for East Kent that had been diverted from Maidstone & District, built in Batch 650, alongside Ribble 2106 (JFR 6W) with body 24953. The latter had been built in Batch 647, comprising the first 31 production Olympian bodies, which had begun with body EX17, renumbered 24948 before delivery as the first of those for Ribble. Similar bodies for NBC fleets, were also built in Batches 652 and 655 in the 1981 programme. This front view conveys the contrast in appearance despite both vehicles being standard 13ft 8in high products and having the BET windscreen in common.

The Olympian body was offered in 'normal height' form, though this came out at 14ft 2in rather than the 14ft 6in of the previous generation equivalent. In this version, the lower deck windows were deeper than those of the upper deck, underlining the affinity to the Titan, though to a less marked extent. In the instance illustrated, as with several others for non-NBC fleets, the use of a vee-form flat-glass windscreen introduced another variation. The example shown was one of ten supplied to Merseyside PTE, of which five (25047-51) were included with 13ft 8in buses for other fleets in Batch 655 and delivered in November 1981, but a further five (25108-12), including 0039 (ACM 711X) with body 25110, seen here in Merseybus maroon and cream livery in later years, were the only vehicles produced in Batch 659 and delivered the following month. This was a significant order, built to a keen price for an important customer yet incorporating various special features such as Formica cappings outside the pillars to simplify repainting and ceiling cove panels with a pattern of the Mersey skyline and waterfront.

The 'normal height' version of the Olympian measured 14ft 2in high, 4in lower than the previous generation standard, this being partly because of the chassis design which was well suited to a lower floor line. Ten such bodies (25047-51/108-112) were built on ONTL11/1R chassis in the 1981 programme for Merseyside PTE, not quite a new customer as there had been a batch of RESL-based single-deck bodies, but no previous double-deckers and again none for constituent undertakings. They were delivered in November/December 1981, and also had the flat-glass windscreens.

With an atmosphere of uncertainty in the British bus operating industry with the prospect not only of increasing deregulation and privatisation, but also the phasing out of the new bus grant, export business was seen as of increasing importance. Over the years, ECW, for varying reasons, had not been involved greatly in exports, being specifically banned from trading thus from 1948 to 1965, but circumstances now signalled renewed attention to such activity. In effect, its role was that of the main bodybuilder

within the Leyland Bus empire, and hence the obvious place to build a series of bodies to attract business for the Olympian as a model, as well as, hopefully, for ECW.

A total of eight export bodies on Olympian chassis were included in the 1981 programme. Five, all of 13ft 8in height, were for the two principal operators in Hong Kong. Three (25042-4) were for Kowloon Motor Bus Co (1933) Ltd, operating on the mainland part of the colony, all of the 10.3-metre type which was the longer alternative available at that stage. Two were on prototype B45/TL11/2R chassis, numbers 8 and 9 in the B45 series, and one was on an equivalent production ONTL11/2R, the third ON-series chassis, ON3. The bodywork was of two-door type with seats for 99 passengers, leaving ECW in April and entering service in July-September 1981.

The other two, again two-door buses, which left the factory in June 1981 and entered service in September, were for China Motor Bus Co Ltd, operating on Hong Kong island, one (25046) being a ONLXB/1R, numbered ON16, of the same 9.6-metre length as the home-market

The first export vehicles to leave ECW for over 32 years were three Olympian chassis with 13ft 8in two-door 99-seat bodies 25042-4 for Kowloon Motor Bus, one of which is seen outside the works before departing in April 1981. The design included a narrow doorway at the front, a wider one to the rear of the front axle and generous provision of full-depth sliding windows to suit the Hong Kong climate. Note also the short bay inserted at the centre of the four main bays to make up the 10.3-metre overall length. Two of the vehicles were on prototype B45-series chassis and one on production chassis ON3, all with TL11 engines. They, and other export vehicles bodied by ECW in this period, were intended primarily for evaluation, having been built in the hope of attracting further orders.

The China Motor Bus specifications for its two Olympian buses of 1981 were basically similar to that of the KMB vehicles in layout, though based on Gardner-engined chassis. Provision of opening windows was slightly less generous, with three-quarter-depth sliders in most side windows. As built, they both had fixed windscreens and hinged vents in the upper-deck front windows, similar to those in most home-market buses though deeper. Body 24045, seen here in its official views before leaving ECW in June 1981, was on an ONLXB/2R chassis, built to the same 10.3-metre length as the KMB trio and had the same seating capacity of 99, with 61 on the upper deck and 38 below. It had yet to receive the fleet number BR2 or the registration CR 4223.

vehicles, seating 89. The other (25045) was on an ONLXB/2R chassis, ON17, and had 99-seat bodywork of similar basic design to the Kowloon buses.

All five, though based on similar basic structure to the home-market versions, were to a specification appropriate to the territory, with much more generous provision of

opening windows, KMB favouring full-depth sliders while CMB chose a three-quarter depth type. Windscreens were of flat glass in the vee formation, but again with variations of opening portions. The longer buses incorporated a short bay just behind the centre doorway. All the ECW-bodied buses which went to these two main operators in the Crown Colony were purchased for evaluation, and whilst large fleets of Olympians were subsequently supplied to Kowloon, unfortunately ECW was not awarded the body contracts, which largely went to Alexander.

Three further export bodies were built by ECW on early Olympian chassis as demonstration vehicles, in this case all of left-hand drive layout and to 10.3-metre length, the two-door body shells being basically opposite-hand versions of the Hong Kong vehicles of this length, though of 14ft 2in height.

The first of the left-hand-drive buses, and the only one of the prototype chassis of this layout was the sixth of the B45 series, type B45/TL11/2L, for Baghdad, where large fleets of British-built buses had been operating since the

The other China Motor Bus vehicle, with body 25046, was on the shorter chassis, similar to home-market models, thus not having the half bay amidships, but was to similar specification in terms of entrance layout and provision of opening windows, seating being for 89, split 56/33. It is seen in service on Hong Kong island as BR1 (CR 4443) – experience had led to the adoption of full-depth sliding windows at the front of the upper-deck and a hinged opening vent over the nearside windscreen – the longer bus, BR2, was similarly modified. The prominent 'Leyland' lettering on the grille had also been added after leaving ECW, but this was doubtless a Leyland Bus initiative related to the fierce competition for orders from the expanding Hong Kong market. All five of the bodies built in 1981 for Hong Kong were in Batch 651.

There had been a long and successful tradition of British-built double-deckers in Baghdad, and the design of ECW body 25057, built on the only left-hand B45-series chassis, though based on a combination of the standard designs for the Olympian, was finished in a way slightly reminiscent of the Park Royal bodied Atlantean buses built for this fleet. The basic body shell was of 10.3-metre length and 14ft 6in height, with similar opening windows to the Kowloon buses though with hinged vents in both decks at the front. It was understood to have operated in Baghdad for several years after delivery in 1982 and is seen here on its return to Britain, looking slightly shabby but basically sound.

'fifties, at first on AEC chassis and then on Leyland Atlantean. Most of the bodies had been built by Park Royal, though Willowbrook built the final 200 bodies on Atlantean chassis to Park Royal design in 1980-1. The ECW body for this operator was 25057, with 86-seat capacity and differing from the other vehicles in having a roof line with slight peaks at front and rear, leaving Lowestoft in August 1981, though returning before departing on its overseas journey in January 1982 – all these vehicles passed through Leyland's Nottingham service centre before being exported. It is understood to have remained in Baghdad from February 1981 until returning to the UK in about 1984 subsequently languishing in Leyland ownership until sold (via a dealer) to Calypso Bus Service, Gibraltar, in March 1990. It had not been registered or used when seen in June 1993, parked with other Calypso buses and apparently in reasonable condition.

It was followed by a vehicle for use by the Carris fleet in Lisbon, an ONTL11/2L, the 73rd production chassis,

with body 25059 of 78-seat capacity, which left ECW in September 1981, though returning before departing again in December. Finally, body 25058 for service in Athens on similar chassis ON52 left Lowestoft also in September.

The Lisbon demonstrator subsequently went to Brazil for the UITP Congress in April 1983, moving to Egypt in March 1984, and returning to Britain via Alexandria in May 1987. It was renovated and modified by Leyland's bus centre in Bristol before being sold in July 1988 to a religious organisation, being inscribed 'The King's Coach'. The Hong Kong and Athens vehicles are all believed still to be working in those cities.

The 1982 production programme for the Olympian consisted of 250 bodies (25113-309/11-43/468-87), delivered between January of that year and February 1983. This was under half the annual output of double-deck bodies for the VRT, Atlantean and Fleetline in the 1977-80 period but was to be typical for ECW's remaining years. However, it is worth remembering that even this

Another Olympian demonstrator, chassis ON73 with body 25059, was for the Carris fleet in Lisbon, another major user of British double-deckers, It is seen operating as this undertaking's 925, registered TA-46-45. In this case the side windows had sliding vents of similar depth to the home market type, though the front-end ventilation was similar to the Baghdad vehicle. It was not retained, travelling on further demonstration duties before being rebuilt and sold as shown at the top of the opposite page.

Barely recognisable as the same vehicle, ON73 returned from its demonstration travels covering three continents and was modified into the form shown, losing the centre exit, lower-deck glazing and receiving dark glass with much reduced provision for ventilation on the upper deck, yet remaining left-hand drive, when sold to a religious organisation in 1988 with the registration NEC 828X.

reduced level would nearly match the entire intake of new double-deckers to British operators in 1993. By this period, the new bus grant was in process of being phased out and uncertainty in regard to legislation likely to alter radically the structure of the industry and its system of route licensing was tending to make operators cautious.

Even so, ECW was fortunate in concentrating on double-deckers, the demand for which was holding up relatively well, and it continued to be among the major builders of such bodywork. NBC subsidiaries were the main recipients, and a fairly wide distribution continued, the 154 vehicles going to twelve operating companies. Most were 77-seat single-door vehicles, though United favoured 76 seats and Southern Vectis 75, while City of Oxford's 24 were two-door with 75-seat capacity. The Scottish Bus Group took 41 bodies (25264-304), 21 for Alexander (Northern), by then using 'Northern Scottish'

as its fleetname, and 20 for Scottish Omnibuses otherwise known as 'Eastern Scottish'. All the above NBC and SBG buses were on ONLXB1/R chassis and to a largely similar specification apart from the usual destination panel differences, with full-width hopper opening windows, though SBG's distribution of these was different. The front upper-deck windows included the top opening portion once so familiar on ECW double-deckers but dropped for many of NBC's Olympians.

Strathclyde PTE took a further 20 bodies (25468-87) to similar specification to its previous batch, these being on ONTL11/1R chassis. All the foregoing 1982 programme Olympian buses were 13ft 8in high, but another new Scottish customer specified 14ft 2in height and 10-metre length. This was Lothian Regional Transport, which took delivery of 35 examples (25172-201/305-9) on ONTL11/2R chassis, with two-door layout and 81-seat capacity. This order, which was awarded on the basis of a special combined Leyland/ECW package deal, caused considerable surprise and some controversy, as the Lothian undertaking and its predecessor, Edinburgh City Transport, had a tradition of purchasing its bodywork in Scotland – its entire fleet of double-deckers at the time had bodywork by Alexander. Similar remarks applied to Strathclyde, though there the policy had not been followed quite so rigorously, but in both cases ECW was competing strongly to broaden its clientele. It was rather ironical that this circumstance had arisen when one of the factors behind the B45 project had been the ability to meet Scottish desire to support body construction in that country.

In addition to the production programme deliveries, four more bodies for Olympian chassis that were numbered in the experimental series were included in the 1982 totals. Three were further export vehicles, the chassis for the first having arrived in September 1981. This broke new ground in having three axles as well as being longer although, rather confusingly, the chassis, number ON119, was again

With the previous generation of double-deck bodywork laid to rest as far as production was concerned, the 1982 programme concentrated on the Olympian. Both NBC and the Scottish Bus Group standardised on the 13ft 8in version on the Gardner-engined ONLXB1/R chassis, generally 77-seat single-door buses, thus coming back into line with each other in basic specification to an extent not seen for over a decade, though the differences in destination display and opening windows continued. As often the case in earlier times, the SBG examples were built first, the 41 bodies all in batch 660, of which the initial vehicle, Northern Scottish NLO12 (TSO 12X) with body 25264, is seen when ready for delivery in January. The 154 bodies for NBC fleets (25113-71/202-63/311-43) followed, being built in Batches 661, 663, 666 and 669 and delivered between March 1982 and February 1983.

The choice of ECW bodywork for 35 Olympian buses for Lothian Regional Transport attracted much attention, partly because of the prestige of supplying Scotland's capital city but more because of the previous support for local industry. They were of 10-metre length with the short bay amidships and two-doorway layout, as well as being to 14ft 2in height – a generous three-panel destination display was another feature. The distinctive madder and white livery suited the design well, though there was a sharp break in the line of the white over the windscreen (of the standard BET pattern) as it dropped to just over side window level. Seen here is 673 (OFS 673Y) with body 25177 – the order was built as Batch 667 and delivered between October 1982 and January 1983.

There was quite a strong Scottish flavour to ECW production at that time for, just as the last of the Lothian order was leaving, a further batch of 20 for Strathclyde PTE was coming through as Batch 668 – indeed the total of 117 bodies on Olympian chassis for operators based in Scotland was only a little short of half the 1982 programme total for the model. The design was similar to the initial ten – Strathclyde was unusual among major urban fleets in choosing the 13ft 8in high version and the single-door layout made its buses basically similar to those for most company fleets. They seated 76 but the use of a flat-glass vee windscreen gave a different appearance. A side route number box was provided, though rather 'lost' in the advertisement display on LO30 (KGG 150Y) with body 25476 seen here – the batch was delivered in January-February 1983. As usual, the Scottish climate was not felt to justify as many opening windows as standard further south. Unusually Strathclyde had some 14ft 2in high Olympians bodied by Roe as well.

designated ONTL11/2R, the extra axle being a steered unit added ahead of the driving axle. It was for Kowloon Motor Bus and body EX18 broke new records for ECW in being 40ft long and seating 104 passengers, 73 upstairs and 31 below, with three doorways. The fast-growing population of the Hong Kong territories had caused the operators to seek larger and larger buses, and the three-axle version of the Olympian was perhaps an ultimate step in that direction.

The completed vehicle left the factory on 7th January 1982, entering service as Kowloon 3BL1 in April. Initially, it was on loan to KMB for evaluation though purchased in 1982. A further generally similar bus, again on a three-axle version of the ONTL11/2R chassis, ON332, in this case arriving at ECW in August 1982, received body number EX19 and was completed in May 1983. This was also intended to be supplied to Kowloon, then reallocated to China Motor Bus, but in fact remained in Britain and in Leyland ownership. It subsequently received a Gardner 6LXCT engine and the body was rebuilt by ECW to a

coach specification, involving some restyling, with one doorway removed and the seating capacity reduced to 71 – air conditioning equipment was also added. It received body number 26236 in this form and was exported to Hong Kong, where it became the first Olympian in the Citybus fleet, entering service as C51 in March 1985.

However, devlopment of the Olympian as a coach had begun in 1982, using a ONTL11/2R chassis, ON281, in an extended two-axle home-market form. The body, EX20, was based on the standard shell, but altered quite dramatically in appearance by the use of upper-deck front windows which were both more sharply raked and extended virtually to the full height of the roof. It was intended as a prototype for National Express, which had become interested in double-deck coaches as a consequence of the deregulation of coach services in the Transport Act 1980. The rear part of the lower saloon was used for luggage accomodation, with access from doors on each side aft of the rear axle. Seating was provided for 65 passengers, with 45 on the upper deck. Initially it was registered SND 50X,

The demand for bigger buses for operation in Hong Kong continued and the first three-axle Olympian chassis was the basis for EX18, which was the longest and highest-capacity bus body then built by ECW, measuring 12 metres overall and seating 104. It is seen above and on the right when ready to leave the factory in January 1982, initially for loan to Kowloon Motor Bus. There were three bays slightly shorter than the standard amidships, and in two of these doorways were incorporated, slightly narrower than the centre door on the three two-axle versions supplied the previous summer. In other respects, the design and specification was very similar to that of the latter, except that the opening windows in the windscreen and front upper-deck windows were incorporated during construction.

A change of livery had disguised the appearance of the same vehicle when this photograph of it in service with KMB was taken – it was purchased by that concern later in 1982. It carried the fleet number 3BL1 and was registered CV 184. A few minor modifications are evident, most obviously the slightly deeper opening sections to the windscreen. The foglamps had gone, and the standard wire-mesh between-decks grille at the rear had been replaced by sets of louvres.

What had begun as body EX19 had looked very similar to EX18 illustrated on the previous page, being also at first meant for loan to the KMB fleet though not completed until May 1983. In the event, it was extensively rebuilt as a coach, in part to a style that had by then been developed and is described in Chapter 14. It was given the production body number 26236, having been sold to Citybus in Hong Kong, for which fleet two all-new bodies, 26237-8, were built, and all three entered service in 1985. They were for use on an express service to Shenzhen in mainland China, and the rebuilt vehicle is seen in service as C51, registered DE 4281. The lettering included the word 'Express' with double-N symbol, exactly as used by NBC. The large grille on the vehicle's side almost suggests a side-engine layout. In fact it was for the auxiliary engine powering the air-conditioning equipment.

evidently for use by National Travel (North West) but entered service in August 1982 as ADD 50Y with National Travel (South West) using the Wessex fleetname, on the Bristol-London service. The seating capacity was later increased to 69 by reducing the size of the luggage compartment. It later passed to Badgerline Ltd but in December 1987 was exported to Hong Kong to join the Citybus fleet as its C101, though it did not enter service until a year later, after air-conditioning equipment was added. Rather remarkably, Citybus had thus acquired what had been EX19 and EX20, despite their quite different design and original use.

The last of the four experimental-series bodies on Olympian chassis in the 1982 programme was EX21, on two-axle left-hand ONTL11/2L chassis ON328, for Saudi Arabia. This had an even higher capacity of 108 seated passengers than the Kowloon three-axle version despite

being shorter, at 36ft, with 68 upstairs and 40 down. Some of the seating was arranged in 'three and two' rows. In accordance with normal practice in Muslim countries, a separate compartment for female passengers and children was provided on the lower deck. It was delivered to Leyland's Nottingham depot in October 1982 before delivery in December.

One further body to the Olympian style was built as part of the 1982 programme. This was a further example of the very rare Atlantean AN69 model, again for J. Fishwick & Sons of Leyland. The chassis had begun life in 1978 as a left-hand 10-metre prototype, type AN69/2L used by Leyland's research department but sold in late 1981. It was converted to right-hand-drive and might have been expected to receive a body of the VRT style, but the vehicle was to be the solitary example of a chassis of its generation to receive a body (25310) of the Olympian

The concept of the double-deck coach was revived in Britain by the effects of the Transport Act 1980, deregulating express services, which had the effect of expanding demand on many of the major routes. The first prototype resulting from this was body EX20, based on a long-wheelbase chassis on which was built a body derived from the standard full-height bus body shell but looking dramatically different, mainly because of the styling at the front of the upper deck, devised on the shop floor at ECW. Whether the overall effect was attractive is clearly a matter of taste, but it differed sharply from the smooth contours of the Standerwick coaches of a decade earlier, possibly being influenced by the German Neoplan design, though the roof treatment was different. The vehicle is seen as operating for National Travel (South West) as its 450 (ADD 50Y), after the front door had been converted to single-leaf form. Initially it had been virtually of bus type, and later, after sale to Badgerline, reverted to that form.

This rear view of EX20, also taken during the period of National Travel (South West) ownership at Victoria Coach Station, shows the way the luggage compartment occupied the rear part of the lower deck, there being access doors on both sides.

When the EX20 body built for National Travel also migrated to Hong Kong to join the Citybus fleet, it was to join EX19, illustrated at the top of the opposite page, a remarkable coincidence, compounded by the way in which the 'Express' lettering and symbol still appeared on the side, albeit reduced in size. The new livery highlighted the bus origin of the side window layout as well as the basically standard cab design. It was numbered C101 and was now registered EB1030 in the Hong Kong series.

The Olympian demonstrator with body EX21 built for Saudi Arabia was on two-axle chassis but had three-door layout, somewhat like the three-axle version for the KMB fleet, though the centre doorway was wider. It was of 36ft (11-metre) length and had five main bays like the home-market coach version and thus had a tidier appearance than previous large-capacity two-axle versions, The opening windows were basically like the China Motor Bus version, though using similar sliders in the deeper lower-deck windows of the 14ft 2in body left a rather deeper fixed portion. It is seen shortly before leaving Lowestoft in October 1982.

The Saudi Arabian demonstrator with body EX21 had an even greater seating capacity, at 108, than the three-axle version despite being shorter, this being achieved by the use of three-and-two seating in much of the upper deck.

pattern. It was built to normal height and incorporated the short bay amidships used to accomodate the 10-metre length. At the rear, the engine was enclosed in a 'bustle' but in this case side shrouds were built in to the body in a manner which had been used by some other bodybuilders but not hitherto by ECW. It was not delivered until 27th November 1983.

The 1983 programme could be regarded as a

continuation of 1982 so far as the output for the Olympian was concerned, with a total of 275 bodies built for this chassis type, and NBC subsidiaries as the main recipients – all but two being delivered within the calendar year. Yet the underlying picture was altering fundamentally, and the future looking markedly less secure. There were no other bodies in that year's programme, the single-deck coach content of the 1981-2 programmes to be described in the next chapter having ended. This was the first time the entire ECW output had been concentrated on one model, but more to the point was the fact that the total had dropped below 300 for the first time since 1945.

A key break with earlier history was NBC's decision in 1982 to sell the half share it held in Bus Manufacturers (Holdings) Ltd to Leyland Vehicles Ltd, which thus owned BM(H), and hence its subsidiaries including ECW, outright. This had been done because BM(H) had made a loss in 1981, and NBC was not in a position to accept the drain on its resources. This broke the link between the Coach Factory, to use the name by which it was still known locally, and the bus operating industry for the first time since its creation by United primarily for its own bodybuilding requirements in 1919.

The final Leyland Atlantean to be bodied by ECW was a second example of the very rare AN69 type for J. Fishwick & Sons, of Leyland, also sold off after use as a development chassis to the local independent operator. It was a 33ft model and this may have been why it received an Olympian-style body, the only example on chassis of another type, for the jig for a 33ft VRT-style body had been destroyed. The basic design of the body, 25310, was to the 10-metre Olympian standard as being built in 1983, but differing mainly at the rear, where the Atlantean engine cover was incorporated, though the provision of side shrouds made this less evident than in earlier cases. At the front, the top part of the grille aperture, slightly deeper than usual, was blanked off and an oval plaque bearing the J. F. & S. initials fitted. This gives a clue to how the need to provide enough internal headroom over the Atlantean rear axle was overcome, for the body design appears to be basically the 14ft 2in type and it seems that it may have been raised perhaps by 4in or so. These views show No. 2 (A462 LFV) in service, the lower view at Preston bus station. The extra height, on this occasion, was in the lower panels (4in) and the lower saloon windows (6in) compared to the normal 13ft 8in body.

Outwardly, the supply of Leyland Olympian buses to NBC fleets continued much as previously, with 197 of the standard 13ft 8in single-door type of body on chassis with Gardner 6LXB engines in the 1983 programme, built in Batches 670, 672, 675, 677 and 678. Behind the scenes, major changes were under way, a sign of this different climate being the closure of the Bristol Commercial Vehicles plant and hence the end of production of Olympian chassis there. The last, ON995, formed the basis of this vehicle, Devon General 1814 (A686 KDV) which received body 25672, delivered in November 1983 and seen in service the following month. This brought to an end 50 years of joint Bristol-ECW involvement in the supply of buses to associated operating companies, but Olympian chassis assembly had already begun at Workington, and some of the latter figured alongside Bristol-built products in the final two Batches quoted above.

It was not directly a consequence of this that Leyland decided to close the Bristol Commercial Vehicles factory, though it was a reflection of the shrinking market for buses, largely due to the growing air of uncertainty about future prospects within the industry. The BCV closure took effect in September 1983, by which date 995 Olympian chassis had been built there, among which 641 received ECW bodywork.

Of ECW's 1983 programme, 244 vehicles, or 89%. were on Bristol-built chassis, 1983 being the last year of the close association between the two factories that had lasted for half a century and provided the majority of buses placed in service over that period by those operating companies which had been controlled by the Tilling group before becoming part of NBC.

The 1983 NBC deliveries of standard Olympian ONLXB/1R buses, all 13ft 8in high, single-door and totalling 197, were distributed among eighteen companies, though this number included some cases of the growing trend for dividing large fleets, with batches for Midland Red East, North and South, and for Devon General, by then once again separate from Western National. All seated 77 except for Southern Vectis, who still favoured 75-seat capacity. To similar specification and included in the same run of numbers (25508-682) as 171 of the NBC buses, all on Bristol-built chassis, were four buses for AERE, Harwell. The last Olympian from BCV, chassis ON995, received body 25672 and was delivered to Devon General in November 1983 as fleet number 1814 (A686 KDV).

The balance of 26 bodies for NBC fleets (25732-57) were on chassis built at Leyland's Workington factory, which was henceforth to be standard for the Olympian. The first such chassis began a new series of numbers at ON1001, this vehicle going to Crosville with body 25732 as its DOG131 (A131 SMA) in September, there having been an overlap of production from the two chassis plants.

There were ten more bodies on Olympian chassis in the

1983 programme for NBC fleets, these (25683-92) being the first production batch of coaches on ONTL11/2R Special chassis (Bristol-built) and derived from the EX20 body. The design was altered somewhat, the luggage compartment at the rear of the lower saloon being dropped in favour of additional seating, the function of the vehicles being different, as they were built for commuter coach duties. The seating capacity became 73, the vehicles being built to 11.6-metre length and 14ft 2in height. Five were supplied to Alder Valley and five to Maidstone & District, all being delivered in May 1983.

The growing uncertainties caused Leyland to decide to have a demonstrator available, and A33 MRN, a 10-metre ONTL11/2R with 14ft 2in-high ECW body No. 25762 performed that function from February 1984 until added to Preston Borough Council's fleet in December 1985. Originally No. 3, though renumbered 33 when seen here in service, it had dual-purpose seating as was as increasingly common.

Lothian Regional Council took a further 34 Olympian ONTL11/2R with bodywork to similar specification to the previous examples in the 1983 programme. They formed Batch 676 and were delivered in September-November of that year. This view of 721 (A721 YFS) with body 25716 shows the frameless upper-deck emergency exit glass which had become a standard feature by this period. These frameless glass upper-deck emergency doors were first found on the production coaches for NBC such as that shown below.

The demonstration Olympian built for service in Athens with the EAS undertaking bore fruit, as an order for a futher nineteen 10-3-metre bodies (25488-506) on ONTL11/2L chassis was fulfilled in February-March. The bodies were to similar design to that of the prototype, though seating 73, one more seat being provided on the lower deck.

Following this delivery, EAS expressed interest in a further order but with bodywork supplied in CKD form. Included in the 1983 programme was a proof body, numbered EX25, and this was built on an Olympian chassis to check alignment early in 1984, though the chassis was then returned. The intention was that 75 bodies would be ordered on this basis for delivery in 1986, but this plan fell through and the body was dismantled and cut up for scrap.

Strathclyde PTE and Lothian Regional Council placed repeat orders for five (25693-7) and 34 vehicles (25698-731) respectively, in both cases to their standard specifications. These were on Bristol-built chassis but two new municipal customers, Grimsby-Cleethorpes Transport and Preston Borough Council received vehicles on Workington-built chassis. The former took four examples on ONTL11/1R chassis with 14ft 2in-high bodywork (25758-61), of which the first two were of two-door layout and the others single-door. They were delivered in December, but Preston's single body (25762) on the longer ONTL11/2R chassis, also 'normal height', delivered from Lowestoft in February 1984, was used by Leyland as a demonstrator until December 1985.

Generally, the attempts to promote export business for ECW-bodied Olympian buses were disappointing in their effectiveness, but an exception was the demonstrator supplied to the EAS concern in Athens in 1981, which prompted an order for a further nineteen built as Batch 671. Maybe the Greek connotations of the model name helped, and it is noteworthy that No. 364 of the production vehicles, with body 25500, bore advertising lettering proclaiming it when photographed in service. The design was basically similar to that of the Lisbon demonstrator shown on page 92, though with more generous ventilation.

The first ten production examples of the coach design for Olympian chassis, built as Batch 674, were of similar general appearance to the prototype but did not have the luggage compartment at the rear of the lower deck, which was akin to the standard bus design. The five for Maidstone & District were in a version of one of the striped liveries then policy for NBC coach fleets and carried the Invictaway brand name, 5442 (GKE 442Y) with body 25686 being shown. The revised design of lower front panel with headlamps repositioned was henceforth standard for bodies of this style.

The first step towards a new coach design was the modification of one of the bodies on Bristol RELH chassis built in 1972 and illustrated on page 55. New front and rear ends gave the impression of a completely new design. Even the sides appeared to have different proportions but this is illusory as the glass remains as used in the original. The vehicle selected was Eastern National 1404 (VHK 177L) with body number 19857, which latter did not alter despite the extensive modifications – it re-entered service in June 1981. New fully-framed domes were fitted at front and rear, and within, the luggage racks were tied into the structure with a new air ventilation system. In recent years the vehicle has passed into the fleet of the Northern Bus Company, of Sheffield, and Mr Duncan Roberts, Joint Managing Director, reports it as being 'a magnificent vehicle' with no structural problems.

Chapter Thirteen: **The B51 saga**

NBC was keen to modernise its coach fleet in the aftermath of the Transport Act of 1980. This was a first step in enacting the policy of abandoning the road service licensing system for bus and coach services that had been in force since 1930, as adopted by the Conservative Government elected in 1979. Its most obvious effect was the opening up of competition on the longer-distance services, in which NBC was able to build up considerable expansion following the deregulation which took effect on 6th October 1980.

Hitherto NBC had obtained most of its requirements for new coach bodywork from other sources, mainly Plaxton and Duple, and ECW had not built bodies of this type since 1972-75. The drop in new bus demand described in the last chapter left surplus capacity available at ECW and it was logical to use this to meet more of NBC's requirements for coaches.

The project for a new coach body to be produced by ECW was given the Leyland code number B51. The need was urgent, so it was decided to modify one of the coach bodies that had been built in 1972, to act as a prototype for the production vehicles to follow. Accordingly, an Eastern National Bristol RELH6G originally delivered from ECW in October 1972 (when it formed part of the Tilling fleet then being run as a sub-section of Eastern National, being numbered 9441) was selected for return to Lowestoft and modification began early in 1981. As the original plan was to rebody RELH, coaches, on the basis of a plan within NBC to work on a seven-year life for coach bodies, this was a logical course of action.

The changes that were made were intended to bring the appearance into line with contemporary tastes, particularly at the front and rear, and the basic structure was little altered. The front end showed influence of Leyland styling trends, for the use of an area of matt black finish below the windscreen to give an illusion of greater depth was being used on a new cab adopted for the Roadtrain range of goods models. At the top, the windscreen was extended upwards virtually to roof level, the destination display being seen through the upper part instead of being mounted in the peak above it. At the rear, although a black surround was again used, the depth of glass was considerably reduced. Detail fittings, trim and finish were all in line with contemporary tastes and the transformation gave the impression of a completely new design.

Rather surprisingly, the vehicle retained its original body number (19857) and registration number VHK 177L, though the fleet number had changed partly as a consequence of operating with National Travel (South East) from 1974 to 1978, having become 1404. It was redelivered to Eastern National in June 1981.

There were plans for further similar rebodying exercises,

On the rebuilt Eastern National RELH, the depth of the rear window was reduced though the black surround gave an impression of greater depth. These views show it in a revised livery adopted some time after its refurbishment.

The plan to carry out a rebodying exercise was altered to one for supplying bodywork to the newly-developed style known by the project number B51 on new Leyland chassis. The first order, included in the 1981 programme, was for 35 on Leopard PSU3G/4R chassis, built in Batch 653 and all delivered in March 1982. The design, to an overall length of 11.28 metres, was largely as set by the prototype, though slightly higher-built, to compensate for which the lower edge of the windscreen was set lower. Although the waistline of the side windows was horizontal, the livery for this initial batch included a sloping moulding under the first bay behind the entrance, giving an effect slightly reminiscent of the contemporary Plaxton Paramount design. The overall external impression was quite stylish if perhaps a little stark, though these vehicles were not intended to compete in the super-luxury class. Seen here is Northern General Transport 7100 (LFT 100X) with body 25091, the last of four for this fleet, originally numbered 5100 as delivered.

and it is known, for example, that Eastern Counties prepared five RELH chassis dating from 1969 – their RE894-8 (SVF 894-86G) – and at least two were ready to go to Lowestoft, the original early-style ECW bodies having been removed by Ben Jordan at Coltishall.

Leyland then intervened and offered new Leopard chassis at a very low price to help increase the volume of production, and the rebodying plan was lost.

Manufacture of the production version of the B51 body was put in hand, now to be based on Leyland mid-engined chassis. In consequence, the design was altered to incorporate a large luggage boot at the rear, an obvious seeming change, but one that was to lead to unexpected problems. NBC specified as much luggage space as possible to meet the growing demands of passengers, and this was supported entirely from the body structure, Leyland's standard practice by that date being to supply coach versions of its mid-engined chassis devoid of any form of frame extension behind the rear suspension mountings. This was accepted practice and in general caused no difficulty, bodybuilders designing their structures accordingly. ECW had been out of touch with this market and, to compound the combination of circumstances, was under pressure to cut costs, adopting the practice of using unsupported glass-fibre mouldings to carry the heavy windscreen glass, for example.

Contracts for a total of 35 bodies (25068-102) were placed for eight NBC subsidiaries as part of the 1981 programme and all were delivered in March 1982. United Counties was the recipient of the largest batch of these, with eight, Cumberland and East Kent taking five each, while Northern General and Lincolnshire took four, and Eastern Counties, West Yorkshire and Yorkshire Traction received three apiece. Most seated 49 passengers.

The foregoing were all based on Leyland Leopard chassis – this very successful model, which had formed the basis of most of the new coach deliveries for NBC fleets through the 'seventies, was then nearing the end of its long production run. The model number was PSU3G/4R, the G signifying the 'rationalised' O.680 engine having some features of the new TL11. The bodies were visually similar to the prototype in most respects, though slightly higher waisted and having quite a marked step-down to the lower edge of the windscreen. A sloping moulding running from the latter level up to the normal waist at the rear of the first side window was a feature of this batch. The front grille lacked the top portion that had been needed to suit the RE's radiator position, whilst double pairs of headlamps were also a feature.

The 1982 programme coach orders, totalling 120 bodies, followed on immediately, deliveries beginning in April, before there had been time to gain any experience with the

United Counties was the first operator to put B51-bodied coaches into service – this vehicle, 170 (CNH 170X) with body 25068, was numerically the first of the breed as well as UCOC's first of a batch of eight. Within a week or two alarm bells began to ring with reports of first one and then further instances of the luggage boot floor collapsing onto the road. Unfortunately, not only were all the 1981 programme vehicles delivered that same month but the 1982 programme orders followed on immediately and the entire build of the type had the same basic defects. Weaknesses of the front end structure also became apparent quite early, and a major programme of rectification had to be put in hand.

1981 programme vehicles delivered the previous month. Production continued to January 1983. There were a further 52 bodies of 11.28-metre length (25344-95) on PSU3G/4R chassis, divided between eight operating companies, including Alder Valley, Oxford, and Southern Vectis in addition to more for some of the companies included in the 1981 allocation. Again, these mostly seated 49, though there were some minor differences, such as the single-panel entrance door on the two Southern Vectis coaches instead of the wider two-leaf folding door usual on the type – the latter had come into favour among many NBC fleets in the 'seventies as a feature of coaches used for part of their lives on stage-carriage duties and thereby qualifying for bus grant. Similar bodies (25396-9) were built on four 1970 Leopard PSU3A/4R chassis that had been rebuilt and given new chassis numbers by Midland Red Express, these also receiving new registration numbers.

The Leyland Tiger chassis was developed, largely in conjunction with NBC, as a successor to the Leopard. It first appeared as type B43 at the 1980 Show, but had gone into production in 1981. It was basically similar in its

general character and mid-engined layout to its predecessor, but incorporated the TL11 engine instead of the O.680 and air suspension as standard, among many other changes. The first and largest number to receive ECW bodywork were 42 on the TRCTL11/2R chassis for London Country for Green Line duty, and classified TL in traditional London style. These also received 11.28-metre bodies (25404-45), basically similar to the Leopard version, although a single louvre over the front grille was added to suit the front-mounted radiator, a feature of the Tiger (and also the Olympian) that adopted Bristol practice. The last twelve of the batch seated 53 rather than the 49 of the rest.

The remaining 22 bodies (25446-67) were of generally similar design but to 12-metre length. This option, permissible in terms of legal restrictions since 1967, had become much more widely used by NBC coach subsidiaries from about 1976. The ECW body design, though similar in most other respect to the slightly shorter version, incorporated five full-length window bays and a slightly longer rear overhang. The entrance was of the narrower inward-opening single-leaf type and the emergency door at the offside rear was also narrower, splitting the rearmost

The major part of the 1982 programme B51 bodies were based on further Leyland Leopard chassis, basically of unchanged design, though some operators specified minor variations and livery variations became common as NBC swung away from the firmly standardised styles of the 'seventies, at least for coaches. Eastern Counties LL882 (XPW 882X) with body 25376, was one of eleven for that fleet with 47-seat capacity and the 'express' style of two-leaf door found on many of these vehicles. This picture shows another livery variation quite apart from the plain 'National' fleetname. Instead of the red/blue bands, one wide grey one has been applied.

London Country took 42 of the B51-type bodies on Leyland Tiger TRTCL11/2R chassis for Green Line duties, using a livery with a broad band of green running completely round the vehicle, and markedly altering the appearance by comparison with the version having the black surround to the windscreen. The example shown was TL22 and, as seen, carried the registration TPC 122X, following on from the earlier examples but this was changed to WPH 122Y before it entered service. After completing five or six years on Gr5een Line duty, the leases under which they were added to the fleet having expired, most were sold off and Midland Red North rebodied a significant number.

This is the rear view of TPC 129X – the unpainted strapping on the rearmost nearside panel suggests something is amiss even now. The vehicle is painted in yet another livery variation, continuing LCBS's ability to cock-a-snook at NBC livery policy throughout the Green Line 'coach era' from 1977. The inclusion of 'GB' plates does not herald an extension of the Green Line network beyond our shores – they were a standard fitment on most B51s.

bay. Seating capacity varied between 50 and 57, these limits being found in one operator's vehicles, for Hants & Dorset took five at 57 and two seating 50. These were on the long PSU5E/4R version of the Leopard, as were four for National Travel West and three for National Welsh, both favouring 53-seat capacity. The corresponding Tiger TRCTL11/3R was favoured for six more similar bodies for National Travel West, and two seating 51 for East Midland.

It might have been expected that a well-proved chassis, such as the Leopard and the new but closely-related Tiger, combined with a body design that was based on a successful predecessor of nearly a decade earlier would be a formula for a sound vehicle but this was not to be. Reports of major failures of the rear end of the body structure began to come in from United Counties, the first operator to put B51 coaches in service, within a week or two of them being put on the road, and this rapidly became a serious epidemic, affecting both 11.28- and 12-metre versions. Some of the vehicles were returned to Lowestoft for rectification, but kits of parts for strengthening the structure were made up and sent out to allow the modifications to be made locally

to the operator, in some case by local bodybuilders – Wadham Stringer is understood to have done some of this work, for example. Similar action was taken to strengthen the front end in some cases.

A sequence of circumstances lay behind what seemed a most surprising design fault from so experienced a firm as ECW, with a generally excellent reputation for structural soundness. Failures in the long overhang at the rear of 11-metre bodies of other makes on mid-engined chassis had not been unknown, but ECW's experience had been almost entirely on the Bristol RE, which had the engine at the rear, leaving room for only a shallow rear boot for luggage, mainly carried in side lockers on the coach versions. The ECW bodies on this chassis undoubtedly benefitted from the close relationship in regard to design between Bristol and ECW, which enabled the resulting vehicles to escape the troubles with the body structure that plagued many early rear-engined single-deckers on other makes of chassis.

This confused creature – with a mixture of several NBC standard vynils but a set of none – is one of the rebodied vehicles (25397) on 1970 chassis for Midland Red Coaches. For an unknown reason the driver's signalling window on this batch was deeper than on any others. It cleaned up the design but how much better if it had been at the same lower level as the windscreen, as per the original vehicle on an RE chassis, shown on page 101. the combination obtained new registrations, somewhat unusually, ROG550Y being WHA251H when in original form.

The 12-metre version of the body was basically similar to the 11.28-metre type, save that there was an extra bay and the rearmost one was split on the offside to include a smaller emergency door. East Midland 32 (SKY 32Y) with body 25447 was one of a pair for this operator on TRTCL11/3R chassis, the only other examples of the 12-metre B51 body on the Tiger were six for National Travel (West). Here again there was a livery variation, with a striped version of the National Express style, also without the black screen surround. This is the 1982/3 season 'Express' livery – with a little local 'forgetfulness' on the part of EMMS so far as the black windscreen apron is concerned!

A variant of the B51 was this 12-metre (25453) on Leopard PSU5. Built originally for Hants & Dorset they had maximum capacity (57) seat bodies for the busy but relatively short Bournemouth-London services. A combination of load factors demanding MCW Metroliners and constant reorganisation of NBC coaching activities saw them pass to Shamrock and Ramster, Pilgrim Coaches and others. this vehicle 9092 (YEL 92Y) – Sir Walter Raleigh – went to Midland Red North and subsequently Northern Bus of Sheffield. This view is at Plymouth in 1986.

The 1984 and 1985 programmes were the last in which standardised ECW bodywork was built for NBC subsidiaries on what could be described as a nation-wide basis. The major part of the 1984 deliveries comprised 186 Olympian buses of the standard single-door 13ft 8in-high type, much as in previous years. All were Gardner-engined and most seated 77, arranged 45 upstairs and 32 down. Southern Vectis 699 (A699 DDL) with body 25824, was one of six for that fleet delivered in February 1984 – it is seen here in Newport in September 1986. They had two fewer seats than standard on the lower deck, a long-standing practice to allow more luggage accommodation in an area with a high proportion of holiday travellers. The NBC vehicles in the 1984 programme were built in Batches 680, 682-4, 686 and 687.

Chapter Fourteen: **The final years**

Bodywork for the Leyland Olympian was to be the mainstay of ECW production for its remaining years, and although output was modest by earlier standards, yearly figures of well over 200 in the 1984 and 1985 programmes were enough to keep ECW among the leading producers of double-deck bodywork in the much reduced overall market of the time.

The 1984 programme was again based largely on NBC orders, with 186 basically standard 13ft 8in high bodies (25766-810, 25817-957) of 9.6-metre length on ONLXB/1R chassis, the latter all coming from the Workington production line. Deliveries of these actually began in December 1983, continuing to December 1984. All were of single-doorway type, and mostly with 77-seat capacity, though with some exceptions. Notable among these were several batches with coach seating, a revival of an earlier trend. Usually the resulting seating capacity was 70, though Ribble favoured 72.

A particularly significant development was the supply of three Olympian models with ECW bodies (25763-5) to London Transport. It had become evident that it would no longer be economic for London buses to be virtually unique to that undertaking and what was called an Alternative Vehicle Evaluation Programme was put in hand, in which various types were purchased for comparative trials. Three examples of the MCW Metrobus, Dennis Dominator and Volvo Ailsa B55 were also ordered (though in the event the third Metrobus was cancelled), and each order included various specifications. The Olympians, numbered L1-3 by London Transport, included one ONTL11/1R and two ONLXB/1R, the latter including one with Voith transmission. The body was basically the 14ft 2in standard with two-doorway layout and 75-seat capacity, though with many features and finish to LT requirements. They were delivered in February 1984.

A further order for Lothian Regional Transport was completed in September-December 1984, this being to the same normal-height two-door 10.2-mtre specification on ONTL11/2R chassis as the previous buses for this fleet. It called for 34 bodies (25968-26001) but the last vehicle was repurchased by Leyland Bus for use as a demonstrator. It was exhibited at the UITP congress in Brussels in April

Not surprisingly, the relationship between the Olympian body and the Titan was brought out most strongly in the London examples. The vehicle shown, L1 (A101 SYE) with body 25763, was the first of the three 9.6-metre buses purchased as part of the Alternative Vehicle Evaluation Programme, and forming ECW's Batch 681. There were numerous London-style features but the windscreen remained the BET type rather than the barrel-shaped design that had been favoured on most London Transport standard vehicles since the 'sixties. The window arrangement on the offside of these evaluation examples is Titan-like, though the window over the offside front wheel is not as short. By this period, London buses had become all-red, the white relief at upper-deck window level associated with Ralph Bennett's influence having vanished, and the plainness was emphasised by the omission of the upper mould normally to be found on the advertisement panels between the two rows of windows. Unusually, they were painted at Workington before delivery in February 1984. Note the central staircase fitted.

1985, returning to ECW for 'tidying up' and remaining until June, only to return again for a further two months in July for conversion as a demonstrator to Bangkok, Thailand, where there were hopes of a massive order for some 4,000 buses. No major structural changes were made but full-depth sliding windows were fitted and the vehicle repainted, being allocated a body number in the experimental series (EX56), leaving the works on 25th September 1985 – unfortunately, again, no order ensued. However, the vehicle went on to demonstrate in Kuala Lumpur and was eventually offered for sale when in Singapore. It was purchased by Citybus, of Hong Kong, in the latter part of 1990 and entered service with that operator in February 1991.

The 1984 programme also included seven more of the 11-metre double-deck coaches with the distinctive raked profile, on chassis which now had their own designation ONCTL11/2R, though Leyland was by no means consistent in such matters. An order for five had been placed by Arlington, the London dealers, and the numbers 25958-62

allocated for the bodies. Only the first two were built, and delivered to Alder Valley in May 1984, but meanwhile a further five (25963-7) had been delivered to London Country as LRC1-5 in April-May.

A further similar chassis, though designated ONTL11/2R Special, was used for a redesigned version of the double-deck coach, exhibited at the 1984 Motor Show. It had been ordered by Ebdon's of Sidcup, and was exhibited in that concern's maroon livery. The design of the body (EX26) was quite extensively revised from the earlier version, with a more upright profile but using curved glass. The driver's windscreen was now almost vertical, though curved in plan at the outer ends, the shape being very similar to that of the Mancunian double-deck design introduced by Manchester City Transport in 1968, though not quite so deep, while the familiar BET screen appeared on the upper deck, complete with wipers. The side windows took on a new look by virtue of the use of bonding for attaching the glass, thus allowing flush glazing with slim

Also adding to the variety of the London scene were the five Olympian 11-metre coaches for London Country's Green Line fleet and delivered in April-May 1984. Similar to the previous examples of the type, they were painted in one of the NBC 'venetian blind' liveries. LRC1 (A101 FPL) with body 25963 is seen in Buckingham Palace Road, Victoria. Unusually for the type, standard destination displays are fitted, as can be seen.

For the 1984 Motor Show, a new version of the double-deck coach body for the long-wheelbase Olympian was produced. The frontal appearance of the resulting body, EX26, was completely changed from the previous style first seen on EX20, becoming more upright but having a smoother profile and using curved glass screens for both decks. At the sides, the use of bonded glazing also helped to give a radically different look. Internally, the staircase was moved to the rear, and there was a roomy luggage compartment. The vehicle was painted in a maroon livery for Ebdon's of Sidcup, appearing on the Leyland stand, but then returned to spend over a year in ECW's yard, where it is seen in this view.

Ebdon's did not take delivery of EX26, and in August 1986, the vehicle was sold to South Yorkshire PTE, becoming No. 100. It is illustrated in the colour section in the form delivered to South Yorkshire PTE.

pillars and brought a reversion to squared window corners. The plug-type door, by then coming into favour on many coaches, was adopted for the relatively narrow front entrance and the second centre door. The walk-in luggage compartment was similar in size to that of the first body of this general type, EX20. The staircase was moved to the rear, thus giving lower-deck passengers an uninterrupted view forward. Luxurious seating was provided for 67 passengers.

Unfortunately, Ebdon's did not take delivery and the vehicle languished in ECW's yard for over a year before being sold in August 1986 to South Yorkshire PTE, becoming No. 100 and registered 4475 WE. It was then altered to 63-seat capacity. Its registration was changed to C259 CWJ as a '1986' vehicle and it was sold via Plaxton's to R. Day (trading as Swallow Coaches) of North Common, Bristol in May 1992, this operator then re-registering it, yet again, to 253 DAF. (!).

A second experimental-series body built on an Olympian chassis was another export venture, this time for the United States, where Leyland had entered into a marketing agreement with Gillig, which was manufacturing smaller buses at Hayward, California. This was on a left-hand-drive chassis, ON1410, fitted with the Cummins LT10 10-litre in-line six-cylinder engine, then beginning to come into favour in Britain and considered more acceptable than a unit of British origin for the American market.

The body (EX32), was derived from the 10.2-metre bus design, but the short bay was repositioned further to the rear to suit the location of the centre exit and staircase. The flat-glass windscreen usual on export bodies was fitted, and in accordance with North American legislation, almost every non-vented window was equipped as an emergency exit.

Stone's air-conditioning equipment was incorporated, this being powered by a Perkins 4.108 auxiliary diesel engine – in place of the lower-deck rear window a longitudinal mesh vent was provided. Again in line with local practice for tall vehicles, groups of three lights were fitted in the front and rear roof domes, as well as single lights at the front and rear corners, the latter facing sideways. It was issued with a British registration number, B 757 UHG, and underwent a series of tests before being shipped from Southampton for delivery to Gillig in September 1984.

No immediate sales in the United States resulted, but the vehicle moved north to Canada, spending some time with Perimeter of Vancouver, and then passed in October 1986 to Grayline Tours of Victoria, before sale to Brampton Transit of Ontario in January 1989. It entered service with this concern in March of that year, the seating capacity being 68. Although the sales impact of this vehicle was yet another disappointment, the order for ten three-axle double-deck coaches for a San Francisco operator supplied in 1986, and described later on pages 118 and 119 may have been a delayed reaction.

A further Olympian export demonstrator was produced, this time for the North American market as a result of an agreement with Gillig, a medium-sized manufacturer producing smaller buses in California. The body, numbered EX32, was based on the 10.2-metre 14ft 2in bus shell but with the short bay further to the rear than usual to suit the centre door position, and extensively modified to suit United States requirements. It was shipped in September 1984 and spent periods with various operators, moving to Canada and then, in January 1989, was sold to Brampton Transit of Ontario, in whose service it is seen, bearing the fleet number 8500 and an Ontario licence plate but still carrying the British registration B757 UHG.

A Danish liaison

Another exhibit at the 1984 Show had been allocated an ECW number in the experimental series (EX36), though it was not built there. The initials DAB stand for Dansk Automobil Byggeri, a concern founded in 1918 and well established as a bus bodybuilder in Silkeborg, Denmark, which began importing Leyland chassis in 1946. Later it became a Leyland subsidiary, though retaining links with other concerns, notably Saurer and Alusuisse, the latter

being specialists in aluminium-alloy body structures. DAB had been involved with the development of the articulated buses of joint Leyland-Saurer-DAB design, of which examples were operated by South Yorkshire PTE in the late 'seventies.

The DAB venture which brought a brief hope of a new source of work for ECW was an integral single-decker, originally advertised to be available in 9.5- or 10-metre lengths, though later publicity quoted 9.48 metres, and it

As a first step in the investigation of the idea of offering a DAB-designed mid-sized single-decker on the British market, Leyland Bus imported this right-hand-drive prototype early in 1984 and registered it as A499 MHG. Its frontal appearance had an obvious affinity with the Leyland National 2, DAB having been the origin of the windscreen of that model, though the destination box, with its bold route number display, was different. It had quite a high floor level and the entrance door was narrow. After testing by Leyland, from September 1985 it spent a brief spell with United, by then already operating the second vehicle shown in the lower picture. It was purchased by Jim Stone of Glazebury, Lancashire, in 1986 and is now lovingly cared for by fitter Steve Mayo. Reregistered BUS 1T it performs schools contract work and the occasional selected private hire

For display at the 1984 Show, a second vehicle was built by DAB and sent to ECW, where it was given the number EX36 though the only work done on it there was trimming, the fitting of seats for 46 passengers and finishing — if the project for producing the model had gone ahead, the hope was that more work would have been carried out there. Significantly, it was placed in service by United, becoming number 1500 as if about to start a replacement series for its large fleet of Bristol LH buses which had numbers which had begun at the same point. The taller version of the curved windscreen encompassing the destination display softened the outline somewhat, but did nothing for legibility of the route number or lettering. The vehicle remained in service until it suffered a serious accident in 1992, after which it was sold in July 1993 once again to Jim Stone. After a full mechanical overhaul and repair the vehicle was returned to DAB in Silkeborg, with temporary windscreen and painted in grey primer. DAB fitted a replacement front and then gave the bus a full repaint. Like its fellow it is used on school contracts.

is thought that this was the figure for the two vehicles built. It was taken up by Leyland as a possible replacement for the sector of the market that had been covered by the Bristol LH. A right-hand version of this was built and is understood to have been imported direct to Leyland early in 1984 for testing, where it was registered A499 MHG – it visited ECW for inspection, though no work was done on it. It was decided to adopt the Tiger Cub name as used for Leyland's lightweight model of the 'fifties. The mechanical units were largely derived from those of the Tiger, with a TL11 engine, derated for this application, and Pneumocyclic gearbox, though the front axle was that used on the Leopard PSU3 series. Inevitably, with such a specification, it came out considerably heavier than the LH or the original Tiger Cub, and indeed more than a typical RE bus. The figure is understood to have been about 8.5 tonnes unladen, though publicity material quoted an 'approximate' figure of 7.62 tonnes.

A second example completed to shell stage was then imported and arrived at ECW's works on 29th August 1984. It was trimmed and fitted with 46 seats and delivered on 11th October for display at the Show. It was relatively high-built and not quite so square-cut in outline. The first imported example had a windscreen of the type familiar on the Leyland National 2 (this item originally having been introduced by DAB for an earlier design), with a large rectangular destination box above. The Show vehicle had a deeper windscreen with destination box seen through the upper portion in the manner then fashionable, and also differed in having four bays rather than five on the offside between the driver's window and the very small emergency exit door at the rear end.

Somewhat amazingly, having regard to its nature, the vehicle was described in some Leyland publicity as a 'heavy-duty midibus', which probably simply confused possible customers. On a more realistic level, NBC may have been fairly receptive to a relatively sturdy vehicle in the light of its whole-life costing studies. The vehicle was placed in service early in 1985 by United as its 1500, registered B500 MPY, and remained in service until 1992, when it was withdrawn as a consequence of an accident. In September 1985, the earlier vehicle, A499 MHG, was

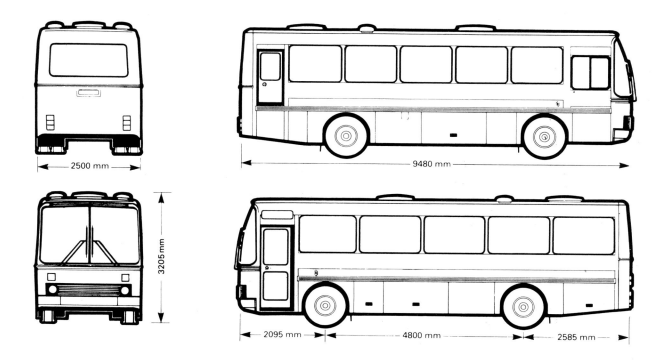

These drawings were included in a leaflet for what was simply called the Leyland Tiger Cub, with no reference to DAB or ECW, issued in time for the 1984 Show. There was no reference to a type designation, a table heading for 'Model' simply quoting a 9.48-metre length, and under 'Bodywork' the entry began 'System Alusuisse M5438...'. With the TL11 engine set to give 170bhp and an unladen weight about one-third more than that of a Bristol LH, this model was hardly in the same category. Note the different pillar spacing on the left and right sides.

also lent to United, becoming 1501, though its stay seems not to have been long.

The project was not taken further and although possibly a little over-elaborate for its suggested purpose, it arrived at a very difficult time for the British bus operating industry, and NBC in particular, with not only further deregulation but also privatisation as a declared aim on the part of the Government. However, it seems possible that had it gone into production, greater participation by ECW might have been possible. The vehicle had a welded-steel underframe, and though described as integral, the description quoted body construction as in aluminium alloy using the System Alusuisse which was to come into prominence in the United Kingdom a little later as being used by Wright of Ballymena and Optare. It seems possible that a suitable structure using this or traditional ECW designs could have been developed, but both the political and operational climates were against such a design. Quite apart from the trend towards lightweight mini and midi buses, the high floor line was out of favour and it would have run into problems when the DIPTAC specification to suit disabled passengers came into prominence.

NBC winds down

The 1985 programme was the last which could be regarded as including a relatively comprehensive delivery to NBC subsidiaries in the traditional way. It had been made clear in the Government's White Paper 'Buses' of July 1984 that its intention was for NBC to be reorganised into free-standing individual companies which were to be sold off. Hence the existing organisation was working on borrowed time as it were, yet, even so, the delivery of new double-deckers was being maintained at what was regarded as a sensible level. In fact the total for that year's programme was slightly up, at 271. Of these, 215 were of various versions of standard bus-outline design for NBC fleets, and the greater part of these were the usual low-height pattern, there being 199 such (26002-186/92-4/6-205/50), largely 77-seat buses but including some with coach seats. The largest single delivery was 45 for Northern General Transport, noteworthy as being ONCL10/1RV chassis having Cummins L10 engines and Voith automatic transmission, some being in full Tyne & Wear PTE yellow and white livery and including eight with coach seating for 72. South Wales also took the Cummins and Voith combination for the chassis of its delivery of seven vehicles, but otherwise the Gardner 6LXB retained its place as the usual engine for what had become the typical NBC double-decker. Other large deliveries included in this group were 32 for Crosville (including thirteen with coach seats for 72), 20 for Ribble, eighteen apiece for West Riding and United, fourteen for West Yorkshire Road Car, plus a

Just as the Government was rejecting such concepts as integration and co-ordination, the Tyne & Wear PTE succeeded in its pressure for local NBC subsidiaries to adopt the full Tyne & Wear yellow and white livery, complete with fleetname, for vehicles operating services within the PTE area, the only identifying feature being the NBC logo. The example shown was one of 45 Olympian models with bodywork of standard 13ft 8in bus outline for Northern General Transport in the 1985 programme, also of interest by virtue of their Cummins engines and Voith transmission, both newly-introduced options – 3657 (C657 LJR) with body 26029 being seen when ready for delivery in the autumn of that year. This had the usual bus seating capacity of 77, but eight of NGT's order had semi-coach seats for 72. Bodies of this type were built in Batches 689, 693, 696-8 and 702-3, deliveries extending from December 1984 to January 1986.

The coach-seated Olympians often had versions of NBC's 'venetian blind' liveries of the period, in line with the new competitive atmosphere, even though deregulation had yet to extend to what were still called stage carriage services. East Midland received five such vehicles built in Batch 696 and delivered in June 1985, including 327 (C327 HWJ) with body 26150 seen here a year later in Mansfield. This is another vehicle with a non-standard destination display.

Some of the NBC liveries were by now more complex than had been seen at Lowestoft since the days prior to the second war! Therefore some of the dual-purpose Olympians were supplied to the customer to finish. Both the East Midland vehicle above and this one, seen left, for Crosville were representative of this category. C208 GTU was to be become EOG208 in the magnificent 'Cymru Coastliner' livery featuring a huge dragon on each side.

Colchester Borough Transport followed up its spell of standardising on the ECW-bodied Atlantean by placing its first two Olympian models in service, choosing Gardner-engined rather than Leyland-powered chassis as might have been expected. As previously, 'normal-height' bodywork was specified, this being of the usual 14ft 2in dimension because of the Olympian's lower build. The vehicle seen here complete but awaiting its fleetname and numbers before delivery was to become 41 (C41 HHJ) with body 26244. The bodies were built in Batch 699, which also included five coach bodies of similar height for Maidstone & District, and were delivered in September-October 1985. Sliding windows have been specified here.

further four for the York-West Yorkshire fleet, and a dozen for Trent. There was also one replacement (26241) for the body of a Crosville Olympian of 1982 that had been damaged beyond repair in an accident.

London Country had obtained normal-height bodywork for its Olympian buses, built to generally similar design to the ECW version, from Charles H. Roe Ltd. This was an old-established bodybuilder, also part of Leyland Bus, and based in Leeds, but the closure of that concern's works led to the 1985 order for fifteen being diverted to ECW. These (26221-35) were on ONTL11/1R chassis and although basically to similar design to the ECW 14ft 2in-high standard pattern, incorporated the Alexander type of curved-glass windscreen that London Country had favoured from its initial batch of Park Royal-bodied Atlanteans of 1982.

One standard 77-seat low-height body (26195) was supplied to Leyland Engineering for use as a test vehicle,

being on a chassis with Cummins engine. This vehicle was delivered in December 1984, the same month as the first of the order of similar chassis for the Northern General fleet. Another (26249), on ONLXB/1R chassis, went to an independent operator, Metrobus Ltd of Orpington, Kent, being supplied via Arlington's.

A further 24 bodies (26252-75) for Lothian, to that undertaking's standard 10.2-metre normal height two-door pattern on ONTL11/2R chassis were included in the 1985 programme and delivered between November of that year and January 1986. Mention can also be made here of one further, and final, vehicle of the same type for Lothian, built to replace that taken from the 1984 order for use as a demonstrator. The body (26280) was included in the 1986 programme but in fact it was built with the others and delivered in January 1986. Colchester took the first of two pairs of normal height 9.6-metre bodies (26243-4) in September-October 1985, these on ONLXC/1R chassis

There was a tendency, completely opposite from that applying in the 'seventies for revivals of old company names. One such was County, of Lepton, near Huddersfield, which had been an unusual instance of joint ownership by BET and independent operators as both Yorkshire Traction and West Riding held shareholdings prior to 1968, though it was absorbed into the former's fleet after both of these concerns became part of NBC, this taking effect in October 1968. Yorkshire Traction owned 666 (B666 EWE) with 26172, but it carried the County name and former livery of cream and blue.

These two photographs, both showing vehicles built in the 1985 programme, provide a comparison of the alternative height versions of the home-market Olympian coach. The Maidstone & District vehicle, like all earlier examples, was to the 14ft 2in height, evidently regarded as desirable to give a more spacious-seeming interior to what was primarily intended as a commuter coach. This view also shows the unusual entrance door design, with unequal panels and a slightly inclined waist strip to suit the lines of the vehicle. The vehicle shown is 5446 (B446 WKE) with body 26190, which was one of a pair of vehicles built in Batch 690 and delivered in January 1985. That batch also included two for Alder Valley and five for London Country. Towards the end of the year, Maidstone & District took four more similar vehicles, plus a rebody, built in Batch 699 along with the Colchester buses illustrated on the previous page.

Eastern National introduced a new variant by having substantially the same design produced in 13ft 8in high form for ten examples which comprised Batch 692, delivered in February-March 1985, the vehicle shown being 4502 (B690 BPU) with body 26213. The lower-deck side windows were shallower, in the same way as applicable to the bus version. The application of the livery helps to disguise the way in which the entrance door and windscreen, unaltered, cause the front panel of the upper-deck to become shallower. Another minor difference was the replacement of the upswept brightwork above the upper-deck windows with this fluted moulding. 'Electronic' destination gear was fitted.

with the less common Gardner 6LXCT turbocharged engine.

Output of ECW's coach body for the Olympian expanded in the 1985 programme, a total of 25 being built. As previously, most were for commuter express routes into London, there being repeat orders of three for Alder Valley (26187-9) and two batches, of two and four, for Maidstone & District (26190-1/245-8), plus one replacement body (26251) for the latter fleet in place of one dating from 1983 damaged beyond repair. These were all to the same basic design of 14ft 2in height as previously, but ten for Eastern National (26211-20) were built to the 13ft 8in dimension, the lower-deck windows not having the extra depth common to both bus and coach models of the taller versions. All the foregoing were on the 'coach' version of the longer Olympian chassis, though the designation had settled down as ONTL11/2R Special.

Three further bodies were built to the modified style introduced by the 1984 'Ebdon's' Show exhibit. Mention

has already been made of the six-wheel Olympian built in 1982 with body EX19, originally for Kowloon but rebuilt in 1985 as 26236 for use by Hong Kong Citybus, which had developed a route from the Hong Kong territories penetrating just over the border into mainland China, to the Shenzan special economic zone in Guandong province. Two new bodies (26237-8) on further six-wheel chassis, now more logically designated ONLXC/3R Special, were also constructed to much the same design, though having fixed windows and forced-air ventilation as well as an increased seating capacity of 77, whereas the rebuilt vehicle retained the original deep sliding windows and seated 71. The first of the new vehicles, which were dispatched from Lowestoft on 28th July 1985, ran for a time in Britain on test registered as B336 YRN. It is thought that originally the order was for five bodies but the other two were not built and numbers 26239-40 remained blank.

A further six-wheel coach body (26242) to similar

The 'Ebdon's' coach built for the 1984 Show spawned a further and final series of ECW double-deck coach styles, though the more angular version was to continue alongside them into ECW's final days. Hong Kong Citybus was the recipient of two new examples on three-axle Olympian chassis as well as the rebuilt EX19 shown on page 96. The appearance of all three was similar but the bodies built from new had a deeper cab side window though possibly the most obvious difference in these views is the modified livery, abandoning the dark surround to the upper-deck front glazing. The upper view shows C104 (DG 7762), which had started life as C53, with body 26238, and that below shows C103 (DG 4817), originally C52, with body 26237 – note the entrance door, similar to the home-market Olympian coach.

design was built on an ONTL11/3R tri-axle chassis as a demonstrator for service in Indonesia, being delivered to Leyland's service depot in Nottingham on 12th September 1985.

Both the operating and manufacturing sides of the bus industry were in a state of turmoil towards the end of 1985. The Transport Act 1985 had passed into law in October, and thus the break-up and piecemeal sale of NBC, as well as virtually unregulated competition outside the London area, was set to take place. These factors in themselves inhibited the confidence needed to place orders. In regard to NBC in particular, the possibilities of management buy-outs also had their effect, as potential buyers did not want the burden of large numbers of new buses which would simply add to the price they had to raise.

Except in regard to minibuses, seen by operators as a means of responding to the advent of unregulated competition, manufacturers were thus becoming even more starved of orders. Economic factors had also hit exports to many countries quite severely. Leyland Bus was making big losses and towards the end of 1985 it was announced that 505 jobs were to be cut across the group. In the event, the total Leyland Bus production of all types

of vehicle or chassis from all factories in the group in 1986 amounted to more than 993, compared to 3,140 in 1981. In addition, the Government, and in particular Mrs Thatcher, the Prime Minister, had made it plain that the nationalised status of British Leyland was to be ended by selling it, whether complete or in parts, to the private sector.

In this climate, the outlook at Lowestoft was beginning to look bleak. Even the relative popularity of the Olympian and what was widely regarded as its standard ECW body was not enough to allay worries. It seems very probable that closure might have occurred earlier than it did but for the decision, announced in June 1985, that 260 Olympians with ECW bodies were to be supplied to what had become London Buses Ltd. This concern had come into operation as successor to London Transport in regard to the operation of its bus services from April that year. The order had come as a surprise in the sense that Leyland had not received an order from London Transport for two years and it was expected that MCW would get at least a share of the business, but Leyland had pressed very hard to win the order, badly needed by both organisations, and succeeded.

This was the largest order for supply to one operator ever received by ECW or its predecessors and it was ironical in the extreme that it was to be the last contract to be fulfilled. It brought the 1986 programme total to 320, the best figure since 1982, though even that was still below any earlier figure since wartime, when the factory had been closed by the circumstances of the time.

When it is remembered that non-London business in the 1986 programme amounted to just 60 bodies it becomes clear that the factory would simply have run out of work early that year, making rapid closure inevitable in the economic climate prevailing. It is understood that the possibility of ECW entering the minibus body market, then rapidly expanding but fiercely competitive, was considered but not pursued. Even if some of the large

The order for 260 ECW-bodied Leyland Olympians for London Buses would have been regarded as a considerable triumph in the early 'eighties, but the demand for new buses had fallen so low that it merely delayed the end by perhaps a year. Output was split, not merely into production batches in the usual way but also in the issue of body numbers, deliveries beginning in January-April 1986 with 26286-351, produced as Batches 704 (34 bodies) and 706 (beginning a run of 32-body batches for this order). Then, from May, came 26382-413 (Batch 709) and 26420-51 (Batch 711), in which the vehicle shown, L105, with body 26423, was produced. It is seen awaiting delivery outside the works in July 1986, yet to receive the registration C105 CHM. Note the outline for the T-shaped advertisement already in place on the offside.

orders for such vehicles placed at that time, notably by NBC, had gone to Lowestoft, the volume of work, much of it related to conversion rather than new construction, and the brief peak in demand seems unlikely to have done other than postpone the closure.

In general, the 260 London Olympian buses were similar to the three supplied in 1984, and thus were based on the ECW standard design for the model in 9.6-metre length and 14ft 2in height, with two-doorway layout. The seating capacity became 68, with 42 on the upper deck and 26 below, a reduction from the 75-seat total of the first three, this and other modifications being related to the 'Human Factors and Design Research Study' that had been commissioned by London Transport in 1983. Perhaps most obvious was the revision in the design of the entrance and exit, the former using a split-level layout rather reminiscent to the system devised by Brighton Hove & District for the rear entrance of its Lodekka FS-type buses in 1960 (see page 115 of the previous volume). The chassis

type was ONLXB/1RH.

Although initially the body numbers for the London Buses contract were allocated in one complete run (26286-545), ECW, faced with so large an order, subsequently decided to take the unusual step of not only splitting it into manageable batches in the usual way but dividing the body numbers into a series of groups. In the event, the first group, 26286-351 was a run of 66 covering the fleet numbers L4-69 and delivered in the first four months of 1986. Then came 26382-413 and 26420-51, two groups of 32 each taking the fleet numbers to L133, completed by October. Then came a longer run of 87 bodies, 26459-545, taking the fleet numbers to L220, the last of which were delivered in January 1987, though not completed in order. The final run of 43, with numbers running from 26558 to the final number 26600 which was London Buses L263, overlapped to some degree and also ended in January 1987.

The other vehicles produced as part of the 1986

Built alongside the London vehicles in the 1986 programme were the last deliveries of Olympians to other operators. The 27 of the low-height bus outline supplied to NBC fleets all had semi-coach seats, being built in Batches 703, 705 and 708 and delivered between January and May of that year. Among the last were three for Midland Red South, of which 964 (C964 XVC) with body 26370 is seen in Stratford-on-Avon in July 1986 – fleetnames were tending to become larger in the run-up to privatisation, but the NBC emblem was still prominent in this case. Note the non-standard destination indicator.

Of the eight 14ft 2in-high bus bodies for municipal fleets in the 1986 programme, five were for Reading Transport, not hitherto an ECW customer but one which had, unusually, chosen the Leyland Titan for part of its intake of new vehicles since 1979, building up a fleet of twelve, switching to the Olympian as its logical successor. In addition, it had grasped the opportunity given by the Transport Act of 1980 to run an express service into London, using 'Goldline' as a brand name, and the Olympians, intended primarily for this duty, had coach seating for 66 passengers. Seen here is the first of the type, No. 80 (D 80 UTF) with body 26452 - note the destination 'Bournemouth' displayed, evidently for excursion duties. These bodies, plus two more to bus specification for Colchester, were built in Batch 712 and delivered in September 1986, among the last to leave the factory, apart from the later deliveries of the London order. During their short lives at Reading, these vehicles were subjected to numerous modifications – to improve their appearance in most instances. These can be seen in the colour section.

programme were interspersed between the London Buses batches. The bodies produced for NBC fleets were subject to various cancellations and revisions before the final version was produced. In the event, only 27 of the standard low-height version, all with coach seats, were built, all on ONLXB/1RH chassis (the H suffix having been introduced to distinguish chassis with Hydracyclic gearboxes after the Voith option had appeared). Eastern National took fifteen with seats for 72 passengers (26277-9/546-557, all delivered between January and April 1986. United took six, also 72-seat (26362-7) in April 1986, these last products of the Coach Factory for that concern being particularly historic since it had been founded by the United company nearly 67 years earlier, largely to supply its own needs when its headquarters were based in Lowestoft. Midland Red South and East Yorkshire took three each of a 71-seat version (26368-73) in April-May 1986.

One further low-height body (26276) with 77-seat capacity was built on ONlXB/1R chassis for the 'A1 Service' fleet controlled by the the Ayrshire Bus Owners Association, the owner in this case being Stevenston Motor Co (Mr Tom Hill) – it was delivered in March, 1976.

There were eight normal-height bodies for municipal fleets, one being the Lothian vehicle already mentioned. Reading Transport became an ECW customer almost at the end of its existence with an order for five single-door bodies (26452-6). They were based on ONLXCT/1RH chassis with turbocharged Gardner 6LXCT engine for use on this operator's Goldline Reading-London express service and had coach seating for 66. All were delivered in September 1986, and one of them shared the distinction with two 76-seat buses on ONLXC/1R chassis for Colchester (26457-8) of being the last standard bodies for other than London Buses from ECW when they left the factory on the 12th.

A total of 24 coach-outline bodies of various types were also built in 1986. London Country and Maidstone & District took five and three examples respectively on

ONTL11/2R Special chassis, together comprising 26374-81, of the original normal-height pattern with the raked front end in May-June. Slightly later, six coaches of the 'Ebdon's' outline and 13ft 8in height were built and delivered in July 1986, three (26414-6) being of 11.16-metre length, 73-seat capacity and on ONTL11/2RH chassis for Eastern National. The other three (26417-9) were unique in being of 9.6-metre length, the only examples of coach-outline bodies (as opposed to bus-outline with coach seats) on the 'short' Olympian chassis, in this case ONLXB/1RH. They had been ordered by Southern Vectis in the hope that they would be ready earlier in the year, but

Double-deckers for coach duties of one kind or another figured surprisingly strongly in ECW's 1986 programme, which included a final eight of the 14ft 2in-high style with strongly-raked upper-deck front windows on the long-wheelbase Olympian chassis. Rather surprisingly, they were built alongside 13ft 8in-high bus outline bodies, including the Midland Red South semi-coach shown on the opposite page, in Batch 708 – ECW's production methods altered somewhat towards the end, and Leyland-style 'build numbers' were introduced. Five of these, all delivered in June 1986, were for London Country, the last, LRC15 (C215 UPD) with body 26378 being seen in Luton Flightline livery with appropriate route number 757.

What tended to be called the 'Ebdon's' outline, first seen on the 1984 Show exhibit, might well have become the double-deck coach standard appearance for ECW, even though only six further examples for operation in Britain were produced, in Batch 710 and delivered in July 1986. Three of these were for Eastern National, and could be regarded as a face-lifted version of the 11-metre commuter coach, with the more rounded front-end grafted on to a bus-layout vehicle with entrance and stairs at the front. They had the same 73-seat capacity (split 45/28) as the previous Eastern National batch illustrated on page 114, sharing their 13ft 8in height. This view of 4511, with body 26418, before delivery shows it bearing the registration C511 HJN originally allocated, but which was changed to D511 PPU before entry into service. Note the rather transatlantic message on the electronic destination display.

The other three vehicles in Batch 710 were unique in applying coach outline to the standard 9.6-metre length double-deck body. They were intended for Southern Vectis and these views show the first of the three, with body 26414, in the metallic grey livery chosen by that concern, though the vehicles had been diverted to Alder Valley and legal lettering showing that concern's name had been applied in this case. The rear view exhibits some relationship to the standard bus body, though the emergency window was set higher to suit the high-backed seats. Noteworthy is the complete absence of destination gear in the Southern Vectis specification.

were diverted to Alder Valley North after completion but before delivery.

The last examples of ECW export bodywork and perhaps the most impressive bodies ever built by ECW were ten on three-axle lefthand-drive ONCL10/2LV Special chassis for Gray Line Tours of San Francisco. This concern is not to be confused with Grayline Tours of Victoria, British Columbia, which had briefly operated the Olympian demonstrator with body EX32 sent over to the Gillig concern in 1984, but the sale was perhaps a delayed consequence of the link with Gillig. The design of the 78-seat bodies (26352-61) was basically similar to that of the Olympian coaches built for Hong Kong Citybus, but incorporated several new features. There were plug-type doors at front and centre positions, a liberal supply of emergency exits to meet North American legal requirements, and an air-conditioning system built into the rear of the vehicle, plus public address facilities and a toilet. The first one left Lowestoft on 5th May 1986 and the last on 24th September.

By that date, the pressure for Leyland Bus to be sold off had reached crisis point, especially as far as ECW was concerned. There had been various discussions with possible buyers but a management buy-out proposal for Leyland Bus reached the stage of an announcement in July 1986 that the Government would be prepared to sell Leyland Bus to its management team, though the deal did not go through immediately. Within the following month, the news came that ECW was to be closed as part of a cut-back which was to require 1,250 redundancies out of a total LB workforce of 2,600 on the basis of forecasts of a further fall in sales.

So the completion of the London Buses contract was to be the end of production at ECW. Clearly, the catastrophic fall in demand would have put Leyland Bus into a very difficult position even if it had been a well-funded company in full control of its own fate. With a modern plant at

The three coaches diverted from Southern Vectis were added to Alder Valley's Londonlink fleet, and thus became the final generation of ECW-bodied double-deckers operated on London services, originally by Thames Valley, since the days of the Bristol K-type. In fact, by the time this photograph was taken, the mantle had moved on again, as Alder Valley was split into what were effectively its old constituents and what was briefly Alder Valley North had been sold off as part of the privatisation of NBC constituents, becoming The Berks Bucks Bus Co Ltd after sale to Len Wright Travel in December 1987. Its buses were given the fleet name Bee Line but the Londonlink name was retained, as seen on 1624 (D824 UTF) with body 26416. Nowadays the bus is part of City of Oxford's Wycombe fleet, fitted with standard upper-deck domes and windows.

Something of a swan song for ECW were the ten three-axle Olympian coaches built in Batch 707 for Gray Line Tours of San Francisco – perhaps the most impressive vehicles ever built by the Coach Factory. It seems sad that they received little publicity at the time. The design was derived from that of the coaches built for Hong Kong Citybus though with many feature to suit United States requirements, such as the multiple emergency exit windows and the array of some seven fans visible through the grilles at the rear for the air-conditioning equipment. These views show 602 and 603, with bodies 26353 and 26354, almost ready to leave the factory in the summer of 1986.

Among projects that did not go into production was one for single-deck bodies on Leyland Victory chassis for which the numbers EX33-36 were issued in June 1984. These photographs dating from May 1986 of one in ECW's yard may well show it in process of being dismantled. It is possible to discern the front cross-member of the chassis and what appears to be part of the engine through the gap in the front panel - evidently the radiator had been removed. The body style appears to be basically similar to that of the rear-engined Tiger shown on the opposite page, but chassis details are quite different. The Victory was an export model, favoured in countries where road conditions, in terms of rough surfaces or dust, favoured a front-engined vehicle. It seems probable that these views show EX35, indicating by the windscreen surround that it never reached completion.

Workington capable of assembling complete buses, chassis and, if need be, bodywork plus the Farington plant in Leyland producing mechanical parts as well as chassis, the remote-seeming Lowestoft works was an obvious target for closure.

Apart from the small Reading and Colchester orders and the remaining Gray Line vehicles, all of which were delivered by the end of September, the factory settled down to complete the London order.

However, before describing the last stage of production, it is appropriate to mention some projects of the final years that were only partially completed before being abandoned or did not materialise at all. All were given numbers in the experimental series. Among the most interesting were EX33-35, allocated in June 1984 to three single-deck bodies for Leyland Victory chassis, a rugged heavy-duty export model which had been introduced by Guy but transferred to Leyland for manufacture from 1982, a final three chassis being assembled at Farington in 1984-5. Its design had affinities with the Guy Big J goods range, and in later years effort was concentrated on the version with engine ahead of the front axle which had found favour in South Africa and Singapore. The ECW bodies are thought to have been designed as prototypes, either for export or for the Ministry of Defence. So far as can be ascertained from the very limited official records, EX33 was purely a 'parts' exercise – possibly for CKD development – no

chassis having been delivered. Chassis for EX34 and 35 arrived at ECW on 20th July 1984. EX34 was completed as a shell only and sent to Leyland for pave testing on 8th May 1985, while EX35 was to seat 35, with standing room for others. It seems doubtful if it was completed, and both bodies are thought to have been dismantled by ECW, EX34 having been returned from Leyland for the purpose. The fate of the chassis is unknown.

Another c.k.d. mock-up for Greece was allocated the number EX60 in June 1985 and was even included in Batch 701 together with four c.k.d. kits but none of these reached the constructional stage.

One of the rear-engined Leyland Tiger chassis on which bodies EX67 or 68 were to have been mounted, in the yard at ECW in October 1985. The basic chassis design is similar to the standard version with mid-underfloor engine, but in this case a vertical engine, probably a TL11 (the turbocharger being visible), is mounted longitudinally at the rear - other equipment in protective covering and mounted on temporary brackets, is visible at the rear. In the background on the right can be seen a Lodekka FLF, Bristol Omnibus JHW68E, intended originally for preservation by BCV then passed to ECW, then to the Leyland Museum and subsequently sold to a private owner

This vehicle, also based on the version of Tiger chassis with vertical rear engine was built in about 1985 in connection with the hoped-for large order from Bankok - the choice of chassis type was related to the climate, with frequent flooding which made an underfloor engine unacceptable. When the order fell through, it was registered Q723 GHG and used by the Leyland-DAF football club, as seen here - reclining seats of the type fitted to the Royal Tiger Doyen were fitted. The vehicle later passed to OK Motor Services, Bishop Auckland, and is in process of being converted to bus specification, with single door. Although no body number plate is fitted, the number EX67 has been found written inside the front indicator flap. The body construction has been found to be poor, with a mixture of welded, rivetted and bolted construction along its length, which seems to suggest it was intended purely as a test vehicle.

Finally, EX66-68 were allocated at an unknown date to bodies intended for Thailand, EX66 was double-deck, presumably on an Olympian chassis, and EX67 and 68 were to be 12-metre single-deck bodies on a rear-engined version of the Leyland Tiger chassis, This was a model never publicised and is not to be confused with the rear-engined Royal Tiger coach underframe, as this version of the Tiger retained a conventional chassis frame and had a vertical engine arranged longitudinally. One vehicle, with body EX67, used for pave testing, is thought to have been the basis for the surviving example used for a time by Leyland-DAF football club.

Returning to events in the last months of production, the uniformity of output was broken to a mild degree when even London Buses adopted the philosophy of including some coach-seated vehicles, with six part-way through the order (bodies 26491-6), delivered as L166-71, which were painted in standard London bus livery, all-red at that

date, and a final four, numerically (26597-600), L260-3, which were painted in a special livery with the upper deck panels below window level in white. The seating capacity was not affected, the relatively spacious layout of accommodation for 42 on the top deck and 26 on the lower deck allowing for this.

The chassis for the last of these vehicles, ON2645, was also the last to be built at Workington at that time – Olympian production had moved again to Leyland's Farington works, though it was to go back to Workington in 1990. It was delivered to Lowestoft on 24th November 1986, and the completed vehicle was delivered direct to Plumstead garage, by then part of London Buses' Selkent district. Before the outer panels were fitted, someone had the idea of the workforce employed in its construction inscribing their names on the outward-facing side of the internal panels, these only becoming visible when the outer panels are removed for repair or replacement.

Production of the London Buses order for Olympians continued. The longest run of body numbers, 26459-545, which were fleet numbers L134-220, was built in Batches 713, 714 and 715 and delivered between September 1986 and January 1987. Batch 715 also included the first nine bodies of the next series, beginning at 26558 which continued to the end at 26600 and fleet number L263. The general pattern had been to produce the buses in batches of 32 each but the final one, Batch 716, covering bodies 26567-600 was of 34, delivered in December-January. The vehicle shown, L259, with body 26596, was noteworthy as the last to bus specification. It is seen at New Addington in March 1987. This view, when compared with that of L1 on page 107, shows how the arrangement of lower-deck windows on the offside was revised, eliminating the short window immediately behind the driver but adding one behind the staircase which improved vision for passengers sitting in the adjacent seat considerably. In standard London fashion, the garage code and running number are carried on the cab side, TC being the code for Croydon, which before 1933 had been a Tilling garage as conveyed by the initial T, and oddly appropriate for buses with bodies built by ECW, so long a Tilling subsidiary.

The coach-seated version of the London Olympian, of which ten were built, formed part of the contract for 260. The first six, produced part-way through the order, were in the normal bus red but the final four, at the end of the contract, were distinguished by white upper-deck side and end panels. This view also shows the split entrance step, based on an idea first used on the rear platforms of Brighton Hove & District ECW-bodied Lodekka buses in 1960. The vehicle shown when ready for delivery is L262, with body 26599, the penultimate ECW body.

In its final days of construction, someone put a piece of cardboard in the upper-deck front window with the message 'Lucky Last' and this proved to be a true prediction, for L263 was selected as one of those sent to rallies by London bus staff, beginning in 1987, and proving very successful. It regularly attended such events until 1990, collecting numerous awards, thanks to the loving care it received from the team at Plumstead, led by Ken Dix, the garage's General Engineering Manager (who has since retired), Fred Mills, his day Foreman, and indeed Mrs Dix and various members of the garage staff, who saw the hard work they put in justly rewarded.

As this chapter is being written, it remains in service, still in Selkent Travel livery, being used on commuter express services and for private hire. Selkent were only too pleased to make the vehicle avaiable for our photographer, knowing that the work they have done is recognised by its use on the cover of this volume, and we thank them for their help.

It seems fitting that this last vehicle from so important a factory in the history of buses in Britain should be properly cherished. The British bus manufacturing industry has had a very difficult time during the last decade but there are many who think that a bus renaissance is long overdue.

When it comes, those responsible could do worse than think of how things were done at ECW and the good service its products have given, and indeed still do, for they remain a familiar sight in most parts of Britain and act as their own memorial.

The last one. London Buses L263 receiving its seat cushions as the Coach Factory closes down for good. Those who built this final body, 26600, had signed its inner panels before the outer ones were attached.

'Lucky last' was the slogan workers had applied to L263 before it left Lowestoft, and so it proved, for specially prepared by staff from Plumstead garage, it was to win many prizes over the years it competed in bus rallies. Carrying the registration VLT 9 which had been that of RM9, it is seen when it had become part of the fleet of the awkwardly-named South East London & Kent Bus Co Ltd, which understandably used Selkent as a more manageable fleet name. As this book closes for press L263 seems set to pass with Selkent to Stagecoach control.

L263 stands proudly behind some its trophies.

Beadle, based in Dartford, on the south-eastern outskirts of London, produced sizeable numbers of bodies for Tilling companies from the 'thirties. Many of those built after the 1939-45 war had a general resemblance to standard ECW designs yet their true identity was readily identified, as in this preserved example, one of a number built in 1950 on Bristol L5G chassis dating from 1940 which originally had Bristol-built bodywork. Slightly higher built than the contemporary ECW body, it has outswept skirt panels, a more rounded outline to the underside of the canopy and a windscreen of a shape typical of this bodybuilder. Western National 333 (DOD 518) is seen in Norfolk in 1989.

ECW Lookalikes

Over the years there have been many instances of bus or coach bodies that resembled ECW products to varying degrees, some to the extent that they could be mistaken for the genuine article, and, even on others where this was less so, the general intention of an affinity was obvious. They fall into three main categories.

1. The Tilling influence

The broadest category was where orders were placed by Tilling companies for bodywork to styles similar to those of ECW. This applied particularly just after the 1939-45 war.

There had been some similar instances in the 'thirties when two bodybuilding firms in particular had augmented ECW output for Tilling-managed operating companies, mainly in the south of England, largely though by no means exclusively in the rebodying of older chassis. These were J. C. Beadle Ltd of Dartford, Kent, and W. Mumford Ltd of Plymouth. These concerns supplied much of the needs of the Western and Southern National companies, while Beadle also built numbers of bodies for Hants & Dorset, and Eastern National. Single-decker buses of both makes were to styles quite similar to those of ECW, and although Beadle's own standard double-decker style was used extensively for rebodying, its bodies on new Bristol K5G for W/SNOC closely resembled the ECW pattern, except for the cab. There were occasional instances further north, where, for example, Northern Counties built some bus bodies in 1934-5 for United to a style resembling slightly earlier Eastern Counties bodies for that fleet.

In the period after the war, Beadle continued much as before for Western & Southern National, though on a more limited scale and concentrated more on

rebodying, having turned much of its attention to new lightweight integral designs using Bedford and other units, also favoured by Tilling companies. It also supplied many of the coach bodies for the post-war Royal Blue fleet on Bristol L-type chassis and rebodied some Leyland Lion buses for Wilts & Dorset.

As in pre-war days, this firm's characteristic windscreen shape, with its lower edge curved downwards, often quite sharply, to the outer corner, was often the most obvious giveaway.

Mumford dropped out, concentrating on other activities but a newcomer to the ECW lookalike category

Beadle's double-deck body, as built for Western or Southern National around 1950-51, was very close to the ECW standard except, again, for the windscreen, of which the shape was quite logical when applied to pre-war Bristol chassis where the original tall radiator was retained. Western National 347 (FTA 639) had entered service with an ECW body in 1941, but was rebodied as shown in 1951.

The Bristol Tramways & Carriage Co had built the chassis and original body of this vehicle in 1933 as well as being responsible for its operation, subsequent modification and rebodying, leaving little but the registration HY 8255 as a clue to its history. It had begun life identified in the fleet by its chassis number J116 in the way then usual for BTCC, being an early example of the J type, with six-cylinder petrol engine and its first Bristol body, of two-door layout and seating 34, was metal-framed, of type AM3/34. It was renumbered 2012 in 1937 and received a Gardner 5LW engine in 1938. It returned to BTCC's Brislington Body Works in 1948, emerging with new 35-seat rear-entrance body and later received the PV2 radiator as seen here. Much of the body was to standard ECW design, but the cab was more angular, no doubt partly due to having been built around the J-type chassis front end and then being modified to suit the much lower bonnet line set by the late-type radiator.

A different version of the BBW-built body is seen on BTCC's 2060 (EHT 98), another rebuilt J-type, which entered service in 1937 as a JO5G, with Gardner 5LW engine from new, and having a BBW two-door 34-seat body. Like others of similar type, it received a PV2 radiator and new BBW body to ECW outline, in this case in May 1950, being one of ten finished to 31-seat express standard. Here side windows were square-cornered at the top, in a manner found on quite a number of BBW bodies of this period, but the cab and other details were as on the Lowestoft-built product.

in the post-war period was Bristol Tramways & Carriage Co, whose bodybuilding department was also known as Brislington Body Works, or BBW for short. This organisation had maintained its own styles, much more angular than those of ECW, in pre-war days. By the late 'thirties, its output was generally confined to BTCC's own fleet or a few instances where Bristol buses with BBW bodies were supplied to municipal fleets. The latter practice ceased in post-war days, when ECW bodywork was supplied to some such customers, but

BBW switched to ECW-like outlines as it resumed building bus bodies, at first largely for its own fleet, and often with more angular detail features than the ECW version. Half of BTCC's delivery of 50 Leyland PD1 double-deckers of 1947-8 was bodied locally, most in the BBW workshops but some by a local firm, Longwell Green, all being built to the simplified BBW version of ECW's outline.

When the family of associated fleets grew as a result of the sales of the Scottish and Red & White groups to

When BTCC took 50 Leyland Titan PD1 buses to augment its fleet, half were bodied locally, most being handled entirely by its own BBW shops, which produced a body style broadly like the 25 standard ECW highbridge examples (see page 35 of the previous volume) but more angular, with no bowing at the front of the upper deck. The first examples had windows with square-cut upper corners where sliders were fitted but the later ones, including C4031 (KHY 400) seen here, had glazing closer to the ECW standard.

The others were bodied by Longwell Green to the BBW design. Seen here is the first, C4001 (KHW 242), which followed the first BBW-bodied example C4000 in 1947, and had the early type of glazing, with fixed glass more deeply inset as well as square-cornered polished frames for the sliders. It is understood that some others of this design were finished by Longwell Green. Two more (C4025 and C4040), recorded as built by Longwell Green and delivered in 1948, were to the modified style with more ECW-like glazing, and further buses of that type were also finished by LG. Bodies to this pattern were also fitted to various pre-war Bristol K5G chassis by BBW.

Red & White Services Ltd had taken delivery of 30 Albion Valkyrie CX13 models in 1946, all originally fitted with Pickering 34-seat bodies to the relaxed utility design – as often the case at the time, this was due to a spill-over of wartime arrangements. As also often so, the poor-quality timber then available and used in their framing did not last well and all were rebodied by BBW in 1951-3. The example seen here was S646, one of those rebodied in 1952, using a style virtually identical to ECW's except for cab details.

Generally, when BBW produced bodywork for Bristol chassis in the post-war period, it conformed to ECW dimensions, but there were exceptions. In 1954, Southern National purchased six Bristol L5G buses dating from 1939 from Eastern Counties, scrapping the original ECW bodies, lengthening the chassis and fitting PV2 radiators etc so that they were largely to LL5G specification. Three went to ECW for new 39-seat bodies (8427-9), which, together with similar 8430-2 for Western National, were the last to the standard design – see page 89 of the previous volume. The other three went to BBW, which produced this special version with higher floor level,

permitting an increase of seating capacity to 43, only two short of the 45 of an LS underfloor-engine model of the period. The seats over the rear wheel arches faced forwards and another row was thereby squeezed in. In most other respects normal design was retained but the overall higher build is obvious in this view of 375 (CVF 844) alongside 377 (CVF 842) of the same type but with standard ECW body – it was taken at Bideford in 1965. It is noteworthy that ECW body numbers 8433-8 initially remained unused, suggesting that these three SNOC buses plus three for WNOC on chassis from its own fleet may have been diverted from ECW to BBW. One number, 8433, was later taken up by a pre-production MW.

Possibly the most surprising rebodying contract carried out by Bristol to ECW pattern was that for Western SMT in 1954-55. The latter had given some rebodying work to ECW from 1951 and was about to begin taking Lodekka buses on a regular basis. The chassis were AEC Regal I models dating from 1946, but they were rebuilt to 16ft 3in wheelbase and thus became equivalent to the Regent II model of the same period. Apart from seating 53 instead of 55, the lowbridge bodywork was almost identical to that produced for Crosville to rebody six Regent chassis in 1948 (see page 45 of the previous volume), even reproducing the characteristic slight inset at the top of the windscreen so typical up to 1950 but rarely found on later bodies. The cab glazing was slightly different and the usual hinged vents at the front of the upper deck omitted, Seen here is GC288 (BAG 86), allocated to Greenock.

Strachans got the contract to build the bodywork for 24 AEC Regal III single-deckers supplied to Tilling companies in 1947-8. They were on the version of that chassis with 7.7-litre engine and crash gearbox, and the bodywork could be described as a reasonably close interpretation of the contemporary ECW standard, though with opening windows of more conventional style for the period. Crosville received twelve and Western and Southern National six each, the last-mentioned's 1076 (JUO 998) being seen here.

United found itself in need of bodies for two Bristol L5G chassis in 1952. This arose as an aftermath of the R-series chassis exercise, in which what were nominally reconditioned chassis were produced as a means of circumventing restrictions on new vehicle production by the British Transport Commission. Twelve chassis produced in this way for United entered service in 1949-50 with Eastern Counties bodies dating from 1934 but it seems to have been decided not to extend this process to the two chassis in question, which were stored for two years but then sent to Roe, which produced a version of its standard half-cab body with Tilling-style destination box and other details. The second of the two, BG14 (PHN 409) is seen at the bodybuilder's premises before delivery.

the BTC, it seems possible that some of the rebodying work was passed on from ECW, then already building about as many bodies as possible, to BBW. In these and some other later cases, they were virtually indistinguishable from ECW products, and are thought to have incorporated ECW parts.

There were other instances where Tilling companies ordered bodywork of other makes in the early post-war period and, to varying degrees, ECW-style features were evident on single-deck bodies built by Willowbrook, Strachans and Roe.

A more specialised case was that of Brighton Hove & District, which had built some of its own bodywork pre-war and inherited a small part of the bodybuilding tradition of Thomas Tilling Ltd which, in the 'twenties, had supplied much of the needs of its subsidiary operating companies in much the same way as ECW did from its formation in 1936. After 1945, no BH&D bodies were produced for new chassis, but two were produced in 1948-9 to a modified and rather more elaborate version of ECW-like style, apparently intended partly to explore possible new ideas for the future.

A more superficial ECW look was given to 50 Willowbrook bodies on Leyland Tiger PS1 chassis supplied to United in 1946-7. The body structure was largely that bodybuilder's standard, higher-built than the contemporary ECW design, but rear-entrance layout and Tilling-standard destination boxes gave sufficient of the corporate look to cause them not to seem out of place, especially in that company's Northumberland area where earlier Tiger buses were largely concentrated. LTO 232 (HHN 332) is seen at Haymarket bus station, Newcastle.

Brighton Hove & District, as successors to the Brighton operating branch of Thomas Tilling, inherited a small bodybuilding facility. Lowestoft influence was evident on some bodies built from 1936, including the well-known open-toppers on older AEC Regent chassis and although output virtually ceased after the last of these was built in 1946, three noteworthy double-deckers based on the standard ECW highbridge design of the time were built at the small Conway Street works in 1948-9. The first was based on a 1931 AEC Regent chassis, 6245 (GP 6245) and although its general conformity to ECW practice is obvious, it was made more 'glamorous' by a combination of feature showing the influence of both the Weymann-bodied buses in the Brighton Corporation fleet and London Transport ideas. The style of front mudguard, with built-in headlamps was quite avant-garde at the time, the nearside one being merged into the body in London RT fashion. The subtle re-shaping of the front, with slightly more vee-effect and Weymann-like flush-fitting cab front and outswept skirt panels, added to the effect.

2. ECW influence via former managers

There were two notable instances where ECW ideas were taken up by other bodybuilders as a result of managers who left. One was that of Bill Bramham, who had brought some ideas from Roe, especially in the style of highbridge double-deckers, when he became ECW's first General Manager in 1936. When he decided to leave soon after ECW became a nationalised concern in 1948, he went to Northern Coachbuilders of Newcastle-on-Tyne, and the typical ECW early post-war double-deck style was reproduced remarkably closely in subsequent NCB bodywork.

J. W. (Bill) Shirley succeeded him but also moved on, in 1953, when he went to Park Royal Vehicles. Here again, ECW influence became evident in the form of construction of the semi-integral AEC-Park Royal Monocoach, which was similar to the Bristol-ECW LS in having an underframe made by the chassis

The second and third BH&D bodies were built on Bristol chassis, that shown being the third, originally built on a GO5G but transferred to a K5G dating from 1937, though modernised with PV2 radiator, 6336 (APN 207) in 1954, as seen here. The standard postwar K-type mudguards were used, though the rest of the front-end was similar to the earlier bus but a new feature was the upward extension of the three centre windows on each side of the lower deck, an idea which seems to show Northern Counties influence.

When Bill Bramham went to join Northern Coachbuilders, he took with him a clear idea of what a double-decker should look like and the 1950 NCB design was remarkably like the ECW pattern as it had been when he left Lowestoft in 1948. The example seen here was the last of a batch of 40 on AEC Regent III 9612A chassis, 350 (NVK 350) — they were 8ft wide.

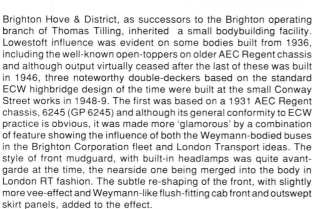

A similar effect was evident when Bill Shirley went to Park Royal in 1953. It was a coach design for the AEC Reliance chassis, first seen at the 1954 Commercial Motor Show, which showed perhaps the most obvious ECW influence on appearance, for it reproduced the front and rear styling of the LS coach as being built from May 1953, even though of curved-waist style and with centre-entrance. Only a few were built, this example being for A.E. Marsh of Harvington near Evesham. Other echoes of ECW practice were found in the slim sides of Park Royal's 1954 double-deck standard product and the LS-like winged emblem used on single-deck buses.

The Hawke bodies built for the Christchurch Transport Board in New Zealand on 54 Bristol RELL and two AEC Swift 505 models were more in the nature of locally-assembled ECW bodies with detail departures from the home-market product to suit local needs than 'lookalikes' as generally understood. Many parts were supplied from Lowestoft though some features, such as the front panel, with the pram hooks characteristic of this operator, a different grille, Leyland National-style light assemblies and separate bumper, were quite different. The rubbing strip on the sides was also set higher. This view of 464 dates from November 1976. The body gradually evolved and was latterly produced using *steel* for the basic framework.

The lookalike concept applied in reverse so far as ECW's body for the Leyland Olympian was concerned, for the upper deck was almost literally 'lifted' complete from the Leyland Titan design, already in full production when the first prototype Olympian was being built in 1979. This London example, T804 (OHV 804Y), was one of those built at Workington after the proposal to produce the model at Lowestoft had been rejected.

Roe was another partner in the Olympian body production team as a fellow member of the Leyland Bus organisation, concentrating on orders for normal-height versions, the basic design being very similar to that of ECW. London Country Bus Services had obtained many of its double-deck bodies on Leyland Atlantean chassis from Park Royal and this allegiance switched to Roe after Park Royal closed, so it was to be expected that its needs for Olympian bodywork would be handled there. The windscreen, originally an Alexander-pattern item, had been standard on LCBS Atlantean buses and was carried over into the Olympian. This example, LR6 (TPD 106X), was one of the first, dating from April 1982. When Roe, in turn, closed in 1984, ECW built one similar batch.

manufacturer and drivable with temporary reinforcement to the bodybuilder. There were also clear resemblences in body design and styling between some post-1953 Park Royal designs and earlier ECW types.

3. The Leyland influence

ECW's relationship within the British Leyland empire at first made no visible impact on body design either to other bodybuilders within the group nor by them on ECW, whose designs still showed continuity from the early post-war period. The appearance of bodywork almost identical to that built on the later home-market RELL by Hawke of New Zealand was more a means of allowing local assembly of what was an ECW design rather than a lookalike in the usual sense.

A more 'centralist' philosophy began to emerge with the development of models such as the B15, which became the Titan, originally intended as a standardised double-decker to replace previous generations of Leyland, Daimler and Bristol chassis. This integral design was planned by Leyland though the prototypes and early production were by Park Royal.

When the Olympian was introduced, as explained more fully in Chapter 12, there was a desire that the bodywork produced for it by concerns in the British Leyland group would have a uniformity of general style, and thus both the ECW and Roe designs for this model took some of the Titan's features – in other words, at that stage the lookalike effect was in reverse so far as ECW was concerned, though the practicalities of designing a low-height body helped to give scope for some originality and, incidentally, what might be widely agreed to be a better-proportioned end result.

When ECW closed, continuity meant that Workington-built Leyland bodywork for the Olympian took on ECW characteristics, and the same was to happen to some degree when Optare was allowed to use a version of this family of designs for a small number of double-deck bodies.

Optare, which set up business in the former Roe premises, was given a short-term licence in 1987 to build some bodies to ECW designs, using ECW tooling lent for the purpose, among them being this vehicle for Cambus, successor to part of the Eastern Counties business. These were orders which had been placed with ECW or customers Leyland wished to retain.

Leyland Bus used the Workington factory to build bodies to almost identical design to ECW products, an example being this one for Colchester Borough Transport, where the continuity is emphasised by livery – compare this view of 45 (F245 MTW) with that on page 113.

A rather curious difference, doing no favour to appearance, was the change to a vertical leading edge to the upper-deck side windows of some Workington-built bodies for Olympian chassis, of which Metrobus F803 NGU is an example.

In 1957, Central SMT gave a contract to ECW to refurbish the Leyland lowbridge bodies of 52 Titan PD2/1 models dating from 1948. Seen here in October 1957 stripped of mudguards and lamps is L358 (DVD 216) which was given the Rebuild number R697. No changes were made to appearance in the ensuing work.

Repairs and rebuilds

Like most bodybuilding concerns, ECW carried out repairs and various types of overhaul and refurbishing. Naturally, many of these were to the firm's own products, and most of them emerged restored to original condition, with little if any change to appearance or finish. This also quite often applied in various cases where vehicles with bodywork constructed elsewhere came to Lowestoft for attention, sometimes because the original builder no longer existed. There were instances where the opportunity was taken to update the specification, and in rare instances, the end-result was virtually a new body.

As explained on page 21 of the previous volume, although an R series of numbers was used for repair work from 1951, running from R501 to R1557 by the time the works closed, other jobs, particularly if minor were not given serial numbers.

Irthlingborough continued to carry out repair and rebuilding work until its closure. This Leyland Titan TD5 with Leyland highbridge body was one of five dating from 1938-9 sent by Western SMT in 1951. They received standard ECW window pans, producing the curious mixture of styles shown in this view of CS 7024, seen after it had passed to Scottish Omnibuses, following sale by Western in 1956 to an independent operator, Lowland Motorways, taken over by SOL in 1958.

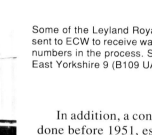

London Transport placed a contract in 1984 with ECW for refurbishing buses of a variety of types, including Routemaster, Leyland National, Fleetline and Titan models. These were not given numbers in the R series and were identified by their fleet numbers. Seen here nearing completion of the work are Routemaster RM1606 (606 DYE) dating from June 1963, and Leyland National LS340 (AYR 340T), one of the 10.3-metre batch of 1979. A total of 74 vehicles passed trough the works – twenty Routemasters, ten Titans and seven Nationals in 1984; fourteen more Nationals and five Fleetlines in 1985, and a final eighteen Nationals in 1986.

Some of the Leyland Royal Tiger Doyen coaches built by Roe were sent to ECW to receive warranty rectification work, and were given R numbers in the process. Seen here awaiting delivery in July 1984 is East Yorkshire 9 (B109 UAG) allocated R1417.

In addition, a considerable amount of work had been done before 1951, especially as operators sought to get their fleets back into good order after unavoidable neglect due to war circumstances in 1939-45 and enforced continued use of over-age vehicles in the post-war years. Tilling-managed companies had applied a policy of updating older vehicles to an extent greater than average in the 'thirties, and thus the same philosophy tended to be applied more willingly in the early post-war years than in most other organisations. Much of that work was either carried out by ECW or was done with assistance from that concern to operators' workshops or local bodybuilders.

The Irthlingborough works was at first primarily involved in such activity from its opening in 1940. New construction was only carried out on a very modest scale – roughly two new bodies per month in the period from 1942-45, though this was to increase to about four per week in the period up to May 1952 when Irthlingborough closed. By that date, the backlog of fleet replacement caused by the war was largely overcome and Tilling companies' normal good standards of maintenance meant that overhaul work became much less common.

In more recent years, work taken on included some refurbishing of London Transport vehicles carried out in 1984-6, when types represented included Routemaster, Fleetline, Leyland National (Mark 1 and 2) and Titan.

Another task which fell to ECW in 1984 was that of warranty attention to Royal Tiger Doyen coaches built by Roe.

Occasionally, what virtually amounted to new bodies received numbers in the rebuild series. United R66 (LHN 266D), a Bristol RELL6G, began life in 1966 with body 15964 of the early production style with rounded windscreen, similar to that shown on page 22 from the same order. Serious fire damage led to the construction in 1970 of the largely new body to the then current deep flat-glass windscreen design seen here, but as parts of the original were retained it was allocated Rebuild number R1058. Note the odd length of the first bay and panel. Doubtless the 19ft 6in wheelbase of the chassis had a bearing on this.

In the early post-war years considerable rebuild work was carried out by Tilling-group operators in their own workshops or on their behalf by other repairers, but under group influence and quite often using ECW parts or techniques. Typical of the type of result was this United vehicle, a Bristol J-type dating from 1935, originally with NW-type petrol engine and having Eastern Counties bodywork to United's standard style of the time. Like others of the type, it received a Gardner 5LW engine, and it was one of 21 which underwent major body rebuild in 1948-9, almost amounting to new bodies, though retaining the original outline, by Woodall Nicholson of Halifax, aided by United's body department. The style of glazing was as used by ECW in 1946, though the original pillar spacing was retained, and another feature often found on post-war rebuilds of J-type chassis was the design of bonnet side seen here, replacing the multi-louvred

original which was prone to cracking as was common with that type. The resulting vehicles could not be called elegant, with an uneasy mixture of styles, but were practical, reliable and economical – BJ0221 (AHN 386), which had begun life as BJ11, seen here in Scarborough in July 1950, remained in service until 1956.

Several Tilling companies still had many of their Leyland Titan TD1 double-deckers with standard Leyland lowbridge bodies dating from 1928-31 in service at the end of the 1939-45 war and quite a high proportion were rebuilt either by ECW or locally, around that time. Some received a new front end to a design giving a profile similar to new ECW bodywork, as seen here on Caledonian 246 (WW 7863), which had begun life in 1928 in the fleet of Keighley Corporation, passing to Keighley-West Yorkshire on its formation in 1932 and sold on to Caledonian in 1939. It had also received a Gardner 5LW engine and a 'modernising' radiator or a type sold by Covrad, and when Caledonian was taken over by Western SMT in 1950 continued in service until 1955.

A less extensive rebuild favoured by United for most of its TD1 buses retained the original 'piano-front' profile but incorporated an ECW-like windscreen similar to that shown.

Colour Kaleidoscope

As 1965 opened, the Coach Factory was still producing derivatives of the same style of bodies common in the 'fifties. That quickly changed, although the differences were often illusory – a good example of the evolution of the company's products.

Alexander (Fife) FPD284 (HXA 404E) was an example of the Bristol FLF chassis bearing an extended body with 78 seats. This derivative was the only Lodekka to have significant body problems – the rear lower saloon floor parted company with the body. The cause was established by ECW engineers after attaching a scribe to the body wall to mark a trace on paper, thereby illustrating the side-to-side movement in the rear body assembly.

The traditional Tilling Lodekka had by 1967 come down to the FLF, commonly with semi-automatic transmission. Crosville DFG257 (SFM 257F) is seen in Delamere Street, Chester on the C84 service to Newcastle-under-Lyme. Cave-Brown-Cave heating had now been deleted, and the glass reinforced plastic dome structure can be seen.

1966 saw the production of the last rear-loading double-deckers. Crosville took 35, of which JFM204D, the first, stands at Sealand Road, Chester. It is in the dismal overall green livery which seemed to demonstrate an NBC fetish for drabness. The cream of the window rubbers at least offers some relief.

The single-deck bus was exemplified by this style of MW and this example for Wilts & Dorset (725 EMR 300D) is seen when new. The mouldings are a blend of LS and later MW styles, although the stainless steel wheel trims were very much *de rigeur* in 1966. Several companies took batches of this body shell in 1966 though, very unusually, the Wilts & Dorset batch had full-size 'lift-up' roof vents.

MW coaches were still entering service up to 1967. PSVs were still restricted to 50 mph for practical purposes at this time and therefore the MW, in some instances with air suspension at the rear, was quite adequate. FRU 873D of Hants & Dorset is seen in the 'seventies carrying the early version of NBC local coach livery. The vehicle has the standard dash panel, although the fixed side windows and simplified waist rail for 1966 build can clearly be seen. The fitment of bus style doors was to facilitate later down-grading for stage carriage use.

This Bedford VAM5, SB664 (NAH 664F) has a body derived from that of the MW. The somewhat clumsy windscreen line demonstrates a foretaste of the early RE style for Series Two chassis. As ever, Eastern Counties Omnibus Company is providing another journey to the village of Service, this time by way of route 2.

The early version of the RE bus had this curved front screen body. The windscreen style had major influence upon ECW's design team led by Stan George, and many, many sketches for Bristol N and RE bodies used it. In practice, Tilling Group engineers baulked at the cost, and curved-glasses were to disappear until 1971 when the BET screen was adopted to avoid reflections. This screen had the same effect.

Coventry was the first non-nationalised customer to take REs and received this hybrid version of the body. Number 521 (KHP 521E) is seen in revised livery.

The Tilling standard RE body settled down to this flat screen variant. Crosville SRG9 (OFM 9E) stands in Chester in 1968. The 1967 build featured green rexine casings in traditional format, and an additional opening window behind the cab. This example has an unusual illuminated 'Pay as you Enter' sign on the front panel.

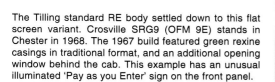

Midland General SRB 67F was one of only two Bristol RESH6Gs to be bodied by ECW. Many of the detail features were, however, repeated on the substantial build of the longer RELH based dual-purpose vehicles.

Pressure from tall drivers led to the introduction of the second RE windscreen as described in the text. This United Auto example No. 4202 (YHN 802H) is seen working a Catchacoach local feeder service contract at Durham University in 1973.

The recurrence of reflections in the windscreen prompted ECW to adopt the BET screen across the range in 1970. In this view an RELH dual-purpose vehicle of Bristol Omnibus, (WHW 372H) shows off a number of RE features some endearing, some less so. Noteworthy are the narrow door fitted to a few 1970 bodies, apparently to increase passenger comfort, and the brightwork as fitted to the Midland General RESH, together with the wheel trims. However, the early BET fronted examples suffered from the low front skirt and the broken corner can clearly be seen, probably after contact with a kerb.

The solution to the skirt problem is clearly visible in this view of brand new United Auto 6075 (SHN 75L) seen whilst also engaged on a Catchacoach contract at Durham railway station. The skirt is now shorter, as denoted by the fog lamps set higher in the detachable cowl. The standard width doorway is fitted and the doors are now air-operated instead of electric – the emergency valve can be seen to the rear of the door pillar. New style light units are also fitted.

The only major changes to bodies for the series 2 RE were those for the 16ft 6in wheelbase RESL. For this variant the window bays were all slightly longer, and the rearmost bay was of full size. The centre view shows 356 (OCK 356K) in Ribble livery with red wheels. The lower view clearly demonstrated the modernising effect of the longer rear bay. Ribble's RESLs had a pleasant red moquette seat covering and, as a consequence, red formica backs rather than the standard autumn leaf to match the casings. The National era has arrived in this view – wheels are now grey.

Large numbers of dual-door vehicles were built for Bristol Omnibus to convert City services to one-man-operation. Number C1199 (YHU 519J) of 1971 is seen operating in Bath in Bristol 'one-man' livery of Tilling green and cream.

The last bodies to be mounted on RE chassis by ECW were five for Thamesdown. Subsequently these passed to a late convert to the RE (although one with an association with some of the first REs sold on the open market). It is seen here in this 1994 view in Blue Buses livery.

The strangest REs of all were the nine built originally for North Western Road Car for the Dunham Massey service. These quickly passed to Crosville and SJA 381J is seen here having lost its NWRCC livery, and with Crosville fleetplates as SRL246 fitted. The service is 140.

The 1963 coach body continued in production with few changes. Both bus and coach doored examples were built and it was necessary to look closely at the fittings to make any judgement on whether they were luxury coach or dual-purpose. Red & White number OAX 4F is a luxury coach and is seen in the livery of Jones of Aberbeeg, prior to the introduction of National liveries.

United retained the livery of Orange Brothers for its Tyne Tees Thames fleet, the very smart olive green and cream. These were probably the most luxurious REs of all, having a mere 43 seats to a very high standard, soft trim to the side casings and other features to make them suitable for what was still a long haul from the North East to London when they were introduced. Number 1257 (NHN 957E) is seen here on the circuitous 203 variant of the service.

Eastern National 1609 (GVW 979H) was a member of the final batch of such bodies delivered to the company. As had previously been the case the order provided a mixture of touring and express variants. This was an express vehicle although many would class it as a luxury coach.

1972 saw the introduction of the Mark 2 RE coach body. Using much of the framework of the earlier coach it combined elements of the Plaxton Elite, the AEC Sabre as well as some ECW ideas. Crosville CRL261 (TFM 261K) stands at Sealand Road in Chester and these views were taken before the delivery driver had even left the premises. The vehicle is to the shorter length (11 metres) and was one of five to be delivered in Crosville colours. Express doors are fitted.

Ribble also had a batch of these coaches. Its vehicles had National livery when new and were built to the longer 11.23-metre length, with coach doors. Number 1018 (PTF 713L) is also brand new in this view and shows the small Ribble fleetname then permitted.

As well as building for its traditional customers, the coach factory had a growing business supplying others. Standard shells were used, albeit with modifications.

Vehicle YRT 898H was an AEC Swift delivered to Lowestoft Borough Council, reviving memories of the 1947 Regents. The standard RE body was used although the rear was modified with the huge and somewhat impractical boot-like flaps with inset grilles, lamps and access points to the rear and side. This arrangement lacked the careful thought of the RE. As the chassis frame was higher than the RE the cantrail beading had to be broken to allow the offside emergency door to rise slightly to achieve its statutory size. This encroached into one of the features which gave ECW bodies their strength, demonstrating the close relationship between ECW and Bristol products.

Leicester 126, TRY 126H, was a Bristol RE. Minor details have been altered to suit the customer – destination screens, fixed windows and lift-up roof ventilators have been fitted. These chassis retained air suspension, by then somewhat unusual.

The 1972 coach body is making its second appearance on a batch of Leyland Leopards. The customer was again SELNEC/Greater Manchester. Reaction to these was mixed and the first group were rebodied very quickly. Number 83 (HNE 643N) shows the new GMB livery, together with the simplified mouldings. The vehicle has luxury-coach-style seats and the destination blind is set to SELNEC Travel which suggests that they were regarded as at least passable coaches, rather than merely dual-purpose buses. The lives of these bodies on certain vehicles were quite short as GMB experienced similar problems to later B51-bodied vehicles. Since they kept this information to themselves, as the warranties had expired, the mistake was sadly repeated through ignorance of the problem.

The first Bristol VRT/SL chassis was shown at the 1968 Motor Show alongside the prototype VRL coach. The vehicle was eventually bodied, and with two others was painted in this reversed livery for use on service X10 from London to Southend. The A27 had an indifferent surface which induced a lively ride. Ride quality was never a selling point of the VRT, and Lodekkas were soon returned to the service. Number 3001 (CPU 980G) is seen here.

Some of the earliest vehicles to be bodied were also the rarest. The 33ft-long VRT/LL could seat up to 83. As with the rest of the VRTs to be found in Scotland in 1971, these were exchanged with the National Bus Company. This former Eastern Scottish vehicle is seen with Eastern National, down-seated to 70!

Prior to the main NBC/SBG exchange of VRTs, Eastern National and Alexander Midland reached a 'private' deal over 15 VRT/SL vehicles. Number SMS 39H is seen here with Eastern National fleetnames on Alexander blue – running on the very service from which the special liveried native machines were withdrawn not long before.

Amongst the first vehicles ordered by NBC was a batch of VRTs for Southern Vectis. They were diverted, before delivery, to City of Oxford, which at the time was perennially in maintenance difficulties caused by a shortage of skilled labour in the car building city. Numbered in the 900 series because they would not pass under the infamous Oxford railway station bridge, No. 903, OFC 903H, is seen here.

Another Oxford vehicle was this Mark 2 VRT. Quite an unusual vehicle, NUD 102L was built to the lower 13ft 5in standard and was also a very early example of the dual-purpose seated variant which later became quite common. Although intended for the burgeoning London services, it is here seen on an Oxford local run.

Production moved on to the Mark 3 VRT chassis and the body also changed. Apart from the grilles necessary for cooling the engine compartment, the front panel was tidied up and, after the first few, the interior colour scheme was changed to one based on various shades of fawn. The other NBC, Northern Bus, of Sheffield has No. 3008, XAK 908T, in its subsidiary Bradfield Bus fleet. It is seen here about to turn in rural north Sheffield.

North Western Road Car had 25 VRTs on order when it was split up. These vehicles went into the SELNEC (Cheshire) fleet. Number 409 (AJA 409L) is seen here. Notice that the board below the windscreen says 'Conductor Operated' and the small label on the nearside screen itself is the 'Keep Out' sticker affixed by ECW to denote a vehicle cleaned ready for presentation to the customer.

Of particular interest were the 50 convertible open-toppers built in 1977/8. Cumberland 2037 (UWV 618S) is a former Southdown vehicle which, unusually for Stagecoach, is not in the customary stripey livery.

Colourful liveries have certainly emerged since ECW closed. Instead of the staid green of the RE for Bristol City service seen on page 136, PHY 697S is in the multi-coloured guise of 'The City Line – Overground'. Quite why the strong emphasis is on Overground is a mystery, as Bristol does not possess an underground.

The most impressive of the ECW bodies on VR chassis must be the VRL coaches for Ribble's subsidiary Standerwick. The features of these vehicles are described in the text and here number 69 (OCK 69K) is seen Blackburn-bound.

Strong sales efforts by Alan Hunton had brought in several significant orders in addition to the one for the VRL coaches. The next few views emphasise some of the variety passing through the coach factory.

Although Leicester took several batches of Bristol RE with ECW body, it fought shy of Bristol's offering for rear-engined deckers. The coach factory took a share of the body order on Atlanteans and number 100 (PBC 100G) is seen. The number plate is mounted above the windscreen, but its normal place is still denoted in the skirt. The skirts themselves are unusual for a municipal order in being of the shallow NBC pattern. Although the latter is more practical, further municipal orders on Atlantean or Fleetline chassis did not follow it.

West Bromwich, too, joined the rush to Lowestoft and took a batch of Fleetlines. These vehicles have an unusual windscreen, although again the moulding for the standard pattern is visible. The side panels are to the municipal pattern, being split half way down. Old fashioned dummy mud wings are also fitted. Sadly both Coventry and West Bromwich were swallowed up by the West Midlands PTE so ECW never had the opportunity to develop these customers, WMPTE being tied to its ex-Birmingham ways. Number 116, TEA 116G, is in West Bromwich livery.

Another group of customers, having rid themselves of VRTs, were not inclined to give the model a second chance. SBG, therefore, took ECW bodies on Fleetlines. Long after BET screens were the norm, SBG's conservative ways specified bodies with the flat version. One suspects that if the Fleetline could have been specified with a manual gearbox that would have been adopted. Number DD692V (KSX 692N) of Eastern Scottish is in fact allocated to the former Victoria garage of Baxters, a company taken over some years before. Vehicles here tended to adopt the blue livery and Baxter fleetname.

The independent sector was not neglected and Harper of Heath Hays ordered two batches of two Fleetlines. The first batch is represented by No. 33, TRE 948L, in original washed out green colours. The first two vehicles passed to Midland Red with the business and the second pair were delivered there in a specification closer to NBC standard.

The biggest order at this time was from Sheffield City Transport for 55 bodies on Daimler Fleetline. These vehicles were quite different to the norm, yet incorporated many standard parts. ECW was still having trouble with its windscreen arrangements and in this case it was the wide pillars which were the source of the problem. The batch was delivered to South Yorkshire PTE in that operator's second livery, although before the politicians had managed to agree a fleetname for the operation. The vehicle had the standard Sheffield blue interior and other features such as substantial front bumpers unique to the batch. Number 813 (GWA 813N) is seen here on service 60 without the pillar windows – a very rare achievement.

Still without fleetnames and advertisements and having that newness which lasts for such a short time, No. 813 has gained the offending pillar windows – for what little good they did. Further modifications inside the saloon included the removal of the nearside lamp units on the lower deck ahead of the door. This necessity should be strictly laid at the door of the Sheffield City Council Transport Department as internal reflections were easily soluble by that time.

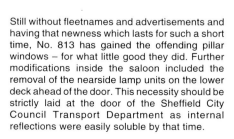

Colchester Borough took one batch of Sheffield-style bodies on Atlantean before switching to the NBC body, albeit with the high cut skirts. Low driving position 69 (TPU 69R) is seen here.

Several NBC subsidiaries took the high driving position Atlantean AN68 and ECW's windscreen problem recurred, tall drivers again having restricted vision. This problem was tackled by the operators themselves and this is Northern General's version. Numbers 3544 and 3541 can be seen in this view. Note that No. 3544 has an experimental Firestone 'Help' bumper designed to absorb low speed impacts. In a strange way it helps to balance up the over high position required for the windscreens.

The Scottish Bus Group remained a steady customer for the lowheight body on Fleetline chassis, later taking the BET-screened version. Here Highland UAS 68T is seen in the new 1994 livery working an Inverness school service.

The Bristol LH in its original 41/5 seat form. This vehicle, No. 204, RRX 995G, was built in 1969 for Thames Valley.

The prototype LH was also used as a demonstrator, passing to Eastern Counties when that task was completed. It is seen here in Norwich showing evidence of how the windscreen modification was completed in this case. Perhaps unusually, the original dome was simply cut down rather than replaced as evidenced by the crude alteration to the cantrail line over the door and windscreen pillar.

This vehicle, WNG 102H, of Eastern Counties was originally built for Luton Corporation and indeed was delivered to Luton. United Counties did not propose to continue with the experimental use and so the batch was passed to Eastern Counties. Seen in Norwich in June 1975, it shows both the effect of relivery into standard NBC style as well as the fitment of the revised front dome. Prior to transfer to ECOC, ECW fitted luggage racks and generally altered the interiors to meet THC specification.

The LH was redesigned in 1970 to take the standard BET screen on vehicles of all widths. Crosville SLL605 (KMA 535N) is seen here when newly delivered to Sealand Road works in Chester. The body now incorporates an extra moulding to ease application of the NBC livery. Notice that the length of the vehicle has grown steadily and the 2.5-metre width is now standard.

The largest single batch ordered was that for London Transport in the BL class. These vehicles incorporated a number of modifications as might be reasonably expected of that operator. In addition to vehicles for main fleet use, four were produced for use on the Hillingdon free service and were indeed owned by the local council. Immediately after withdrawal the batch passed to OK Motor Services of Bishop Auckland and were refurbished in that operator's customary way. The former BL93 stands in its home town and demonstrates a feature peculiar to the Hillingdon quartet – an offside destination box, now used for a fleetname. The original registration OJD 93R was surrendered as OK adopted an electronic ticket issue system that demanded entry of a vehicle identity in each machine:

OK does not use fleet numbers hence no two vehicles now have the same registered **numbers.**

The end of LH production came just before the midibus revolution of the 'eighties, although the high steps were to remain a problem. NBC requirements towards the end were for the 26 and 35-seat versions. The livery on well-travelled GTX 760W is a variant of the much-reviled PMT privatisation livery. Notice that the moulding for the white relief band of its former NBC livery had been deleted on the last of the LH family as that feature was deleted from NBC liveries

The DAB shelled Tiger Cub model was a peculiar interlude. Leyland Bus must clearly have had thoughts of marketing the vehicle as the second prototype appeared at the NEC show of 1984, yet it was not a practical design, nor indeed one which was well thought out. The floor line and hence the steps were high and the coach-type door narrow – as well as flimsy – with no real opportunity for improvement on either score. The size niche is now handsomely filled by the Dennis Dart.

The B51 was primarily intended for medium distance express services such as Oxford to London as well as National Express operations generally. In this view Oxford 29, VUD 29X, is seen at Oulton Broad prior to delivery. These were the times when NBC subsidiaries were breaking ranks over liveries. Group reaction was the Venetian blind liveries.

United Counties 175 (CNH 175X) was a member of the first batch of B51s. It is seen here reversing onto the forecourt at Charlotte Road garage in Sheffield. Ominously the vehicle is but a few days old in this view but the problems which were about to descend upon the coach factory were already gathering.

The B51 could have been developed into an attractive vehicle, with a sympathetic livery style, had its weaknesses not sealed its fate before even 20 had been built. Ambassador's CAH884Y is seen at Victoria Coach Station, complete with curtains and a particularly attractive livery.

How the B51 will be remembered by so many. This example was built as part of an extra batch on Tiger TRC/TL11-2R chassis for Green Line use. In this view the former TL6 (standing for 'Tiger Lowestoft') is seen at Cannock prior to the final removal of its body and despatch to East Lancashire Coachbuilders for a service body. The registration, DJN 25X, had replaced the original TPC 106X. Unusually, this vehicle had seen limited service with Midland Red North, as a result of the Stafford fire.

The final bodies of the traditional style were those produced for South Notts on Fleetline chassis – also amongst the last of that line as well. Number 116 is seen here in Lowestoft prior to registration and delivery. Two more bodies were to be produced to traditional lines in 1983 on VRT chassis.

The first few Olympian bodies were produced alongside the last VRTs and here United Counties 609 can be compared with Eastern Counties VR290 immediately prior to despatch.

The first Olympian body was produced in 1978 on chassis number B45-01. This latter had been hand-built at Leyland. It was ultimately brought up to service standards as a single-door bus – still showing many of its VRT lines.

The second and third vehicles finished at Lowestoft were respectively the 'demonstrators' aimed at NBC and SBG. Of these the Scottish example was put to work as TB4 in a series of comparative trials. Although seen here as Midland Scottish MR01 (OMS 910W) it soon transferred to Northern Scottish alongside a production batch. Today it can be seen in the guise of a 'Perth Panther' in the Stagecoach fleet.

Leyland Bus zeal to sell the new product extended to taking on an order for special Olympians for both Merseyside and Greater Glasgow PTEs. Here one of the Merseyside vehicles is seen prior to delivery in the now customary sylvan setting for ECW's official portraits.

Not to be outdone, Lothian regional Transport was taking the first of many Olympians with ECW bodies to grace Scotland's capital. These orders, whilst good for ECW, were to prove controversial by provoking Alexander's retaliation in going into partnership with Mercedes Benz to produce double-deckers for certain overseas markets. For once, however, ECW was a beneficiary of a Leyland strategy and it retained Lothian's confidence until closure of the plant.

NBC steadily took Olympians and this one for Northern General Transport had a Cummins engine and Voith gearbox. The destination screen aperture has been enlarged slightly although standard blinds are fitted.

155

The general standardisation of the Tilling and NBC era was soon replaced when orders were being taken from the PTEs. Greater Glasgow received both ECW and Roe-bodied Olympians at this time. The interior trims were in entirely different colours and these vehicles had back-to-back seating over the rear wheels in the lower saloon.

NBC was also entering the final years of central buying, and as close to a standard vehicle as maybe is seen in this view. North Devon was created out of part of Western National in 1983, and shortly afterwards decided to call itself Red Bus. Number 1818 (A989 XAF) is a standard 77-seat NBC vehicle built on a Workington produced chassis. The front upper-deck opening ventilators were only found on a few vehicles.

There was a conscious move to improve the standards of vehicles allocated to longer services. Midland Red South had revived the old Stratford Blue Buses image in that town and No. 964 (C964 XVC) of 1986 is seen in Birmingham. Apart from the dual-purpose seating, different destination indicators are fitted as is a safety rail across the upper-deck front windows.

The standard product is seen here in Northern General Transport JTY 372X. The vehicle is shown in Tyne and Wear PTE colours, signifying its use on services under the control of that organisation. The interior shots show how the standard NBC product appeared. Opinion is always subjective but apart from the upholstery, whose brightness soon faded with sunlight and dirt, little opportunity was taken to provide cheery surroundings for the passenger. The rearward-facing seat of the offside lower deck was necessary to accommodate the upsweep of the chassis perimeter frame. This also intruded severely around the rear wheel boxes.

To entice customers away from other coachbuilders Leyland Bus had ECW produce various vehicles for both home and overseas. Preston Corporation was the ultimate customer for A33 NRN, built to 74-seat dual-purpose specification in 1984. The body was to 14ft 6in height and 33ft long which was becoming increasingly common amongst ECW production. The interior shows a further variation with wood-effect casings and Duple-style patterned roof.

ECW began to enjoy some success in supplying to independent operators – although the real orders were to go to Workington later. The fast expanding Metrobus of Orpington took C395 DML in 1985. This was a fairly standard 77-seater bus.

Home Market Curiosities

ECW now tended to take on the role of meeting Leyland Bus' needs for one-off bodies. One very peculiar vehicle was this 10-metre body on Leyland Atlantean for Fishwicks. Standing 14ft 6in tall, this was the highest variant ever built. As ever, ECW used as many standard parts as possible and in typical fashion, the extra height was in the lower panels. In these views number A482 LFV is seen before delivery.

The interior of the lower deck shows the forward ascending staircase, as well as the very spartan interior for a bus produced at this time.

London Country had managed to develop considerable originality during the few years of its existence. Even into the Olympian era, when one might have expected it to follow the party line, it had Roe create a special body for its use, 14ft 2in tall and fitted with Alexander style windscreens. When Roe closed ECW maintained the breed and this vehicle, LR75, B275LPH, was the result. It is seen here as a London and Country vehicle after the forced division of LCBS.

EX20 was built as an 11-metre prototype Olympian for medium distance National Express services. This view shows the coach, provisionally registered SND 50X, standing at the Leyland Technical Centre in the days that this organisation's facilities were available to Leyland Bus – albeit on payment of a fee. The view below shows the vehicle posed immediately prior to its first delivery to the customer as ADD 50Y. The body has been subject to a number of modifications – as was to be the case during its short service life in this guise. It was, to say the least, adaptable. When its time with Wessex was complete, it passed to Badgerline, re-converted to bus doors, and with part of the rear locker added to the saloon. It did not find favour and was resold to Citybus of Hong Kong in late 1987. Prior to departure an additional door was fitted to the offside to facilitate operation in China and, after a short while in Hong Kong, it was fitted with air conditioning – in the remains of the locker area. However, in 1991, it received the ultimate in air conditioning – conversion to open top form with bus seats ! It continues thus today. The vehicle was built for a market which Leyland Bus elected not to pursue, yet it was one which MCW exploited. Whether profitably or not has to be discovered but nonetheless that company took its Hong Kong Metrobus design and sold 130 high specification coaches to NBC and SBG at a time when orders were becoming scarce.

The publishers are not offering a prize for those who 'Spot the Changes' but nonetheless the two views are worthy of the basis of such a competition. For those pitting their wits against our expert the changes are summarised in the caption below.

The changes: the radiator grille is now deeper and has a removable centre section for access to the radiator itself; the destination screen has been inverted; the upper-deck cantrail trim now rises to the top of the dome; the door glasses are both deeper and now square; the step has a new safety edging; a luggage locker door has appeared over the rear nearside wheel; additionally seats and wheel trims have been fitted. The large mirrors would have been required for motorway use.

The production versions were essentially very similar. However, the front grille was tidied up and altered to conform to the bus pattern in fitting. The luggage lockers were also not required. This view shows Alder Valley 1502 (YPJ 502Y) when new. There were minor changes in the brightwork fitted to the various batches and the rear panels were restyled slightly.

There was a vain attempt to restyle the coach body and the first UK example was the 'Ebdons Olympian' shown at the 1984 NEC show. Although a high specification vehicle, the order was cancelled and nearly eighteen months later it was delivered to South Yorkshire PTE as No. 100 (4475 WE). The vehicle could be used in various formats and is seen when 'new' with tables. Unfortunately, a series of rear-end fires earned this vehicle the soubriquet 'The Olympic Torch'!

More workaday examples were built for two NBC subsidiaries, Alder Valley (9.5-metre models diverted from Southern Vectis) and 11-metre vehicles for Eastern National. Number 4512 (D512 PPU) is seen here in current colours and showing the modifications done over the years. Electronic destination screens have been removed and extra opening windows introduced. Sadly, the livery has been applied with no sympathy for the body – ECW designers were traditionally adept at using subtle paint applications to enhance appearance.

Reading Borough Transport had successfully competed with Alder Valley for the London commuter traffic. It too had been steadily improving the calibre of its vehicles and this batch of five Olympians were an anachronism in that they had many high specification features – and yet the bus shell! Externally there is the coach grille panel, and wipers to the upper-deck front windows. Fixed tinted glazing hides the full soft trim within as well as overhead luggage racks sporting individual reading lights and blowers.

Unusually, another view of the Reading vehicles shows No. 84 (D84 UTF) after refurbishment into London Line livery – the name given to the combined Alder Valley and Reading London services. Although the upper-deck wipers have gone and limited opening windows have been fitted, the new metallic livery and Vultron destination display combine to enhance the opulence still further.

London Transport was one obvious target for the Olympian. For ECW, coming so soon after the Titan fiasco, it eventually proved to generate the largest single operator order – as well as the swansong. Three trial vehicles were built for comparative testing and ECW's biggest single-order was the result. This order was also its last. L263, the final vehicle, is well illustrated within this volume but this is L12, C812BYY, a more humble member of the batch.

Exports were seen as one outlet for the traditional double-deck bus at the time of declining home demand. A number of demonstrators were produced but the biggest success was the order for twenty vehicles sent to Athens.

Baghdad had been a traditional customer of Leyland and its associates over many years and this vehicle was prepared for that market. It had peaked domes intended to resemble earlier Atlantean deliveries and the grille panel was not repeated on any other vehicle.

Another long-standing customer was Carris of Lisbon and this vehicle was built for this endeavour. The vehicle stands outside the coach factory awaiting despatch.

Saudi Arabia too was seen as a potential market and this 11-metre vehicle is seen at the Leyland Technical Centre awaiting its opportunity to promote its builder's skills. Those in the bodyshop at ECW had good cause to remember its return – the upper-deck was full of goat droppings and its windows had been removed!

The vehicle intended to be Lothian 770 was bought back by Leyland Bus. Prior to departing for overseas sales demonstration, beginning in Thailand, it was returned to the Lowestoft factory and revamped as seen here. This vehicle continued its wanderings and was offered for sale by Volvo Bus (Singapore) as successors to Leyland Bus in 1991. It ended up in the Citybus fleet in Hong Kong with several other of the EX series vehicles. The body was yet again adapted to its new home, with revised destination equipment and flat windscreen. Happily that home seems somewhat more permanent.

The last remaining part of the British Empire was not forgotten and various sizes and styles of vehicles found their way to the crown colony. This tri-axle seen in KMB's original livery, was experiencing snow for the first and last time, in this Leyland suburb

Three of the revised coaches were built for T.T.Tsoi's Citybus cross border services into China. The first vehicle was body EX19 in heavily revised form. This differed from the later two by having gasket, as opposed to bonded glazing, and sliding windows. These windows have since been removed. The vehicle is seen here before shipment and now has local registration DE 4281.

APPENDICES

Body number allocations – annual production programmes

Prog Year	Body numbers built in year's programme*	Totals
	Total carried forward (1946-64)	13,446
1965	14698-14913/14919-15135/15139-15380	675
1966	15381-16054/16080-16085, Ex 10/11	682
1967	16055-16079/16086-16222/16225-16378/16383-16618/16623-16754, Ex 12	685
1968	16755-17235/17264-17387/17389-17436	653
1969	17437-18136	700
1970	18137-18786/18798-18838	691
1971	18839-19158/19163-19779/19846	938
1972	19780-19845/19847-20320/20846	541
1973	20321-20845/20847/20858-20907/21473/21474/21483/21497/21498, Ex 13	582
1974	20848-20857/20908-21472/21475-21482/21484-21496/ 21499-21505/21567	604
1975	21506-21560/21568-21587/21594-21977/21983-22038	515
1976	21978-21982/22039-22384	351
1977	22385-22882/22887-22905/22907-22920	531
1978	22921-23458/23463-23508/23599-23607/23638-23648/23657-23662/23667- 23678	622
1979	22883/22884/23509-23550/23552-23598/23608-23637/23649-23653/ 23663/23679-24206, Ex 14	656
1980	23459-23462/23654-23656/24207-24761, Ex 15/16	564
1981	24762-25057/25059/25062-25102/25108-25112	343
1982	25113-25401/25404-25487, Ex 18-21	377
1983	25058/25488-25506/25508-25762	275
1984	25763-25810/25817-25959/25963-26001, Ex 26/32/36	233
1985	26002-26235/26237/26238/26241-26275	271
1986	26276-26280/26286-26600	320
	Overall total (1966-86)	25255

Notes: 1981 Programme   Ex 17 renumbered to 24948
        1983 Programme   Ex 25 renumbered to 25058
        1985 Programme   Ex 19 renumbered to 26236

*Actual year of build was quite often the following year to that quoted and occasionally was the previous year.

APPENDIX 2

ECW production 1965-86 by programme year and body type

Prog. Year	Bristol Lodekka Double-deck			Single-deck on non-Bristol u/f or rear-engined chassis			Bristol MW Single-deck			Bristol SU s/d	Bristol RE Single-deck				
	LD	FS	FLF	Leyl'd Leop Bus	Leyl'd Leop Coach	AEC Sabre Coach	Bus	Exp	Coach	SUL Bus	RELL Bus	RELH Exp	RELH Coach	RESL Bus	RESH Exp
1965		102	351				135	14		12	61				
1966	1**	94	279	5			81	28	57	28	36	29	36	6	
1967			287						22		183	43	15	94	2
1968			85								272	28	43	58	
1969											305	13	54	27	
1970						1					348	23	44	9	
1971											441	29		161	
1972											125	44	57	14	
1973					10						15	43		7	
1974					6						8	37	28	6	
1975					6						5			23	
1976															
1977															
1978															
1979															
1980															
1981															
1982															
1983															
1984															
1985															
1986															
Total*	2180	890	1867	5	22	1	1095	234	584	118	1840	340	347	405	2
Grand Total#	5218						1913				2934				

* Included examples built in programmes up to 1964
# Includes examples and other variants built in programmes before 1964
**This was a replacement body – the total for production of this type up to 1965 in the previous volume should have been 2179, and that for the Lodekka to that date 4472.

ECW production 1965-86 by programme year and body type

Prog Year	Bristol VR Double-deck				Double-deck (VR style) on other chassis		Bristol LH Single-deck				Single-deck on other light chassis		Single-deck (RE style) on AEC Swift	Single-deck on Ley. Nat.
	VR Proto type	VRL/LH Coach	VRT/SL	VRT/LL	Fleetline	Atlantean	LH	LHS	LHD Midi	LHS Coach	Bedford VAM	Ford R1014		
1965														
1966	2													
1967					18		1				20			
1968		1	55	25	7	14	62	3						
1969			157				128	12					4	
1970		11	82		81		92							
1971		10	130		76	13	74						4	
1972		8	220		2		69						2	
1973			269		85		66	23		1		50	12	1
1974			344		10	6	129	30						
1975			105		10	87	251	8	20					
1976			273			10	55	2	11					
1977			452			6	59	14						
1978			550		34		38							
1979			469		59	74	42	11						
1980			506			42		8	6					
1981			187		2				3					
1982			2											
1983														
1984														
1985														
1986														
Total	2	30	3801	25	384	252	1066	111	40	1	20	50	22	1
Grand Total	2858				636		1218				70			

168

APPENDIX 2

ECW production 1965-86 by programme year and body type

Prog. Year	Leyland Olympian Double-deck	Double-deck (Olympian style) on Atlantean	B51 coach body Leop'd	B51 coach body Tiger	Leyland-DAB Tiger Cub (Trim and seats)
1965					
1966					
1967					
1968					
1969					
1970					
1071					
1072					
1973					
1974					
1975					
1976					
1977					
1978					
1979	1				
1980	2				
1981	116		35		
1982	254	1	70	50	
1983	275				
1984	232				1
1985	271				
1986	320				
Total	1471	1	105	50	1
Grand Total	1472		155		

APPENDIX 3

Bodies built under EX (experimental) numbers

Number	Chassis or vehicle type etc	Operator	Date
EX1	Bristol Railbus RBX1	British Rail	8/58
EX2	Bristol Railbus RBX2	British Rail	11/58
EX3	Bristol Lodekka LDS (LDX.003)	Crosville DLG949	9/58
EX4	Bristol Lodekka LDL (LDX.004)	E. National 1541	3/59
EX5	Bristol SC (glass-fibre body)	E. Counties LC565	3/60
EX6	Bristol RELL (REX.001)	United BR1	9/62
EX7	Bristol RELH (REX.002)	South Midland 867	3/63
EX10	Bristol VR prototype (VRX.001)	Central SMT BN331	9/66
EX11	Bristol VR prototype (VRX.002)	Bristol livery	9/66
EX12	Bristol LH (LHX.001)	Bristol-ECW demo	1/68
EX13	Leyland Nat. underframe (C27)	Leyland prototype	2/74
EX14	Leyland B45 (Olympian) (B45-01)	Leyland prototype	10/79
EX15	Leyland B45 (Olympian) (B45-02)	Leyl'd/Ribble 2100	2/80
EX16	Leyland Olympian (B45-04)	Alex. Midland MRO1	9/80
EX17	Leyland Olympian (ON1)	Ribble 2101	3/81
EX18	Leyland Olympian (three-axle) (ON 119)	Demo/Kowloon	1/82
EX19	Leyland Olympian (three-axle) (ON 332)	Demo, orig. for Kowloon	5/83
EX20	Leyland Olympian (coach) (ON 281)	Nat. Travel (SW)	8/82
EX21	Leyland Olympian (left-hand) (ON 328	Saudi Arabia	10/82
EX25	Leyland Olympian (left hand) (ON 1238)	For Greece	/83
EX26	Leyland Olympian (coach) (ON 1362)	For Ebdon's	9/84
EX32	Leyland Olympian (left-hand) (ON 1410)	Gillig demo, USA	9/84
EX33	Leyland Victory (single-deck)	(Parts)	c1984-5
EX34	Leyland Victory (single-deck)	(Shell)	5/85
EX35	Leyland Victory (single-deck)		c1985
EX36	Leyland-DAB (Tiger Cub) (8301216)	Leyland/United 1500	10/84
EX56	Leyland Olympian (ex-Lothian) (ON 1538)	Demo for Bankok	9/85
EX60	Leyland Olynpian (CKD mock-up)	For Greece. Not built.	
EX66	Leyland Olympian? (double-deck)	For Bankok. Not built.	
EX67	Leyland Tiger (rear-engined)	For Bankok. to Leyland	c1985
EX68	Leyland Tiger (rear-engined)	For Bankok.	c1985

The entry under 'Operator} relates to the vehicle's initial status or livery. EX10-12 were all initially operated by Bristol Commercial Vehicles as demonstrators. No chassis was delivered for EX33.

Chassis for EX34 and 35 were delivered in 1984, EX34 being completed as a shell and delivered to Leyland for pavée testing in May 1985 and EX35 appears to have been at least part completed before both bodies were dismantled. EX 67 went to Leyland as a shell for pavée testing and was retained for use as the Leyland-DAF football coach. EX68 is thought to have been completed but then dismantled.

EASTERN COACH WORKS
– A RETROSPECT

A final volume, to complete the story, and to record the endeavours of those who spent all or part of their working lives in the Coach Factory will be published early in 1995. Fully illustrated, largely in colour, it will complement the previous three volumes whilst providing the opportunity to set the record straight once-and-for-all as to how a factory employing highly skilled craftsmen with a reputation second to none for its products could be placed in a position where despite its profitability it had no place in its owner's plans. Based largely on first-hand interviews conducted over the last 25 years and brought up to date since the closure of the factory the book will be compelling and essential reading for all those involved with Eastern Coach Works as employees, customers or enthusiasts.

Send a stamped addressed envelope to Venture Publications Ltd at 128 Pikes Lane, Glossop, Derbyshire, SK13 8EH for advance details and an order form nearer to publication.

INDEX – Previous Volume 1946-65

EASTERN COACH WORKS 1946-65

Published by Venture in October 1993, ISBN 1 898432 01 5
is available from your transport bookshop or direct from

Venture Publications Ltd, 128 Pikes Lane, Glossop, Derbyshire SK13 8EH

at £19.95 post free

INDEX – This Volume 1965-87